MW00634421

**E40°**

# E40°

# An Interpretive Atlas

**Jack Williams**

University of Virginia Press | Charlottesville and London

Publication of this volume was assisted by a grant from Furthermore: a program of the J. M. Kaplan Fund.

University of Virginia Press
© 2006 by the Rector and Visitors of the University of Virginia
All rights reserved
Printed in China on acid-free paper
*First published 2006*

9 8 7 6 5 4 3 2 1

Library of Congress
Cataloging-in-Publication Data
Williams, Jack, 1941–
  East 40 degrees : an interpretive atlas /
Jack Williams.
    p.   cm.
  Includes bibliographical references and index.
  ISBN-13: 978-0-8139-2524-0 (cloth : alk. paper)
  ISBN-13: 978-0-8139-2585-1 (pbk. : alk. paper)
  1. Appalachian Mountains—Geography.
2. Appalachian Mountains—History, Local.
3. Cities and towns—Appalachian Mountains.
4. Appalachian Mountains—Environmental
conditions.  5. Appalachian Mountains—Social
conditions.  6. Social ecology—Appalachian Mountains. 7. Landforms—Appalachian Mountains.
8. Geology—Appalachian Mountains.
  I. Title.
  F106.W67 2006
  911'.74—dc22

                                    2006004628

For
Frances G. Williams

*"No, no! Bring me apples from the tree of Life!"*

—Henry David Thoreau, *Wild Fruits*

**On Exactitude in Science**

In that Empire, the Art of Cartography attained
such Perfection that the map of a single Province
occupied the entirety of a City, and the map of
the Empire, the entircty of a Province. In time,
those Unconscionable Maps no longer satisfied,
and the Cartographers Guild struck a Map of
the Empire whose size was that of the Empire,
and which coincided point for point with it. The
following Generations, who were not so fond of
the Study of Cartography as their Forebears had
been, saw that that vast Map was Useless, and
not without some Pitilessness was it, that they
delivered it up to the Inclemencies of Sun and
Winters. In the Deserts of the West, still today,
there are Tattered Ruins of that Map, inhabited
by Animals and Beggars; in all the Land there is
no other Relic of the Disciplines of Geography.
Suarez Miranda, *Viajes de varones prudentes,*
Libro iv, Cap. xlv, Lerida, 1658

—Jorge Luis Borges

Geology map of the eastern United States showing the great sweep of the Appalachian Mountains east 40 degrees from Alabama to the coast of Maine. (Courtesy of Auburn University Library Map Collection)

This extensive mountain cordillera begins north of the parallel yellow and green arcs of the relatively flat, sedimented soils that curve from the Carolinas to the Mississippi River valley. The rich cotton-growing region of the Old South is contained within this area of low relief, as are the courthouse-square and river towns of Alabama. Red, blue, and tan indicate the folded ridges and mountains that continue eastward through the entire continent to the coast of Maine. Geological formations rendered in light blue hold the extensive shallow beds of bituminous coal from Alabama to Pennsylvania. Dark blue marks the deeply eroded Appalachian Plateau of West Virginia, which furnishes much of the runoff to the Ohio River. Just west of New Jersey the cordillera bends sharply: northeast of this deformation lie the deeper veins of Pennsylvania's anthracite coal. Off the fragmented, heavily glaciated coast of Maine sit the many underwater banks and shoals that define the Gulf of Maine, with its rich fishing grounds.

Many of the soil and rock formations of the Appalachians are far older than the mountains themselves. Plate tectonics warped and tilted these formerly horizontal layers into the complex topography of the entire range. This massive wrinkling of the earth's crust stretches over two thousand miles and provides the armature for this book's study of small towns.

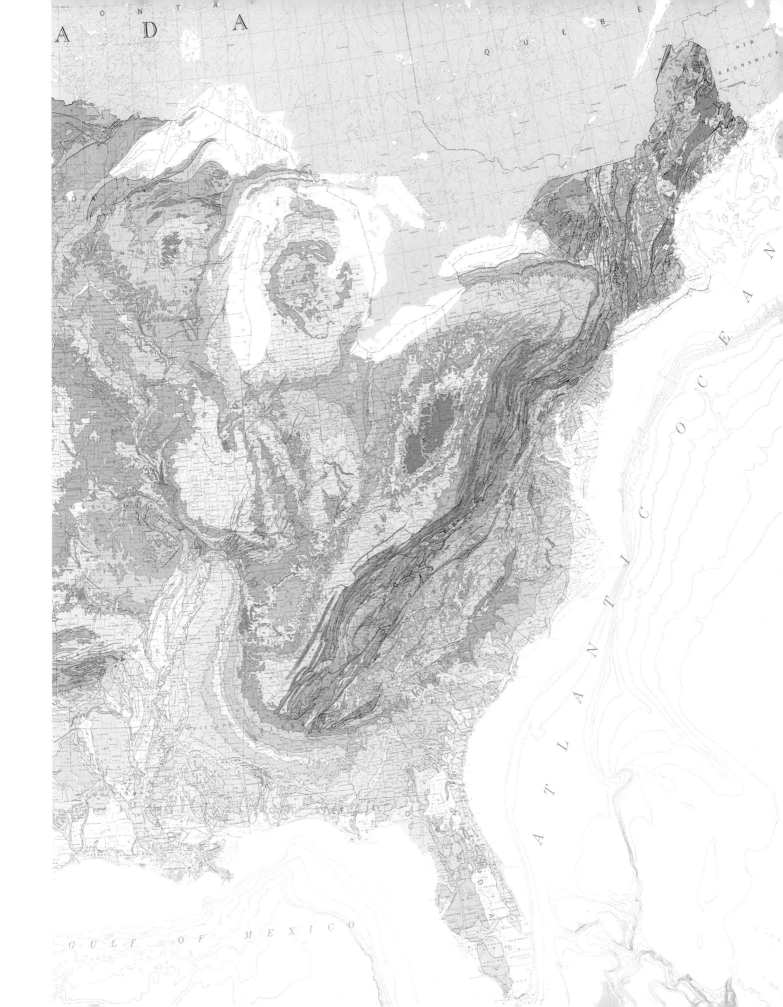

# Contents

# Acknowledgments

I wrote this book for the students, graduates, and faculty of the Landscape Architecture Program at Auburn University. During courses I have taught, in independent studies, seminars, and studios, wonderful young students have provided energy and commitment to many investigations beyond those contained within these pages. I thank them all for many delightful years of shared explorations. Without their enthusiasm and encouragement, I would not have had the fortitude to complete such an overwhelming task as writing a book.

These written words summarize many of the discussions and talks within the Landscape Architecture Program, so students will recognize the words, phrases, and concepts they have heard often in reviews and classes. In this sense the book belongs to all of them, friends and colleagues, as they now devote their young lives to other searches for meaning. I truly hope that as they read these words they will smile at the familiar ideas. I can receive no greater compliment than that my students share authorship with me. I only ask that they take responsibility for a future that I can only see dimly but that they must influence. This is not a legacy that I leave lightly,

nor is it the one I would necessarily have chosen for them. But a teacher can only teach; it is left to his or her students to implement change. As they are of the future, I hope they discover the journey to be as satisfying as I have found it to be.

Several graduate research assistants made significant contributions to the graphic studies of this book. I owe much to Richard Amore, Keli Davis, Ben Farmer, Michael Franks, Randy Morgan, Chad Sands, and Anne Wallace. They have done beautiful work.

My writings owe much to conversations with my fellow faculty about urban form and the history of cities. Professors Charlene LeBleu, Cheryl Morgan, David Pearson, John Pittari, Michael Robinson, and Kim Steele have been generous with their insights and tolerant of my constant diversions from the established academic curriculum. Professor John Gaber coached me through the publication process with humor and indulgence. I thank especially my good friend Chris Calott, professor in practice at the University of New Mexico, for his many trips with me as we searched for the perfect courthouse square, plaza town, or other examples of collected form. These colleagues are all steadfast and warm friends.

I owe my discovery of small southern towns to a Canadian, John Pratt, professor of history. He arranged field excursions with his students to places I had never been and graciously asked me to accompany him. He was a lovely person, full of laughter and life. Frank Setzer, a passionate urbanist and director of the Urban Studio in Birmingham, shared his knowledge of the history of that city and the coal and iron industries of Alabama. They are both missed, and I wish they could have read this book.

The School of Architecture, College of Architecture, Design and Construction, Auburn University, provided me with release time and funding at crucial periods that allowed me to finish individual chapters. I thank Bruce Lindsey, head of the School of Architecture, for his support and Associate Dean Sharon Gaber and Dean Daniel Bennett for their constant encouragement. Dwayne Cox and Joyce Hicks, librarians of the Special Collections, Auburn University Libraries, allowed me access to rare documents and maps and provided me with space in which to work. Boyd Childress, head librarian of the College of Architecture, Design and Construction, found rare and obscure maps and resources for me and was very generous with his time in explaining them. Chris Pyron advised me wisely about the uses and limits of technology in the preparation of the digital images. Cindy Hammonds fixed every impossible mistake I made during the preparation of the final manuscript.

During the course of researching and writing this book I visited many small towns and talked with members of their historical commissions and librarians in their public libraries. Always across the twelve hundred miles of the Appalachian Mountains I was met with warmth and offers of assistance. The many generous encounters proved beyond anything that I could write that these places are true repositories of our common cultures. I only wish I could have included every town, photograph, and map that was shared.

The staff of the Library of Congress Map and Photographic Collections provided me with images and prints of exceptional quality. The professionalism and assistance of the Library of Congress as the custodian of such wonderful and extensive resources never ceases to amaze me.

Many public libraries and local historical societies provided photographs for this book and wherever possible confirmed their dates. I have acknowledged their significant contributions in the illustration legends. The uncredited and undated color photographs and maps are from my own collection.

The Alabama State Council on the Arts awarded me a fellowship that enabled me to write the studies on Alabama's heritage that became chapters 3 and 4, "Shared Realities" and "*Urbis* Alabama."

I gratefully acknowledge a grant from Furthermore, a program of the J. M. Kaplan Fund, which assisted publication of this volume.

My two daughters, Megan and Tamsen, never gave up on my efforts to reinvent myself as an academic. Megan, a teacher and successful author in her own right, edited the many draft manuscripts for each chapter. Her reassurance, guidance, and sound advice carried me through periods of indecision. It is indeed delightful when one's daughter becomes a valued colleague.

I thank my wife, Clara, for carefully listening to all of my ideas—even those justifiably discarded. There is hardly a sentence in my writing that she has not winnowed from my hubris. Her patience and humor as I struggled to articulate yet another concept allowed me to maintain perspective.

My appreciation to Rayo, my constant companion in the gray empty hours of the morning when inspiration would not come. He would follow the cursor on the computer screen with his white gloves or purr upon my rejected drafts.

**E40°**

# Introduction

This book explores places, those small towns of America whose sedimented layers of history connect us to our past and attach us to this earth. The great cordillera of the Appalachian Mountains, which runs east 40 degrees from Alabama through fifteen states to the coast of Maine, forms the spatial armature for these investigations. This sutured record of continental collisions begins each town's history with the shaping of the earth's surface more than 300 million years ago. Each town included in this book sits either within the folds of these mountains or beside a river nourished in their moist uplands. Those same ancient geological forces tossed and kneaded, in the wide mixing bowl of plate tectonics, land forms and mineral deposits. The extractive process for these resources brought into existence each town: cotton from the rich black soil of Alabama, coal from deep veins in narrow Appalachian valleys, and fish from the cold waters and shallow banks of the Gulf of Maine. These towns differ in form and content, in origins or futures, in almost every way, yet they are all real, full-of-time, narrative places that give meaning to everyday life. And it is these common narratives that imbue their form, their urban patterns, with such beauty. We cannot expropriate their realities, for the exigencies of the past dissipate swiftly, yet the compelling stories revealed in the beauty of their urban forms deserve to be told so that we may better understand ourselves and the places we so carelessly inhabit today.

The points of the compass have served to locate us in history as well as in space. The title of this book, *East 40 Degrees,* refers to the deviation of the axis of the Appalachian Mountains from true north. This continuous, eastward-leaning range of mountains and valleys is more than two thousand miles long and contains both the locations and the histories of those towns included in this study. *Cordillera,* from the Latin *chorda,* meaning "braided rope," is a geological term for a great range of parallel or intertwined mountains. During the extended period of their complex formation the Appalachians were the highest and most dramatic mountains on earth. Worn down over eons, they still hold some of the most varied climatic zones and most singular geological formations of any existent mountains. That they run 40 degrees east of north across the entire breadth of North America ensures a wealth of different conditions that required an equal richness of settlement responses. As we today homogenize our settlement patterns into repetitive and standardized regularity, regardless

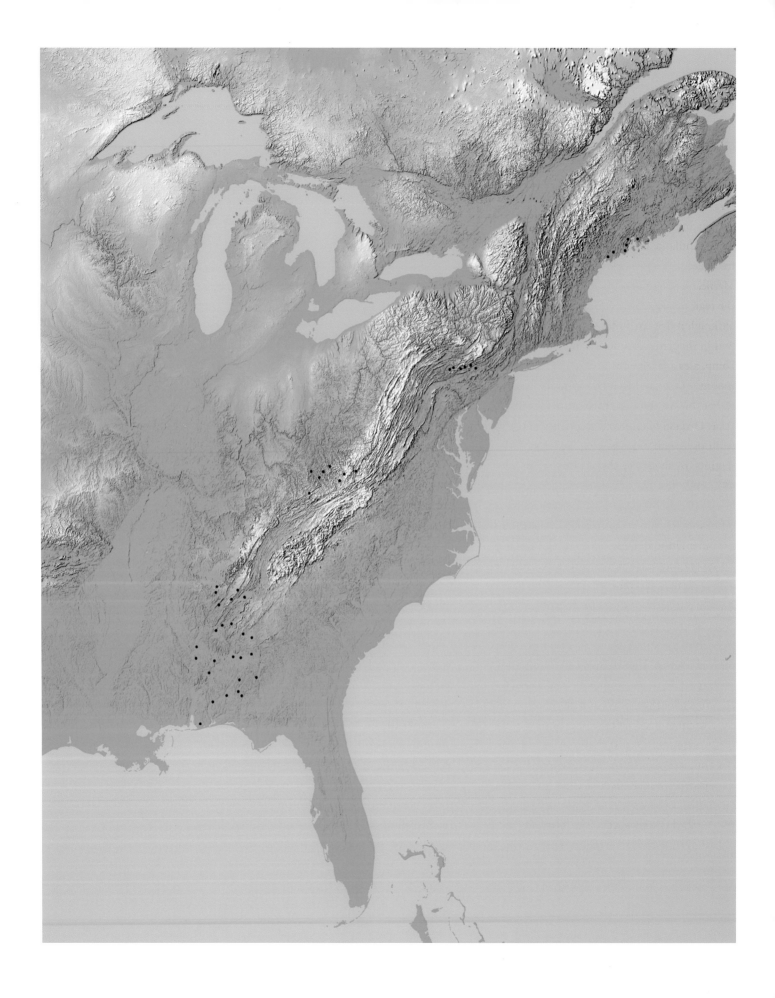

of topographies or histories, these past examples of urban form instruct us with their prolific and sensible accommodations to the earth's mantle.

While the Appalachians actually run from the Ozarks in Arkansas up the eastern quarter of the United States, through Nova Scotia, and on into Newfoundland, this book limits its investigation to that part that begins in Alabama and ends in Maine. It should be understood that this is not the region commonly referred to as Appalachia, although it does include certain towns clearly within that cultural construct. This study encompasses a far greater area and considers these mountains a historical and spatial armature rather than a uniform economic development zone. Diversity of urban form arises because of a multiplicity of factors beyond financial constraints. By following the Appalachians north and south, these investigations present more varieties of towns than those of the economically depressed central highlands.

Other authors study urban form and have presented their ideas in writing. John Reps compares the typologies of western railroad settlements in his early book *Frontier Towns*. His study *Tidewater Towns* concentrates on the history of a specific geographical region. *Spanish Urbanism in America,* by Susan Couch, follows the spread of a cultural frontier in America's Southwest. Warren Boeschenstein's well-documented book *Historic American Towns along the Atlantic Coast* offers detailed studies of nine familiar and lovely villages with an emphasis on distinctive residential architecture. The advantage of the Appalachian Mountains as a frame is that they slice through so many distinct cultural regions, encompassing radically different ecotones. They provide an extended time sequence from the sixteenth-century discovery of New England, through the settlement of the newly formed State of Alabama in the early nineteenth century, to the development of coal in the West Virginia mountains in the twentieth century. Although our geological explorations extend much further back for reasons that become apparent in the individual chapters, our European cultural history includes the most recent five centuries superimposed on at least ten thousand years of Native American inhabitation. In short, the Appalachian cordillera includes layers of history and geography that make this comparative study of places both richer and more informative by allowing us to see the tenuous web of connections between ourselves and the natural processes that shape this earth. A topographical map of the entire eastern half of the United States generated for this book illustrates the placement of the towns of this study within the spatial armature of the great sweep of the Appalachians. The usual cultural clues, such as state and county boundaries, have been removed to emphasize the links between these tiny urban centers and their immense context.

Because the Appalachians formed such an impenetrable barrier to our westward expansion, they have been surveyed and documented exhaustively. Whether for mineral deposits, for more direct routes, or for railroad rights of way, the complex geological formations of the Appalachians are well known, as are their many different ecotones. Three of the country's oldest and most heavily visited national parks—Great

(Opposite) Relief map of the Appalachian Mountains. The black dots represent the towns of this study.

(Above) Great Smoky
Mountains National Park
(Below) Baxter State Park,
Maine

1. The map on page 6 was
brought to my attention
in McElfresh, *Maps and
Mapmakers of the Civil
War*, 163.

Smoky Mountains, Shenandoah, and Acadia—
as well as many state parks, such as Baxter in
central Maine, are in these mountains. All are
places of great beauty. In addition, these mountains hold at once some of the most intractable
pockets of poverty in America and some of the
most desolate, barren, industrial landscapes on
earth.

A wonderful example from the Library of
Congress map collection illustrates a historical
concern for the strategic shielding aspects of the
Appalachians.[1] A former schoolteacher in Virginia, Jed Hotchkiss (1828–99), drew beautiful
maps for the Confederate cause while serving as
a civilian topographic engineer on the staff of
the Army of Northern Virginia. After the war he
was influential in developing the coal resources
of Virginia and West Virginia, and his railroad maps appear in chapter 5. His map of the
Shenandoah Valley shows the eastward ridges
of the Appalachians from Virginia through
Maryland into Pennsylvania. At Harrisburg the
mountains turn east at the Susquehanna River
into the great anthracite coal seams of Pennsylvania. This map is especially germane to this
study, not for what it was intended to show or
for its accuracy (the mountain ridges are much
too narrow), but for the way it discloses General Robert E. Lee's ability to conceptualize and
utilize the space of the Appalachians. He clearly
understood these mountains as a spatial armature within which he could move northward relatively protected on his right flank to carry the
war above the Mason-Dixon Line. He turned to
go through the Cashtown Gap and approached
Gettysburg from the northwest. After its defeat,
the Army of Northern Virginia retreated southward along the same valley.

Arrayed along the two-thousand-mile length
of these mountains, our sampling of towns com-
prises an amazing range of urban forms—from
the courthouse squares of Alabama agricultural
towns, the crescent shapes of West Virginia coal
communities, and the linear grids of Pennsylva-

nia coal patches to the weblike centers of Maine coastal villages. Each town's character is the product of both its cultural and social circumstances and the geological history of the region. These histories contain vast complexities of economic contingencies that shaped each town down to the tiniest detail. The granite lintels above windows in Maine mercantile buildings, the gilded tiles on the onion domes of Pennsylvania's Eastern Orthodox churches, and the red clay bricks of an Alabama courthouse all trace their origins back through circumstances that began with shifting continents eons ago. Thus this great cordillera offers up answers to most questions we might ask about place making.

Small towns contain all the richness of our experience: the hushed conversations in a barbershop, a child's savings account, the cornucopian clutter of a hardware store—all the small human transactions that occur within its buildings and along its streets during the years of its existence. Those same streets witness dreams of the future, hopes for a winning baseball season, a safer job, equality of justice, even aspirations to leave for distant cities and better opportunities. A town is the locus of these multiple events gathered over time into an identifiable place; it is those hidden stories and lives that play themselves out within its confines. A town's content remains an abstraction, the accumulated wealth of tiny or momentous decisions. Content is ourselves, our hopes, disappointments, failures, and triumphs made manifest by a place. Because any town, by its complexity, holds so much for so many, towns and cities become telling reminders of our culture. Anyone who has walked across

an empty courthouse square or climbed the mellow oak stairs in a discarded high school understands the evocative power of all those who dwelled before. We cannot escape this tight grip of the past. We can try to erase it, but never successfully, for it transcends physical boundaries. We may alter these boundaries, repair or build anew. Different interests or different needs may demand new settlement patterns, but everyday happenings, some good, some bad, persist in our collective memory.

Three hauntingly beautiful photographs show better than any words the people who inhabited the places described in this book. The first is of a chilly December day in Selma, Alabama, taken in 1935 by Walker Evans. The store's merchandise—bags of salt, pickax handles, washing buckets, mule collars—spills out onto the public sidewalk under the protecting arcade supported by thin cast-iron columns. Three seated men turn toward a fourth lighting a pipe. The shoes of the nearest man catch the slanted rays of the sun, which highlight their worn, thin soles. An elegant woman in a long coat and stylish hat turns away. It is a remarkable urban composition—until one realizes that it is so obviously racially segregated.

The photograph of coal breaker boys in Kingston, Pennsylvania, ca. 1900, by an unknown photographer, shows a group of young boys at the base of a breaker, a great structure for grinding and separating coal. At about age ten children started working in the collieries sorting coal into different sizes before moving into the deep mines, and families depended upon their income to survive. The photograph

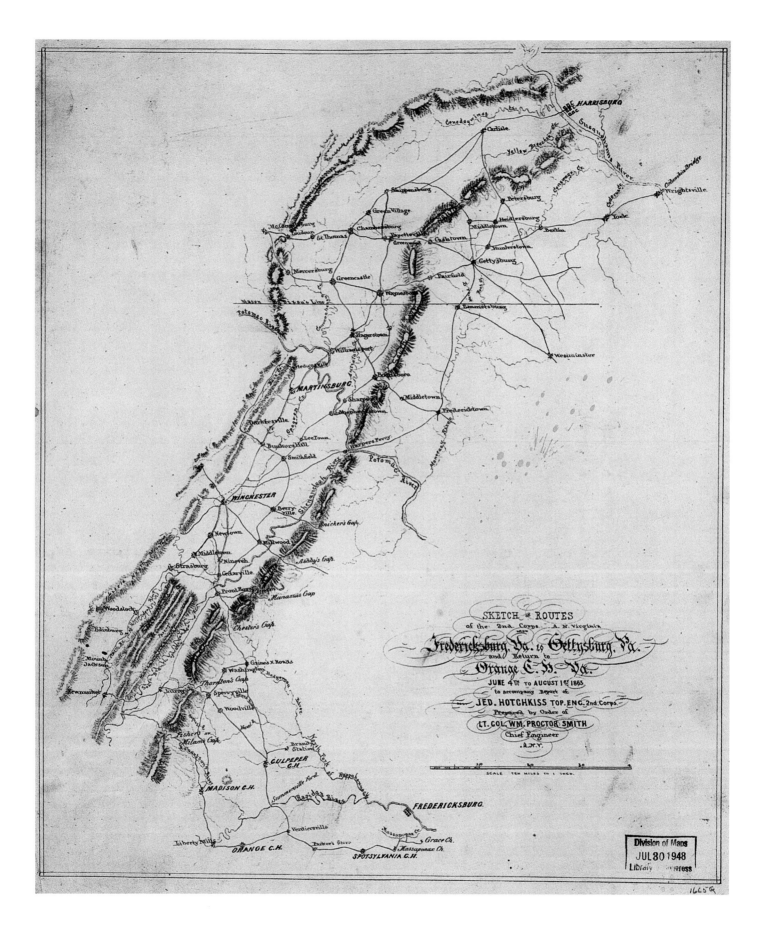

SKETCH of ROUTES
of the 2nd Corps A. N. Virginia
from
Fredericksburg, Va. to Gettysburg, Pa.
and Return to
Orange C. H. Va.
JUNE 4TH TO AUGUST 1ST 1863.
to accompany Report of
JED. HOTCHKISS TOP. ENG. 2nd Corps
Prepared by Order of
LT. COL. WM. PROCTOR SMITH
Chief Engineer
A. N. V.

SCALE TEN MILES TO 1 INCH.

1665 G

Sidewalk scene in Selma, Alabama, 1935, Walker Evans, photographer. (Library of Congress)

(Opposite) Jed Hotchkiss's sketch of the routes of the Second Corps, Army of Northern Virginia, from Fredericksburg, Virginia, to Gettysburg, Pennsylvania, and return, June–August 1863. (Library of Congress)

was taken at the bottom of the breaker where the railroad cars entered; the two boys at the extreme right sit on a railroad car. The metal pieces on their hat brims hold lamps that are in place on the hats of the boys to the left and at the top of the stairs. Two boys carry metal lunchpails, and one holds the remains of a partly eaten sandwich in his small hand. All the boys' faces are covered with grime from the always present black coal dust.

The third photograph was taken by Harlan Hurd at about the turn of the century just off Rockport Harbor, Maine. The men are brailing the pocket of a herring weir. *Brail* comes from the old French word *braiel,* meaning "strap" or

"belt." A brail is a dip net resembling a small purse seine with which fish are hauled aboard a boat after being gathered in a larger net. It was cold, wet labor, and both men wear rubber bibs and heavy woolen shirts. The photograph captures both the fecundity of the Maine inshore fishing industry and the extremes of weather and work etched deeply into the two men's faces.

All three photographs, separated by both time and distance, remind us that any town has been inhabited by ordinary people whose lives of toil and hardship deserve our respect and admiration. In each photograph something more than the setting or context is captured. The segregated cluster on a southern street, the defeat in

**Breaker boys, Woodward Coal Mines, Kingston, Pennsylvania, ca. 1900. (Library of Congress)**

the eyes of the young boys, and the lined faces of the fishermen all evidence a common humanity memorialized in the places they struggled to inhabit.

The reader who would seek here a panegyric on small-town values will be disappointed. Towns have no such privilege, no exclusivity, to a mythic American consciousness. Some of the towns included in this book are not beautiful in any picturesque sense. They show instead a gritty determination to endure against all odds. Some barely survive, their populations leaving and their retail spaces empty. Nor is this book a sentimental, idealistic reflection upon the past. These towns arose for very pragmatic and mundane reasons. The histories of some contain disastrous episodes or the disenfranchisement of an entire race, but these are nevertheless their histories, their content. As the chapters ahead show, many of the southern towns embedded racial segregation in their physical form. History, however, chooses not only the romantic and nostalgic for preservation. This book tries instead to be a way of looking, of rediscovering that which we already have but which we somehow fail to recognize or appreciate. Rather than just another lament for what we have lost, it is an exploration of what we may yet find.

We take measure of a culture by its art, its literature, its music, all the traditional artifacts exhaustively examined in any time period, including the almost daily analysis of our most current efforts. This book suggests that we must also use a culture's communities as a way of understanding its place in the world. The groupings and associations of dwellings, churches, and civic structures give us a clear indication of what a culture values or valued. These communities indicate former social and economic constraints. The way a community orders its resources clearly tells us its priorities. We find, for example, in the very poorest towns in the anthracite coal region wonderfully grand churches—even as many as a dozen in a town of a few thousand. Unlike literature or poetry, whose words are created by an individual and are thus fixed in the author's time, communities result from the ideas of many people and are re-created continuously over time. Towns adapt, change in response to a whole spectrum of influences, grow or shrink in population—all aspects that are evident in their physical form. Like the individual buildings of which they are composed, these towns experience cultural corrosion as all their structures behave in aggregate and grow old together. The churches of Pennsylvania coal towns mentioned above still exist, empty or boarded closed, as mute testimony to better times with far larger populations; their rich architecture, together with their surrounding residential neighborhoods, is a reminder of the vicissitudes of change and shifting values.

Before examining the particular towns described in the chapters ahead, let us first investigate more deeply the meaning of place. The well-known Gettysburg battlefield serves as an apt beginning to the discussions for several reasons. A beautifully rendered map by S. G. Elliott drawn after the battle clearly places Gettysburg within the Appalachian cordillera. This singular location determined much about those tragic events, including where they would actually transpire. Every possible topographic detail is noted, along with vegetation and watercourses. The town's relationship to the surrounding topography shows how the battle stretched away south and west of downtown. The rendering of Gettysburg's center is a beautiful example of an urban form that collects roads and railroads from the region into the concise space of its main square. Notice how the seven roads drawn

in Elliott's map converge on the town. Gettysburg's gathering of these roads into its core caused two mighty armies to converge onto this place in our history. The accurate and detailed rendering of the varied topography is especially relevant to our study. Every ridge, every depression shaped the battle and holds our memory of each engagement within the beautiful rolling hills of this place. This is a landscape populated by ghosts.

In his Gettysburg Address, delivered on 19 November 1863, Abraham Lincoln said that "in a larger sense we can not dedicate, we cannot consecrate, we can not hallow this ground. The brave young men, living and these dead, who struggled here, have consecrated it far above our power to add or detract. The world will never note nor long remember, what we say here, but it can never forget what they did." Ironically, the

Brailing the pocket, ca. 1900, Harlan Hurd, photographer. (Courtesy of the Carroll Thayer Berry Collection, Penobscot Marine Museum)

Map of the battlefield of Gettysburg, made from an accurate survey of the ground by transit and chain by S. G. Elliott, C.E., published in 1864. (Library of Congress)

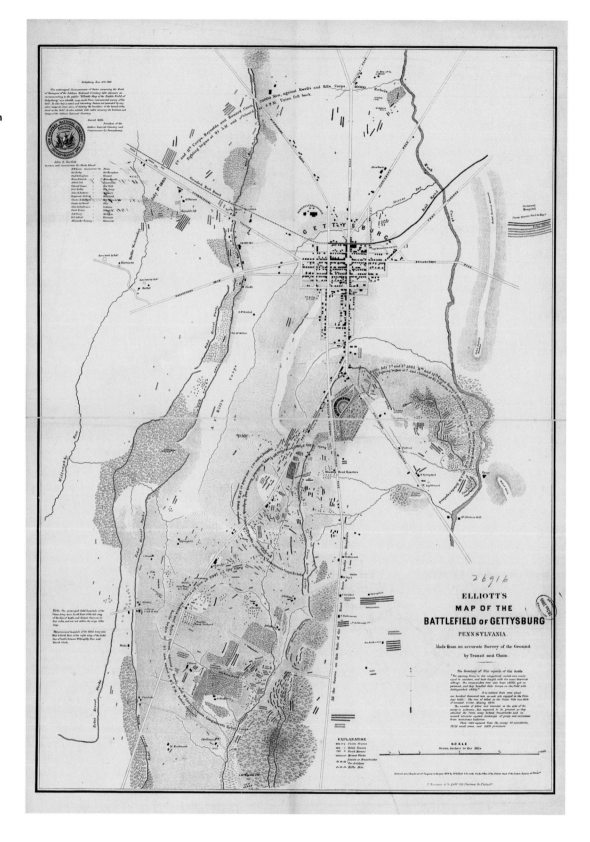

world does well remember what he said that day. The Gettysburg Address contains some of the best-known and most beloved words in the English language. And those words elevated Gettysburg from the carnage of a pivotal battle into such a special place and "hallowed its ground" into one of the most sacred locations in the American consciousness.

Gettysburg is a real place and as such has several necessary components. First is its landscape, today covered with Victorian monuments and interpretive markers. On that awful morning in July 1863 it must have presented a typical if unremarkable pastoral agricultural landscape of southern Pennsylvania—open fields and orchards between a series of gently sloping ridges. The location for the battle was chosen through a sequence of seemingly unrelated troop movements and maneuvers that by chance brought these two armies together. Having confronted each other, both sides, North and South, sought even the most minute advantage in topography: rock outcroppings, irregularities in the undulating slopes, or extensive tree canopies. Over three days the Gettysburg battle became the most thorough search for accommodations within the irregularities of the earth's surface possible as desperate men took cover for their lives. Men fought for and hid within the tiniest depression or reinforced the slightest elevation as the fighting ebbed back and forth. To visit Gettysburg today is to appreciate and comprehend all the named places, such as the Peach Orchard, Devil's Den, the Wheat Field, and Little Round Top. S. G. Elliott's remarkable map indicates troop concentration by dark lines upon the to-

pography and draws the cuts in the earth's surface as breastworks that no longer exist. However, all the erasures of words and men on a map can never return this landscape to its bucolic beauty, no matter how much time passes.

Thus Gettysburg holds the first component of a place: a physical presence that we can measure by walking through its entirety. This presence is actual and sensory in that we can experience all of it: the slopes of the fields between the ridges, the whisper of wind in the trees that hid Lee's forces, the warmth of the sun on open slopes, the songs of birds in the silence of Devil's Den. Second, an event of momentous consequences took place within this physical reality. In actuality it was many thousands of small events over three days that, added together, became what has since been called the battle of Gettysburg. Individual acts of courage, of cowardice, movements of companies and regiments, occurred in this landscape night and day until at the end thousands of young men lay dead.

We shall debate the reasons behind these horrific events as long as our history lasts. That they occurred is etched forever into the American psyche. The place of Gettysburg has two components, then: the form of the landscape and the content of the event. Or, as will be explored further, it has structure and meaning, the structure of the topography and other physical realities and the layers of meaning imposed upon that location by all the individuals who took part in that interminable and wasteful battle. Abraham Lincoln clearly understood this and thus gave Gettysburg one more attribute, the one most necessary for a real place: he made the battlefield a repository for collective memory. He said it so forcefully and eloquently when he used the words "hallow this ground." With that phrase, he gathered all events, both past and future, upon that location. For all who visit today or tomorrow, he made it as personal a place as humanly possible.

Not every place witnessed such historic or cataclysmic occurrences as Gettysburg, but all places contain form and content together gathered into our collective memory. Most places are brought into existence not by a single event but by many layers of small or even insignificant happenings over an extended period of time. A place is like a container, a vessel, which has form or structure and can be filled many times over with different kinds of liquid—corresponding to its content or meaning. As the liquid may drain away or evaporate, leaving an empty jug, so too may the content leave a place not once but many times, not only quickly but often slowly, over its temporal existence. Content may dissolve, form may disappear, but the place remains.

Words speak. In common usage events or acts "take place." We admit in our daily speech that any happening must have a physical reality, a location, in order to exist. A place is therefore a totality composed both of spatial dimensions and the multiple acts that occurred within its boundaries. Our ordinary experience tells us that different actions need different environments in which to "take place." A building, a group of buildings, or a town consists, then, of a multitude of particular places. A town too must have its place within a larger reality, the natural

world of geography and topography. As soon as we enlarge the boundaries of a town into this greater context, we must also, by extension, include all the actions of its inhabitants outward into an extended space. For example, as chapter 7 illustrates, it is impossible to consider a coastal fishing village separate from the wind and tides that follow its fishermen as part of their journey out into the wider fishing grounds of the open ocean. It is instructive that we refer to these areas of the watery deep as "grounds"; they are places that we can never see but that a fisherman can know intimately from the feel of "depth" in the dragging of nets and fishing lines.

While settlements are closed entities with boundaries, as places they have limits that reach out to gather in all that sustains them. A southern courthouse gathers within its walls all the deeds and birth, marriage, and death certificates not only of the town but of the surrounding county as well. These documents become markers of a larger place, an abstraction upon the earth's surface that we call the county, yet we understand this abstraction as a community within which we dwell. It should be clear that place is not synonymous with location. Location is neutral, without a history or an act to bring it into being. The earth's crust, however, has an unlimited richness of attributes and characteristics that we expropriate for ourselves when we "make a place" and anchor ourselves to its surface. The chapters ahead explore in detail the variety and richness of natural locations that settlements have appropriated for their "placement."

Language allows us to express abstractions

such as duty, honor, and community through comparisons. Metaphor becomes the vehicle for attaching the physical world to the emotional or abstract world. Shakespeare refers throughout his plays to our lives as actors upon a stage. Macbeth has but "his hour upon the stage."[2] In *As You Like It* Jaques says, "All the world's a stage / And all the men and women merely players. / They have their exits and their entrances."[3] For ordinary people, our stage is where we dwell, our home, our work, our community. It is there that we play out our lives, in a place that is both real and illusive. The sum of all these lives, births and deaths, our entrances and exits, are marked by our places of dwelling. A town becomes both a place, full of many narratives, and, through its form, a metaphor for those lives. Communities are cultures before they can be built, constructs of the imagination projected upon a site or actual topography. Once the community, an abstraction, establishes itself in our minds, it takes on a reality of its own, and the metaphor can become more real than its referent, for it allows us to imagine who we are. To be born in a certain place is to be born into a time, a color, and a destiny. We cannot change an individual's time nor race; whether one's destiny can be freed from place is a question this book cannot answer. It is certain, however, that the destiny of any town can never be removed from its place.

These places have distinctive form, and it is the thoughtful aggregation of many structures that brings urban form into being. Urban form is like a tapestry, a whole woven of many strands. But like a tapestry, it is the whole we must comprehend. To remove a block of build-ings is analogous to cutting out a section of the tapestry: it destroys the whole composition. Even removing a small piece, such as an individual building, fragments a town. Remove many buildings, and the town's fabric disappears. Like fabric, urban form depends upon interrelationships. The towns in the pages ahead were chosen because they still have their fabric intact. Each chapter in this book investigates a different example of urban form and through comparisons formulates a more comprehensive definition of this elusive concept.

This discussion of urban form highlights a central dilemma of this book. It argues that towns are real places and that places have three essential components: content, form, and memory. Furthermore, it proposes that the more successful a town is as a community, the more content and form become inseparable in our memories. As it attempts to explain and compare the different configurations and patterns of many towns, however, this book analyzes form separate from content. This problematic and risky approach in dealing with any urban complex leads us into mapping abstractions that could weaken our initial definition of place. Succinctly put, the best map of a town is the town itself. The wonderful quote from Jorge Luis Borges at the beginning of this book beautifully evokes this dilemma.

The process of dissection proposed does, however, permit an analytical and comparative study that supports the basic premises of this book: that urban form of and by itself has aesthetic value and that the construction of concise urban form is the most sustainable action we

2. *Macbeth*, 5.5.24.

3. *As You Like It*, 2.7.139.

can take to protect the future of this earth. By gathering dwellings and structures together into tight groupings, we preserve the largest amounts of undisturbed natural habitat. Since habitat fragmentation represents the greatest threat to our planet, these settlement patterns of the past contain lessons very applicable to our contemporary world of urban sprawl. This book argues as well for another measure of sustainability that is perhaps even more important than habitat preservation: the sustainability of our culture. Density or conciseness of urban form equates with density of human interactions, and we must have diverse and constant exchanges with one another to preserve and transmit all that is uniquely human.

These two concepts of sustainability hide many assumptions. To aid in the discovery of the relationship between sustainability and urban form, the book is organized into seven chapters. Chapter 1 begins with a comparison of the "two Camdens," located like bookends at either extremity of this study—one in Alabama, the other in Maine. Using these two towns as examples, this chapter explains maps both as sources of information and as methods for comparison. Many new interpretive graphics have been generated for this book, so the reader needs to be aware of the wealth of sources behind their creation. The simplicity of these new maps should not mask the many layers of research beneath their representations. In an effort to map new territory, several unusual graphic mapping conventions require further explanation, so chapter 1 delves more deeply than later chapters

into specific kinds of maps, like figure-grounds or layered axonometrics.

A narrative drawn from the Civil War establishes a connection between the two Camdens. The choice of this time period is not capricious; the end of the Civil War began seventy years of growth and prosperity for the United States, and so much of what we now experience in these small towns' built form came into existence during those years. The development of a national railroad network, along with the demands of the two world wars, especially spurred growth. Almost without exception the flourishing of these towns took place from 1870 to the 1940s. Why they thrived will be the subject of the following chapters.

All towns register the circumstances of their founding cadastral or individual boundary surveys in their final form. Most of the towns discussed in this book, with the exception of the Maine coastal towns, contain a street grid or fragments of one. The coastal towns' "long lots" for water access provide a second, contrasting example of "anchoring" abstractions—ways in which we mark ownership. Chapter 2, "The Ubiquitous Grid," reviews the origins of both anchoring systems, grids and "long lots," as organizing devices and as a means for measuring our accommodations to the exigencies of the earth's surface.

Chapters 3 through 7 each correspond to a geographical region. The regions move from south to north along the Appalachian Mountains, beginning with the agricultural towns of Alabama and then moving to the coal and mountain towns of Kentucky, Virginia, West Virginia, and Pennsylvania. The coastal towns of Maine terminate the explorations at the farthest reaches of the Appalachians in the United States. This book depends heavily upon a comparative method for its discussions, so each chapter builds upon those that precede it to buttress the argument of a consistency of concise urban form across disparate regions.

Chapter 3, "Shared Realities," focuses our journey east 40 degrees on the courthouse-square towns of Alabama and on a discussion of civic hierarchical spaces. Remaining unspoiled in these towns are some of the most exquisite courthouses and surrounding spaces in America, unknown outside of this region. Chapter 4, "*Urbis* Alabama," groups other southern towns into three common typologies—river, wagon, and railroad towns—and explores their transformations over time in response to each new transportation shift.

Chapters 5 and 6 move northward into the two coal-producing regions of the central Atlantic states: the bituminous coal belt of Kentucky, Virginia, and West Virginia and the anthracite mines of eastern Pennsylvania. Chapter 5, "Volatile Matter," concentrates on the region of the more highly volatile bituminous coal seams and investigates the influence of geology on topology and urban form. Economic exploitation underlay much of the settlement of this region and, sadly, remains its most enduring legacy. Nevertheless, these mining towns retain a gritty, haunted beauty. Chapter 6, "Harvesting Sunbeams," shifts eastward into the anthracite

coal hills of Pennsylvania. These mines and towns lie within one hundred miles of New York City and Philadelphia, yet they exist as distant worlds. The development of anthracite coal corresponded with the emergence of a national transportation infrastructure, so these towns reflect this influence in their linear and compact urban form. Little known outside their deep valleys, these communities provide examples of the most condensed urban form in America.

Chapter 7, "The Search for Norumbega," turns farther eastward to the coastal fishing villages of Maine. Of the towns included in this study, these villages have the longest histories. Several predate the landing of the Pilgrims and the settlement of Plymouth Colony in Massachusetts. One of these towns is, of course, Camden, so with this chapter our study comes full circle, concluding with a summary of those physical characteristics most common to all towns included in the study. Compactness and order are the two most salient characteristics. Every ordinary town condenses our expectations and presents a succinct summary of a region's culture. A "conciseness" of urban form is prevalent throughout our examples as a distinctive feature that should have enabled these towns to sustain both themselves and the surrounding landscape. Few did; many failed.

A town or any settlement is a concentration within a larger unity, and we need to understand both that unity and why it disappears. So my conclusion returns again to the issue of cultural sustainability; these towns gather us together and anchor us to the earth. But it is the gathering that is so necessary to sustain ourselves and our cultures. These towns serve as repositories of our humanity, both the exultant and the exploitative. We should respect their completeness as works of art.

My aim in writing this book is modest. I ask only that we see these towns for what they are: complete and integrated complexes with regional commonalities, each with its own individual characteristics. These many responses to the world hold a unique beauty, and beauty of urban form at any scale is not to be squandered lightly. If these essays give pause to the further erosion of this cultural heritage, if these writings render the meaning and value of these towns more legible, if only in recollection, then I will have succeeded. At the core of my argument is the obdurate belief that the new spatial order imposed upon our landscape by our obsession with the automobile and our consumer-driven universe, where convenience and price are the only measures of value, is not sustainable.

As an architect I have been fortunate indeed to bring into existence new communities of substantial size and complexity. I have tried to confront the issues described throughout this book through my designs of compact urban form. From experience, then, I would always choose not to dwell in a mindless world devoid of community and metaphor, where our physical environment no longer reflects our highest aspirations. I cannot contest the reality of this change; rather, I wish to reveal the richness and complexity of our past efforts to dwell together and to explain what we may have lost. Like any history, this book on urban form cannot be a plan for action nor a recipe for the future. The future will be formed by similar but different forces than those that formed these towns, and it will become its own record of our values. Instead of solely planning for the future, I invite the reader to reflect upon our common places and the immense reservoir of meaning and memory layered beneath their physical form.

# The Two Camdens

## A Comparative Study of Mapping

This chapter compares two towns with the same name located at opposite ends of our spatial armature of the Appalachians: Camden, Alabama, and Camden, Maine. This comparison introduces ways of graphically representing the urban form of both places. Conventional and especially unconventional mapping techniques are used to illustrate the different characteristics of the two towns. Because urban form should only be considered in its totality, new mapping methods that enable such a syntactical approach are introduced throughout this book. These two towns serve as useful examples of their applicability.

Like many other places in the United States, both Camden, Alabama, and Camden, Maine, are named after Lord Camden, a member of Britain's House of Lords in the eighteenth century. As a member of English Parliament, Charles Pratt, the future Lord Camden, discouraged inciting Native Americans against the rebellious Colonies. One of the few in England who publicly supported aspects of the American Revolution, he was considered a hero by the Colonists. The name of Camden, Alabama, came by way of Camden, South Carolina, also named for Lord Camden. Although they share the same name, Camden, Alabama, and Cam-den, Maine, are as different in structure and history as possible. One is the county seat of Wilcox County and contains a lovely courthouse square surrounded by shops and stores in the cotton belt of the Deep South; the other is a beautiful coastal fishing and shipbuilding village clustered around a secure harbor. While the two towns are separated by time and distance, ironically fate brought together young men from both towns for a brief moment upon a fold of the eastward-flowing ridges of the Pennsylvania Appalachians. Both towns must have contained something of great value to lead those soldiers to travel so far and risk so much. These towns held both meaning and structure for the soldiers, and this chapter begins our exploration of form for what it tells us about content. By doing so we add to the third component of place—collective memory.

Turn back with me again, but briefly, as the hot July afternoon sun cast longer shadows among the dark boulders and dense oaks, and determined men tensed for the battle certain to come. Officers spoke softly to their men, telling them to check their cartridges again and make ready their extra ammunition. Thoughts turned to the ordinary, the heat, the thirst; many turned to their friends nearby for encouragement and

1. Joshua Chamberlain, "Dispatch to General Barnes, 5 July 1863," in Nesbitt, *Through Blood and Fire*, 81.

2. Chamberlain, from Brunswick, Maine, recruited most of the men in the Twentieth Maine from the surrounding area, including Camden. See Reuel Robinson, *History of Camden and Rockport*, 370, for a detailed discussion of Maine regiments at Gettysburg. General Law's brigade comprised five regiments from Alabama: the Fourth, Fifteenth, Forty-fourth, Forty-seventh, and Forty-eighth. The Forty-fourth was mustered in the spring of 1862 from Wilcox County, of which Camden is the country seat.

3. McPherson, *For Cause and Comrades*, 80.

shared words of remembered homes, of coastal harbors and spruce headlands, of white clapboard structures and weathered shingles. All from Maine, these young men were to play out their short lives upon a forgotten bubble of granite on a distant Pennsylvania ridge south of Gettysburg.

Concentrated fire from the right announced the advance of attacking Southerners, as the Fifteenth, Forty-seventh, and Fourth Alabama regiments drove steadily into the waiting muskets of the Twentieth Maine. Again and again the two sides clashed as each attempted to gain possession of that pile of earth and rock known to us now as Little Round Top. The brave Confederates did not waver; time and again they came within yards, if not feet, of the Union position before retreating from the appalling fire of the determined Yankees. There seemed no end to the fighting as line after line of Rebel troops pressed forward. Exhausted and out of ammunition, the Northerners mustered for one last charge against their fellow countrymen. "I saw that the defensive could be maintained not an instant longer, & with a few gallant officers rallied a line, ordered 'bayonets fixed,' & 'forward' at a run," wrote Joshua Chamberlain, colonel of the Twentieth Maine Volunteers, in his report a few days later.[1]

And thus for a few awful moments of that slowly ebbing day of 2 July 1863, men from coastal Maine and their fellows from the rich farmlands of Alabama mixed and fought within paces of each other. They came from towns such as Castine, Belfast, and Wiscasset, Maine and Selma, Elba, and Eufaula, Alabama.[2] And in one of those tragic ironies of that terrible battle, men from both sides came from towns named Camden. Originally separated from each other by over a thousand miles, these men from different Camdens fought that day for country, for home, for ways of life that were imbedded both in their memories and in the places from which they came.

In his thoughtful book *For Cause and Comrades: Why Men Fought in the Civil War,* James McPherson articulates, through his readings of actual soldier's letters and diaries, the reasons why they endured the horror and depravation of that terrible conflict. According to McPherson, their motives for leaving their homes and families were bound up in abstractions such as honor, duty, vengeance, and peer acceptance. Most men in a volunteer company or regiment came from the same region or even the same town; they knew each other, and if they survived, they would see each other again. They would miss those who did not return. These men maintained constant correspondence with their homes through letters, shared newspaper articles, and furloughs home.[3] As groups of young men they collectively carried their places with them. Most regiments incorporated their state name: the Fifteenth Alabama; the Twentieth Maine. Shared pride of place was important.

But place must have physical form, if only in recollection or memory. It is difficult for us to conceptualize or visualize abstractions such as duty or honor, so we bring them into existence either through metaphors or through mental images. Thus duty becomes duty to family, to home, or to country. This abstraction *duty* requires the physical realities of either persons or places. When we speak of home, we conjure up concrete images of rooms, houses, streets. When we talk of country, we mean our region, the landscape with which we are most familiar.

By the second half of the nineteenth century, Camden, Maine, clustered around a deep water harbor on the west side of Penobscot Bay. It was one of several original fishing villages placed upon what was once the eastern boundary of the British territories in North America—fragile outposts against the French Empire to the north and east. Strung along the broad reaches of this enormous bay, Camden and its neighbors Rockland and Belfast provided ready access to the rich fishing grounds of the Gulf of Maine to the south. The earliest fishermen had chosen Camden harbor because its approach allowed unobstructed sailing along the westerly winds and because it had an abundant supply of fresh water tumbling into the sea from Megunticook River and from Mount Battie beyond. Even before Europeans settled on the Maine coast, the native Wabanaki used this location for their summer encampments because its gently sloping beach and flat settlement areas were protected from cold northwest winds by the Camden Hills. These Native American settlers especially favored the two peninsulas guarding the bay's entrance for their temporary villages. Permanent European settlement of this naturally advantageous harbor began in the mid-eighteenth century and continued to expand slowly through all the vicissitudes of the French and Indian War, the American Revolution, and the War of 1812. Almost continuous warfare across the Atlantic

between Britain, France, and the United States characterized the first quarter of the nineteenth century. Camden, like other coastal villages dependent entirely upon the sea, suffered greatly. With the advent of peace after the close of the Napoleonic Wars in Europe, America's seaports, both large and small, burgeoned into maritime centers. Camden, Maine, was no different and grew into a small but dynamic shipbuilding and manufacturing town.

A photograph taken during the last decade of the nineteenth century shows Main Street and Monument Square with its Civil War monument. (The Civil War statue has been moved across the street into the park beside the Camden Public Library to protect it from automobile collisions.) Most of the structures in this photograph remain and still define the same public space of the street. Megunticook Stream flows beneath the street just beyond the single automobile on the right. Camden, like most Maine coastal towns, had public transportation in the form of electric trolleys that ran on tracks down the middle of the street. Another photograph, from a slightly later time period, looks toward the intersection with Main Street across Elm Street to the harbor beyond. To the right, tall elm trees spread over the road. (The Bay View Hotel occupied this space when the photograph was taken. Today the hotel is gone, and the space is a shady village green.) The prominent Opera House still remains as a national historic landmark. Even small towns in nineteenth-century America had opera houses for the many traveling troupes of performers.

By the close of the nineteenth century

Camden had become a thriving town of five thousand. Shipping concerns lined its harbor; the H. W. Bean Ship Yard provided rigging, oakum for caulking seams, and spars for straight masts of native white pine. Opposite stood the Camden Anchor Works, whose hot forges melted out cast iron for the flukes and rings of deepwater anchors. Everywhere were docks and warehouses for lumber, hay, and grain; coal was stockpiled for the cold Maine winters; and other goods were stored that moved in quantity up and down the Atlantic coast in boats of all sizes. Coombs Yard and the Bean Ship Yard built hundreds of vessels of all types. Captain

Stetson, of Coombs Yard constructed more than seventy vessels from 1819 to 1853, including full-rigged ships, barks, brigs, and schooners.[4] Their ships carried products throughout the world, including cotton from Mobile, Alabama, and undoubtedly from Wilcox County and Camden, Alabama, to English mills.

Just one block up from the harbor, at the intersection of Elm, Main, and Bay View streets, stores standing in tight rows filled with fruit, fish, and hardware were located next to banks, a barbershop, a tailor's shop, and several hotels. Stretched farther along Bay View Street were lime kilns and warehouses for processing

4. Dyer, *More Memories of Camden, Maine*, 61.

Elm Street, Camden, Maine, 1915. (Courtesy of Camden Public Library, Frank E. Claes Collection)

the highly flammable barreled quicklime from nearby quarries. And rising above it all was the white steeple of the Chestnut Street Baptist Church. It was a thriving commercial core from which radiated broad elm-lined streets and residential districts with large Greek Revival homes. Gabled ends met the sidewalks as the rows of houses telescoped backward into outbuildings and barns. It was an easy ten-minute walk downhill from most homes to the town center. The street names described the very structure of the town: Commercial Street led from the bustling docks; retail establishments lined Main Street; Bay View Street stretched along the ridge

to the neighboring town of Rockport and provided unobstructed views of Penobscot Bay, blue in the sun. Tall arching elms punctuated Elm Street, which was lined with stately homes of retired sea captains.

Civic pride was evidenced by the many beautiful churches and the Opera House at the corner of Washington and Elm. The halls and rooms of the Masonic lodge occupied the space over the shops on Main Street. Camden had its own fire station, its own post office, and municipal rooms for its many contentious town meetings. Its civic and financial strength allowed it to survive and quickly rebuild after a disastrous fire that destroyed its commercial center in 1892.

Much of Camden's economic robustness came from the Megunticook River, which drops 150 feet from Megunticook Lake into Penobscot Bay and runs directly through the center of town. Today it still flows under Main Street into a pond before splashing into the bay. Its current provided water power for the Camden Grist Mill and for other types of mills that ran along its banks and ponds. A cleverly engineered series of dams pooled its waters into reservoirs that then rationed it out to drive the looms of complexes such as the Knox Woolen Company, the Camden Woolen Company, and the Knowlton Brothers Foundry and Machine Shops. Farther upstream the large Megunticook Mills manufactured woolen feltings for the warm coats necessary for the long, cold winters. While Camden had strong ties to the sea through trade and fishing, it was also a small manufacturing center providing a diversity of employment for its inhabitants. Its tight urban core supplied an assortment of goods and services, all those things necessary for daily life in the nineteenth and early twentieth centuries.

Camden, Maine, has been able to reinvent itself through periods of economic change; first a fishing village, it became a shipbuilding town and then a mill and manufacturing center. Through it all, it has retained its scenic and picturesque qualities; in fact, in the 1960s it was chosen as the setting for the notorious television series *Peyton Place*. Today a large national financial-services institution has renovated the old mills into offices, and it is hoped that

this marks the beginnings of another successful reinvention. The harbor is full of boats, and the streets are crowded with shoppers and tourists—the new and demanding industry of coastal Maine. Camden's inhabitants are no longer confined to the shores of Penobscot Bay. People from all over the world are drawn to its downtown and waterfront, its shops and restaurants. Camden retains its vitality year-round, even during the twilight months of a Maine winter. On an October day, as the red and orange leaves of the sugar maples cover the ground in front of the lovely library, the harbor is filled with the masts of luxury yachts and pleasure boats. At the same time, a continuous line of cars and campers edges up Main Street to turn eastward at Monument Square. This is perhaps a different future than the soldiers imagined on that hot July day in 1863. In form Camden remains much as it was then. It is still a lovely town, having managed to secure a series of successful futures. Will its latest prosperity overwhelm its beauty and detach its older form from a new but perhaps less authentic meaning?

Far to the south, at the other end of the Appalachians, Camden, Alabama, came into existence several decades after its northern counterpart as the county seat of Wilcox County. It is situated on a high ridge in the approximate center of the county amid the coils of the Alabama River. Built in 1858, the imposing Greek Revival brick courthouse sits today in the middle of a beautiful tree-canopied square. Retail stores group around the courthouse and continue one block west. These were formerly small, more generalized "dry goods" stores sell-

ing everything from cloth to cooking ware. In the farming economy of the Deep South, with its long growing season, everyone raised their own food, so there were few grocery or food stores, although just north of the square was a steam-powered gristmill for flour and cornmeal. Two barbershops, a few boarding houses, a sturdy county jail, and a small shop for books and "fancy goods" completed the square.

An enormous livery complex for stabling horses and mules fronted directly onto the courthouse square on the southeast side and took up most of the block. The courthouse was a day's ride or drive from many places in the county, and horses and mules needed to be watered and fed during the long days of town business. The many single-story office buildings around the square for lawyers and surveyors attest that this was a place of property transactions; both law and surveying were necessary

services in a plantation economy based primarily upon large landholdings. For those needing several days to complete their transactions, the Wilcox Hotel on Broad Street provided nearby accommodations. An evocative photograph from 1936 captures the public space of the street and the deeply shaded porches. Running north from the square on the aptly named Church Street were three places of worship, a school, and a Masonic temple. Large homes lined two streets leading out of town that connected to ferry crossings and landings on the nearby Alabama River, Camden's lifeline to the greater world. Camden was a tiny seat of government serving the county with all its necessary offices and other facilities to gather people from outlying areas.

Most plantations in the South had river frontage for loading cotton bales directly onto riverboats. Those around Camden were no ex-

**Wilcox Hotel, Camden, Alabama, 1936. (Library of Congress)**

ception, with landings on the twisting Alabama River, which flowed south to the Gulf of Mexico port of Mobile. Any heavy goods or furniture, such as a plow or a piano, would have been shipped directly upriver to the specific plantation or farm. Consequently, downtown Camden did not have the kind of bulk storage or diversity of commercial ventures of a Maine coastal town, where all things came by boat into the harbor.

Twenty years after the Civil War, the arrival of the Louisville & Nashville (L & N) Railroad had a major impact upon Camden, Alabama,

doubling its population to over a thousand. The railroad installed both a depot and numerous sidings to serve the lumber warehouses along a spur that connected Camden to the main line between Selma and Mobile. Rail service changed Camden's downtown dramatically. Besides the addition of the Liddell Power Company, an ice plant, a ginnery for cotton and a gristmill by the tracks, the downtown now had another gristmill, indicating the switch from cotton to corn, a steam laundry, and the exclusive Baltz Hotel. Soon the courthouse square was surrounded by

several drug stores, a telephone exchange, gro-cery and meat stores, and a new post office, and later in the twentieth century a fancy art deco theater was built. While there was still a black-smith, the liveries had disappeared, replaced by automobile sales rooms and garages. The large livery opposite the courthouse became a filling station and garage. The exclusive residential sec-tion continued up Church Street toward Miller's Ferry, but now there were large, stately Victorian homes with deep porches set within spacious grounds. These elegant homes were for whites, while down by the tracks much smaller "shanty" dwellings occupied the less desirable land. Af-rican Americans had their separate Antioch Baptist Church, while outside town, on Oak Hill Road, was the all-black Women's Board of United Presbyterian Church School. Unlike in

Camden, Maine, in Camden, Alabama, segrega-tion was imbedded within the town's physical form.

Camden, Alabama, retains its elegant neo-classical courthouse, although it has been added to symmetrically on both sides. A photograph taken in 1938, shows the building before these additions. Today a library, instead of a court-room, can be reached by climbing the handsome black wrought-iron stairs. Most civic functions have moved across the street to a bland annex. Law offices occupy many buildings around the square, and the brick county jail remains empty, gathering vines rather than inmates. Gone are the continuous arcades that protected the store display windows from the burning southern sun; gone too are the two hotels, the Baltz and the Wilcox. More than half of the remaining

structures are empty, victims of the move to larger superstores outside of town, although fresh peaches can still be purchased from the back of a pickup truck parked in the deep shade of the courthouse. Down toward the site of the vanished railroad tracks, new trees reclaim the old warehouses and storage facilities of the People's Gin Company.

A walk out Broad Street, which changes to Church Street, transports one to another era. The grand Masonic hall still guards the triangular intersection with genteel Clifton Street. Farther along, two lovely Presbyterian churches, the Baptist church, the original school, and arching trees line the road with tranquil shadows.

In the cemetery, a Confederate soldier stands sentry over his fallen comrades, an affront to the predominantly African American population of Camden. Large houses on wide lots, well removed from the street, continue out Church Street, now interspersed with modern low ranch homes and the occasional empty shell of a magnificent mansion slowly dissolving under the weight of luxuriant vegetation. Timber is now the big industry in Wilcox County. Across the Alabama River, dammed and tamed by a series of locks, Weyerhauser's enormous Yellow Bluff's Plant harvests trees from the region and employs most people from Camden.

On a parching hot summer's day Camden,

Alabama, remains fixed, undecided whether it will dissolve into nostalgia or move elsewhere; its tragedy and its haunting beauty lie in the fact that it cannot prevent the destructive pull of the easy mobility of the highway bypass. Despite their struggles at Gettysburg 140 years ago, those young men could not secure a future for Camden. Perhaps they realized that they fought for a doomed way of life and that Camden's lovely structures and streets would forever whisper their stories with elegant architectural phrases.

In both Camdens the cemetery is located on a main street, within short walking distance of the town center. In the Camden, Alabama, cemetery the final remains of Confederate soldiers and cavalry officers are marked by tilted and fractured headstones beneath the ever-spreading shade of live oaks. Older by two generations, the cemetery of Camden, Maine, slopes gently downhill from Center Street. Its black slate markers are splashed orange with lichen nourished by the damp fog. The act of interment grounds a community to the earth and brings closure to its many individual histories. These cemeteries become the most important witnesses to a town's past, giving each generation a deeper connection to its place. They allow us to attach each name to a time, often to an event, but always to a dedicated, dimensioned space. Perhaps more than any other civic structures, cemeteries imply permanence, row upon row of mute records that can never be moved. In later chapters we will encounter towns without cemeteries. Those towns have lost the opportunity to record their dead, to name them and their places, and are cast adrift in a restless world,

unable to mark those same histories that once brought vitality and life to their streets.

A beautiful park designed by the talented landscape architect Fletcher Steele overlooks the quiet harbor of Camden, Maine. On this green, as in so many New England town parks, a monument stands to those who gave their "lives to put down the rebellion." Seven members of the Twentieth Maine came from Camden. Similarly, between white Doric columns at the entrance of the haunting Greek Revival courthouse of Camden, Alabama, hangs a small weathered plaque that reads, "Enoch Hooper Cook, CSA, 1803–1877, Who gave more sons to the war between the Confederate States of America and the Union than any other man." The plaque lists his eleven sons and two grandsons, all of whom died in the Civil War.

The narratives of the two Camdens serve as examples of the kinds of stories behind all small towns. Many sources provide information for these narratives, such as writings, photographs, and maps. Maps of many descriptions and the mapping process itself elucidate the physical histories of communities. As the discussions that follow utilize different kinds of documents, the comparison of the two Camdens introduces examples of many new maps developed specifically for this book.

Before elaborating on these sources, however, let me offer a cautionary note about maps generally. Maps tell us more about ourselves and our expectations than about the actual world, for mapping is how we imagine *a* world as opposed to *the* world. The very choice of the map implicates us in a particular existence to the exclusion of other, equally true realities. We desire possession of that singular truth that lies behind the scrim of surface cartography. Therein lies our predicament: we constantly use maps to find our way, to explore new terrain, yet we must recognize their limitations as only partial realities. There can never be a map equal to reality—only fragments of an unimaginable whole. Yet both Camdens, as we have seen, are far more than fragments. Each contains enough buildings and structures grouped together to be called an urban form. This book takes the idea of urban form, a hidden territory that we know exists yet that eludes the cartographer's grasp, and, by cutting and segregating many of its components in a process of dissection, attempts to argue for its acceptance as an enduring aesthetic value. To accomplish this I first separate content and form, a dubious approach in dealing with any urban complex. A work of art—and I propose that these small towns are works of art—combines or synthesizes content and form in differing amounts. The more successful the art, the more inseparable content and form become. The conundrum of this comparative study of small towns is that we peel away layers hoping to discover the integrated whole.

We emphasize the importance of physical form in the formation of place, yet few mapping conventions allow this. How do we describe a town's physical dimensions, the reality of its overall form, so that we may begin to discuss its success as a place? Or put differently, how do we know what world we are bringing forth, and how do our maps help us? Maps are always abstractions and can easily become graphic plates in their own right and finished works of art, so let us take some of the maps available to us of the two Camdens and illustrate how each gives specific information about the town's form and, by inference, explains our explorations of other towns in this study.

We begin with the larger context: where and how a town is placed within the landscape. For this information we turn to the most conventional of maps, the United States Geodetic Survey (USGS) maps. These contain a wealth of contextual information: contours, topographic features, roads and watercourses, buildings and building complexes. These maps are published in quadrangles of several square miles at a consistent scale of one inch equal to twenty-five thousand feet. By connecting contiguous quadrangles one can construct a mosaic of a very large area that tells much about a town's founding circumstances. For example, one can tell that Camden, Alabama, sits on high ground amid a series of great loops in the Alabama River and its tributaries. Six roads come together at Camden, connecting Selma and Montgomery to the west by Miller's Ferry across the wide swampy Alabama River flood plain. (The Alabama River is dammed and flooded in this part of the state. Miller's Ferry now lies beneath Miller's Ferry Lock and Dam.) Two other roads stretch southward to Monroeville and the earlier Federal Road and east to Greenville. Easy travel across the high ground of this wet part of Alabama was established by the Native Americans long before European settlers arrived. Camden's location usurped these well-worn trails and continued to reinforce their importance. All these roads came together at Camden's courthouse square, giving it both traffic and trade. Sadly, a modern bypass redirects Route 10 around the downtown and deprives it of the necessary congestion so vital to a healthy commercial center. As with many southern towns, Camden's location as a crossroads within a much larger network reinforced its importance. Camden's placement also reconciled spatial requirements: access to the Alabama River, security from flooding by that same river, and centrality within Wilcox County.

The USGS map of Camden, Maine, places the town at the convergence of many roads radiating outward from the center. These roads connect the town to Rockport in the south and Belfast in the north. U.S. Route 1 travels from Key West, Florida, to Canada, through the middle of downtown Camden. Several other roads lead along the shores of Lake Megunticook directly to the harbor, evidence of the ice industry before the days of refrigeration. The USGS map reveals the dramatic siting of Camden at the head of the harbor, clustered around a freshwater source on a gently sloping "bowl" down to the water's edge. Easy access to the water without interference from excessive tides or storm waves was necessary. Mountains wrap around Camden to the north and west and afford protection from winter winds. Imagine sailing into Camden for the first time in the seventeenth century on a fair wind from the south and discovering so many favorable topographic features. And finding too that Native Americans had enjoyed these same attributes for thousands of years.

Four hundred years later, twenty-first-century journeys provide different images. The familiar photograph of this blue earth floating in the blackness of space taken from an Apollo spacecraft headed to the moon changed the way we view our planet. Since that voyage a bewildering wealth of information has become available from satellite imagery. Maps of entire regions, maps of the bottom of the ocean, and infrared photographs of metropolitan areas are all readily available. Examples of this imagery are used throughout this book, especially when illustrating an entire region, such as the Gulf of Maine or the Allegheny Mountains of Pennsylvania. At the beginning of each chapter a digitally manipulated image positions that chapter's towns within a broader context of regional topography. These maps intentionally delete all cultural references, such as state and county boundaries and highways and other roads. This omission serves to emphasize one of the central arguments of this book: that the form of a town is rooted in its region and topography. More standardized black-and-white aerial photography gives information about the two Camdens not shown on other kinds of maps, such as structures, buildings, and vegetation. Low-altitude aerial photographs taken especially for this book provide detailed views of courthouse squares in chapter 4.

Old photographs, samples of which are included in each chapter, help us to understand the public spaces of these towns. A contemporary photograph of the same space is inevitably filled with automobiles, drive-through tellers, and parking lots. Throughout this book are many sharply focused contemporary color photographs, generally of architectural details or

Camden AL             USGS                          aerial photograph                         1888

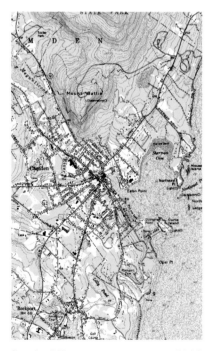

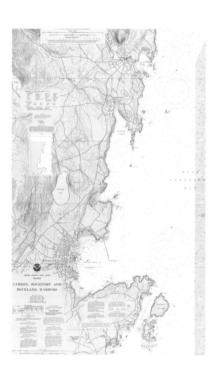

Camden ME            USGS                          aerial photograph                      nautical chart

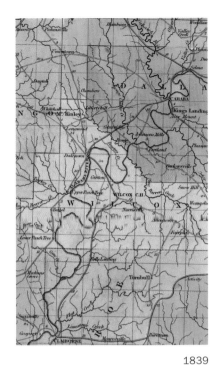

1839

1938

The two Camdens in maps.
(Library of Congress and
Special Collections, Auburn
University Libraries)

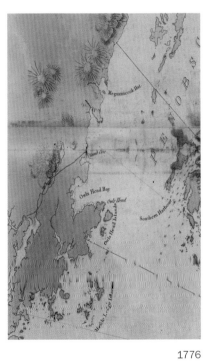

1776

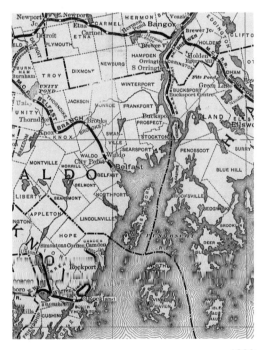

1899

31

abandoned industrial implements from specific towns. These photographs serve as antidotes to the more abstract maps, for they illustrate textures, materials, and uses and are reminders of the layers of richness in every place.

Nautical charts provide information that is very different from the information provided by a photograph of a small detail. Nautical charts are abstractions of a landscape we can never see, one that lies beneath the ocean. They delineate the other half of the context of a seacoast town, for a map of the surrounding land shows but part of the history of Camden, Maine. The approaches from the open ocean, hazards such as submerged ledges or shoals, and water depths are as important as approaches by road or rail. Since Camden, Maine, and many other coastal towns were originally settled from the sea, contemporary nautical charts allow us to infer the many practical concerns and safety issues of the sailors in the early days of exploration. All coastal towns originated during the days of sail, so a knowledge of wind and tide and coastal weather were, and are, necessary to an understanding of their histories. Sailors came to these waters long before the existence of charts or even crude recordings of water depth or local conditions, so our interpolations must be tempered by the information gaps between twenty-first-century and seventeenth-century charts.

A nautical chart of the approaches to Camden shows it to be a fine deepwater anchorage facing southeast into the broad reach of Penobscot Bay with direct access to the fishing grounds of the Gulf of Maine. A fair southwest or southeast wind made Camden an easy reach by sail. The land protects anchored boats from the northwest cold fronts and the fierce gales of a northeaster. After leaving dangerous shoals to leeward, one took a north–northwest course directly into Camden harbor between Curtis Island and Sherman's Point. Most shipbuilding took place not on the town's shore but across the inner harbor from Camden, on Eaton Point. A ship launched in the inner harbor would have run aground on the opposite shore. From Eaton Point the construction ways pointed southeast into broader and deeper waters. This water is fourteen to sixteen feet deep at low tide. By waiting for another eight to ten feet of depth at high tide, one could slide a ship into twenty-five feet of water.

Nautical charts and USGS quadrangles are contemporary maps constantly revised and updated. Many historical documents provide information lost because of subsequent changes in the landscape. A detail from an 1888 map of Alabama and Wilcox County shows the town's relationship to the river, information unavailable today because the Alabama River has been damned and flooded so that its original channel is submerged beneath recreational lakes and navigable locks. Camden connected to Canton Bend by road along a ridge. This high ground protected both the town and the road from flooding but made access to the water difficult. There are many bluffs on this map— Prairie Bluff, Yellow Bluff, and Walnut Bluff— indicating that the Alabama River originally flowed between deeply cut banks and that ferry crossings were important for their graded access down the steep banks. This map also shows that the railroad had not yet extended to Camden.

A detail from an 1839 Alabama map of Wilcox County underscores Camden's significance at the convergence of three roads. (On this early map Camden is referred to as Wilcox C.H.). These roads are like a network connecting county seats across the state: one from Greenville in Butler County, another to Linden in Marengo County, and a third south through Claiborne, the former seat of Monroe County. It also suggests that a circuit judge needed an easy day's ride from court to court. There is a ferry connection across the Alabama River to Cahaba in Dallas County. Cahaba was important because it was briefly the capitol of Alabama, before Montgomery, but was abandoned due to persistent flooding. This map emphasizes that Camden's importance came about as part of a larger political landscape.

Early explorers sailed the coast of Maine in the seventeenth and eighteenth centuries, so there are many maps that locate the earliest settlements. A 1776 map names Camden, Maine, as Megunticook Harbor and Rockland as Owl's Head. Megunticook remains the name of the lake and the river that flows through present-day Camden. This map accurately renders every island and harbor of Penobscot Bay. Of most concern to a ship sailing these waters would be the edge conditions, so where water meets land is drawn in great detail. Inland only the Camden Hills are shown, more as landmarks for navigation than as topographic features.

Most U.S. railroads have disappeared, so we turn to maps of the late nineteenth and early twentieth centuries to discover which tracks served which communities. An Alabama rail-road map from 1938 indicates that the L & N had pushed a dead-end spur up to Camden from the main track traveling south between Selma and Mobile. This same map also shows that Selma had superseded Cahaba as the county seat of Dallas County. The railroad gave Camden a more dependable means of transportation than the constantly flooding Alabama River and dramatically changed the town's form.

By contrast, the railroad never reached Camden, Maine, even though it connected north at Belfast and south at Rockland. Consequently, Camden maintained excellent steamship service to Portland and Boston well into the twentieth century, with an impressive terminal on its harbor. A Maine railroad map of 1899 does show a streetcar connection between Rockport and Camden. (Note the small railroad loop at Rockland. This is the Lime Rock Railroad, discussed in chapter 7.) If one examines the two photographs of Camden earlier in the chapter, one sees the trolley tracks and overhead wires down the middle of town.

The Sanborn Map Collection in the Library of Congress consists of a remarkably uniform series of maps of the commercial, industrial, and residential sections of more than twelve thousand towns and cities in the United States, Mexico, Canada, and Cuba. The Sanborn Map Company published surveys of these towns and cities, building by building, in amazing and very accurate detail. Since these maps were for the specialized and exclusive use of fire-insurance companies and underwriters, they contain such information as construction materials, building heights, building use, window and wall openings, and fire-protection systems, all brilliantly color coded.

D. A. Sanborn, a young surveyor from Somerville, Massachusetts, began his career with the Aetna Insurance Company in 1866, just after the close of the Civil War. In 1867 he established his own company, the D. A. Sanborn National Insurance Diagram Bureau, in New York City. From this modest beginning grew the specialized Sanborn Map Company, which compiled and published maps for the fire-insurance industry for more than seventy-five years. Over the course of the firm's existence it surveyed and produced more than seven hundred thousand of these beautiful maps. Each map was drawn to a uniform scale, generally one inch equaling fifty feet. Each used standard symbolic notations for the detailed information necessary to assess the risk of insuring a particular building or property. Usually at ten-year intervals, the Sanborn Company would revisit towns and cities and revise and update their maps. For most towns and cities these maps constitute a continuous historical record of urban growth and change from 1867 into the late 1940s.

Sanborn maps indicate no topographic context, no contours or other natural features. Since they were published on individual sheets, usually twenty-one inches by twenty-five inches, they must be spliced together to show a complete town. Fire-insurance companies were mainly interested in individual buildings and fire zones. These maps represent, then, financial-replacement value or what was worthy of underwriting risk at any given period in a town's history. As these maps were periodically revised,

they often record the passage of time in fascinating detail; for example, livery stables were frequently renovated to automobile garages. This accommodation or resistance to change becomes a major component of a place.

Documented change tells much about our efforts to inhabit this earth. By reading these maps as serial episodes in a town's physical history, we gain information about the layering of cumulative human adjustments. The Sanborn map of Camden, Maine, dates from December 1884, eight years before the fire of 1892. Buildings colored yellow are wood frame structures, so it can be seen that the downtown was mostly combustible timber except for three buildings at the intersection of Commercial and Main streets and a storage structure in the Anchor Works. Most of these wooden buildings were destroyed in 1892 and rebuilt in brick shortly thereafter. What is important about this map is the consistency with which Camden maintained its compact retail and commercial center through the years. Six streets join in a wonderful public space that continues to guarantee Camden's identity today.

The Sanborn map of Camden, Alabama, asserts the primacy of the courthouse in its public space. The courthouse is brick (replacing several wooden ones also destroyed by fire), as are buildings on two sides of the well-ordered square, a bank, a general store, a dwelling, and a county jail. Almost all building fronts are shaded by arcades. Unlike the apparently random street layout of Camden, Maine, the surrounding street grid of Camden, Alabama, frames the courthouse in its square. Arising from different circumstances that produced contrasting urban forms, both Camdens are compact and concise.

A close reading of both Sanborn maps reveals much about building construction and function. Both towns contained a richness of uses that have disappeared over time. Other aspects too have disappeared: Elm and Chestnuts streets in Camden, Maine, retain their names even though both species of trees have gone from all New England towns and forests. Smith Place, in Camden, Alabama, recalls the nineteenth-century blacksmith's stone shop. Claiborne Street leads to the vanished town of Claiborne's Landing, now flooded beneath the locks and dam of the Alabama River.

These are but a small representative sample of the maps available and the wealth of information obtainable. These are "texts" to be read, each with a different content, that together give a town's history and growth. Each may contain but a single clue that leads to other discoveries that unravel the past and explain a town's placement upon the earth's surface.

But this is a book about urban form, not about maps, even though these maps argue for a particular point of view: that urban form means more than isolated episodes of good design, that it includes the whole composition, the larger landscape, the entire settlement, the streets, the back alleys, the spaces in between, the empty lots, the less distinguished buildings—everything that makes a town both functional and legible. To explain this totality, I have developed abstractions or new maps specifically to compare different communities and to explain

the richness of form found in these many towns. I take all the different information contained in the maps, historic, contemporary, or Sanborns, and layer it onto composite maps of each town. These composite maps can then be computer separated into three distinct layers. One layer contains just the topography as it might have been prior to any settlement; this allows an examination of the care and attention given to the siting of each town. Using topography as a starting point, we can connect backward to those larger geological forces that shaped a given region, with all its distinctive characteristics. In Alabama we observe the alluvial systems of its rivers draining from the Appalachians into the Gulf; in the deep valleys of the coal belts we can see the steeply folded ridges; and on the coast of Maine, the advantages of gently sloping shorelines. We can illustrate the continuity from the grandest history of the earth's surface down to the most local decisions of building placement. It is this continuity, this sense of the historical and ecological whole, that underlies all these explorations and buttresses the argument that a profound and considered connection to the earth renders a place meaningful.

The topographic map of Camden, Alabama, shows the flat area on the ridge between deeply eroded gullies and watercourses that drain to the Alabama River. Camden, Maine, by contrast, sits in a shallow bowl that drains Megunticook Lake down the Megunticook River. Behind the town looms Mount Battie, a hill whose southern face has been deeply plucked by glaciation.

The second layer separated out from the composite delineates the street or road grid, showing

(Following spread, left)
Sanborn map of Camden, Maine, December 1884.
(Library of Congress)

(Following spread, right)
Sanborn map of Camden, Alabama, April 1910.
(Library of Congress)

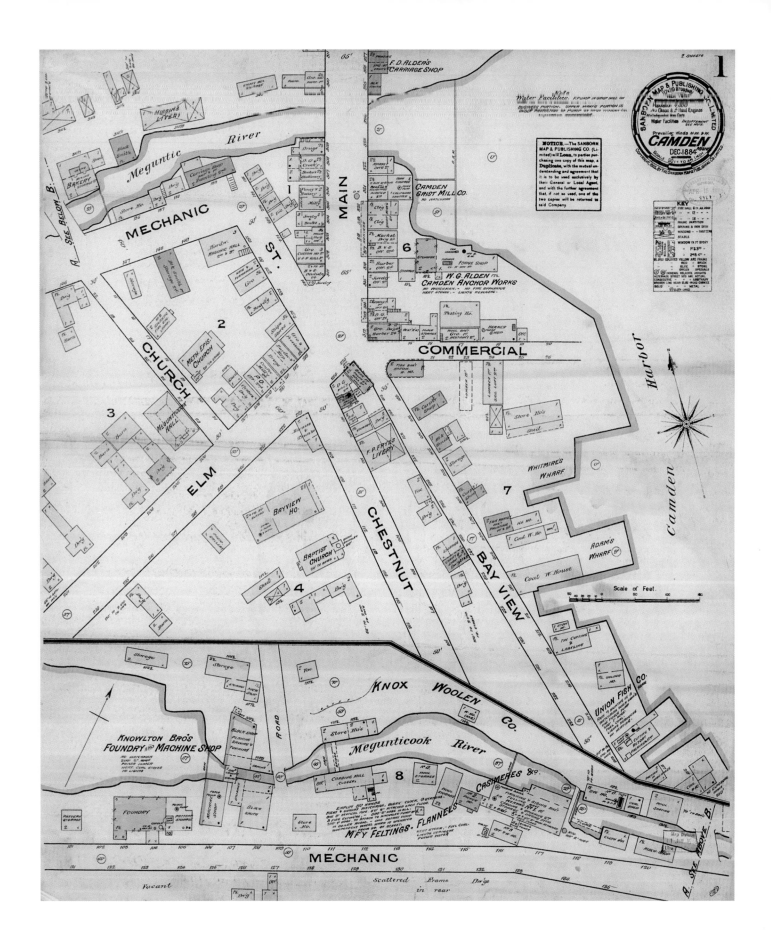

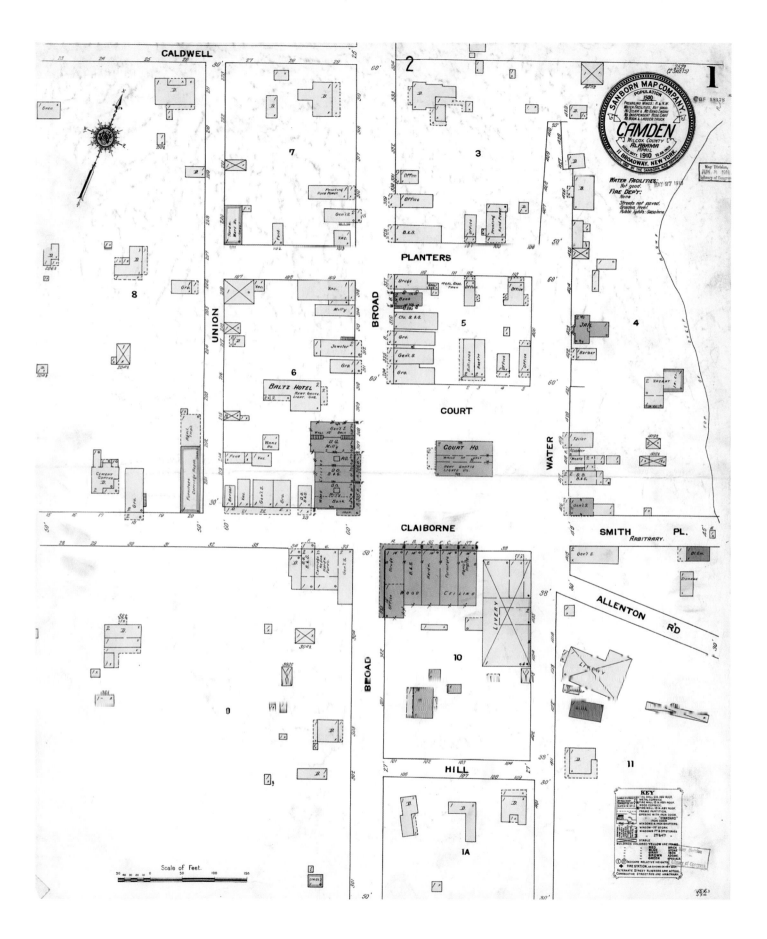

**Layered maps of the
two Camdens**

no buildings or topography. Streets are essential and important public spaces, so we use these abstractions to compare and measure civic awareness and pride. This book emphasizes streets as the most important spaces within an urban fabric, yet streets remain mostly invisible to contemporary American culture. Chapter 2, "The Ubiquitous Grid," explains this methodology of modeling streets as three-dimensional spaces without reference to the enclosing buildings.

A close examination of Camden, Alabama's downtown and courthouse square reveals the two small "ladders" of streets that form its center.[5] These streets are uncharacteristically shifted off of true north because the town could not fit the topography along the ridge line to the Alabama River. A single straight street does orient true north–south just to the left of these "ladders." By contrast, Camden, Maine's streets all run downhill to the harbor, but they most likely grew the other way, radially away from the harbor, since access to Camden for its first one hundred years was from the sea, with nothing but footpaths penetrating inland.

The third layer of these maps, called a figure-ground, shows the buildings as solids, or figures, without any of the normal contextual clues of topography or roads, what would normally be considered the ground. While a figure-ground is an abstraction, figure-ground studies allow comparisons of the forms of communities unencumbered by the overlays of other information. One might think of a figure-ground as a radiograph, a picture produced upon a sensitive surface such as a photographic film by a form of radiation other than light. A figure-ground, like

a radiograph, measures densities: the density of buildings or mass or, by interpolation, the density of economic, retail, or civic activities, and the density of human activity. So we search these studies for patterns of clustering or coalescing. To illustrate the usefulness of these studies, let us compare the two Camdens using just figure-grounds. Both patterns coalesce towards a center, although Alabama's Camden is slightly more structured than Maine's, implying a planned growth sequence. Camden, Maine, wraps around a natural feature, the sea, emphasizing its importance as a magnet for the town's placement. Both patterns lose density and coherence as they move outward from the center. Camden, Maine, is more radial; Camden, Alabama, emphasizes Church Street, stretching to the river. Obviously these towns are self-organizing systems created by a multitude of decisions over time rather than resulting from a larger order imposed at once. Both exhibit a fascinating ability to draw us into their center, to equate density with order, and they force us to discover those ordering devices that seem to go in and out of focus.

Our readings of these figure-grounds of the two Camdens reveals other things about their physical form that we will explore further throughout this book. Besides compactness, there is a hierarchy of public space, with important buildings given priority of place. The courthouse in Camden, Alabama, sits isolated within a larger space; its churches, Masonic hall, school, and cemetery elegantly punctuate the wide avenue leading out of town to the Alabama River. Pride in public space and in the buildings that enclose these spaces is embedded within

5. I am indebted to the book *Ladders* by Albert Pope for the identification of these street grid fragments as "ladders." His book deals more comprehensively with grids of larger contemporary cities.

Camden ME

**Figure-grounds of the two Camdens**

Camden AL

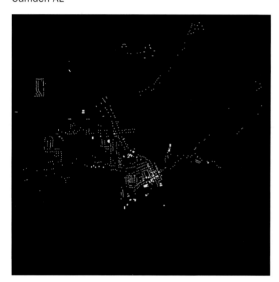

the town's overall structure. Camden, Maine, places its church in an equally prominent place, next to the open village green opposite the Opera House. In the most prominent location, on the hill at the head of both the harbor and Main Street, sits the Camden Public Library, repository of books, knowledge, and history.

Thus we talk of the two Camdens as abstract compositions with qualities, both organizational

and perhaps aesthetic, inherent in their figures. While these maps are abstractions and we can use them as effective tools for study, we must always remember that ultimately they stand for genuine places brought into being by real forces and histories. By illustrating the diversity and similarities of the towns explored in this volume, we discover the richness of urban form in its many permutations, which argues for an

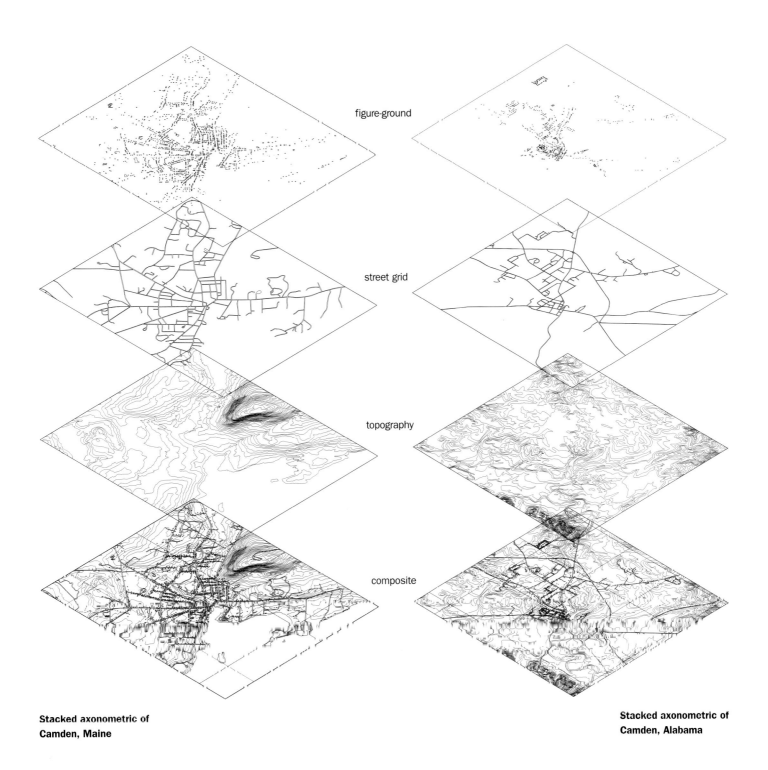

figure-ground

street grid

topography

composite

**Stacked axonometric of
Camden, Maine**

**Stacked axonometric of
Camden, Alabama**

41

aesthetic of urban form complete within itself, worthy of both study and emulation.

To summarize these discussions about mapping the two Camdens, we generate a stacked axonometric that allows all layers to be separated but also shows their relationship to one another. These clearly indicate how all parts of a town work together to become a single composition: the siting within the topography, the public space of the streets, and the clustering of structures all combine to make their urban form an identifiable place.

Both Camdens were perceived by those young men fighting in 1863 and by their other inhabitants as places worthy of civic pride. Their inhabitants agreed that their places of dwelling had both a past and a future, a future worthy of investment beyond expediency and personal gain. This collective perspective enabled both communities to see aesthetic consequences in every act of building. Over the years, in spite of self-organizing and singular decision making, these towns continued to foster and maintain a sense of an aggregated whole. Discrete pieces of architecture like the Alabama courthouse or the Maine public library consistently attest to the importance of civic pride. But these towns today are more than a few significant structures; every part of the existing composition was once valued by its inhabitants. From the rounded corners of buildings at intersections to the continuous arcades, all were part of a common endeavor to make a beautiful aesthetic organization. Both Camdens remain physical evidence of the collective, an abstraction difficult to articulate except through its physical realization.

This book explores many towns as self-organizing systems, towns that maintain their coherence through a long history of contested individual actions that appear to work toward the common goal of an ordered composition. The opposite organization will also be found: planned communities such as the company towns of the coal-producing regions, which initiated their structure through a few overarching design decisions or through a strict regulatory process. This book studies instances of both extremes as it journeys east 40 degrees, yet no town remains a simple example of either totally planned or completely episodic approaches. Every urban configuration contains aspects of both, and it is the tension between the two poles played out over a town's history that makes the study of settlement patterns so compelling. The urban designs of these small towns become microcosms of the balanced constituent elements found in larger cities and in American democratic culture generally.

This summary of maps and other graphic devices uses the two Camdens as examples. As representative towns, they both suggest a definitive and compelling aesthetic that results from a study of the whole composition rather than from studies of individual parts. Chapter 2 reviews the cadastral organizations common to most settlements. The following chapters then begin the exploration of other towns by starting at the southern end of the Appalachian cordillera with the courthouse-square towns of Alabama. At the end of this journey northeastward, chapter 7 returns to other Maine coastal towns.

# The Ubiquitous Grid
## The Cadastral Origins of Urban Form

To take possession of this earth, we first inscribe our desires on paper and then incise them on the land. This process of establishing ownership, so central to the Western mind, sets in motion a whole series of transcriptions that ultimately become the physical demarcations that impart character to our landscapes and form to our cities. Anyone who has flown over the Great Plains of the United States has seen these patterns of property painted the rich greens of agricultural prosperity. To fly over our cities and towns is to recognize the prevalence of structured and ordered settlements.

This telluric marking of ownership is as old as civilization and its permanent settlements. The word *cadastre*—from *capitastrum,* the name of the Roman registry of property, for the purpose of collecting the *capitatio terrena,* or head tax—means the marking of lines or boundaries and the recording of quantities. After the invention of the compass and early measuring instruments these apportioning lines took on an accuracy that could be described by a survey and officially registered on paper. Land became a commodity transferable from one party to another; property could be bought, sold, inherited, freely exploited, and of course contested.

The discovery of the land that was to become the Americas resulted in cadastral disputes beyond anything ever envisioned.

Usually the first mark made upon the newly claimed American continent by Europeans was some kind of property division. During the early years of exploration land could only exist as property of the crown. Royal grants allocated vast tracts to the king's favorites as payment for services. Soon, however, commercial ventures speculated in tiny settlements on these faraway coasts. Beginning in the early seventeenth century as one of the greatest migrations in the history of human existence, the settlement of a seemingly empty wilderness moved inexorably forward until North America's apparently unlimited spaces joined together in a network of public and private ownership from coast to coast.

The colonization of the Americas was also a great land usurpation, as one culture's fixation with possession collided with another's more expansive view of dominion. Native Americans looked on with amusement, then with dismay, as their lands were divided and then "improved" by Europeans. Improvement changed ownership of the landscape from an abstract or emotional attachment to a specific matrix of legal rules that would eventually destroy Native American culture.

One forgets—now that 250 million people inhabit the United States and overdevelopment threatens much of our environment—that there was a time when improvement to land was actively encouraged as necessary for survival. Habitation with all its changes, such as the clearing of forest for agricultural use or for fuel or transportation infrastructure, increased the value of land and was often considered a moral imperative. Unimproved land was essentially limitless and of little value; speculation followed by settlement could make fortunes. Great tracts were bought and sold with little understanding of their boundaries or contents. When one considers that early grants such as Virginia, Pennsylvania, or Massachusetts extended as far as the "South China Seas," one can grasp the absurdity and greed of early land ownership in America.

All this began to change, however, as boatloads of settlers arrived on the shores of this unexplored world. Europeans brought with them different but very determined views on ownership and property rights. Lines were drawn, markers placed, and boundaries walled as immigrants claimed their piece of the new Eden. With the rush to possess land came the inevitable disputes, and so legal restraints and requirements developed to regularize the immense endeavor of settling an entire continent.

The history of urban settlement contains examples of many inventive geometric shapes to regulate ownership. The most universal figure across time is the grid. As an organizing frame for towns and cities the grid traces its history back into the obscurities of earliest human inhabitation. Many civilizations claim the grid's antecedents—China, pre-Columbian America, Europe. Its obvious simplicity of measurement and ease of duplication make the grid ubiquitous in all urban cultures. The rapid unfolding of settlements across previously uncontrolled land contains many examples of gridded plans, from the earliest Roman military camps or the French bastides to the Spanish Laws of the Indies, which governed the establishment of early communities in Latin America. The size of the territory and the speed of its organization, however, were unprecedented in seventeenth- and eighteenth-century America. In the wilderness of this new continent difficult terrain and dense forestation made the clarity of a gridded plan especially pragmatic. Its employment will be found to be universal throughout most of the towns explored in subsequent chapters of this study. Thus, this chapter's organization follows the general outline of the book as a whole— from Alabama through Pennsylvania to coastal Maine. As a region settled according to the Land Ordinance of 1785, Alabama provides the most extensive and detailed illustration of cadastral arrangements.

When applied to thousands of towns stretched across a continent, the grid's repetition in settlement patterns can become monotonous. This repetition, however, gives another, more compelling advantage to the study of urban form. Rather than seemingly abstract and neutral nets placed upon the landscape, unsympathetic to local conditions such as topography or

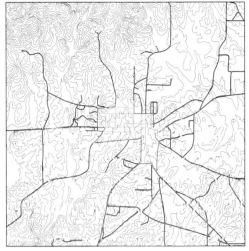

Ashland

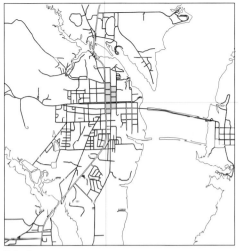

Eufaula

(Left) The grid as datum in Alabama towns

(Right) "Ladders," or fragmented grids, of Alabama towns

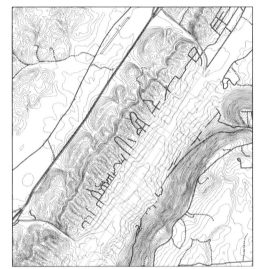

Fort Payne

Demopolis

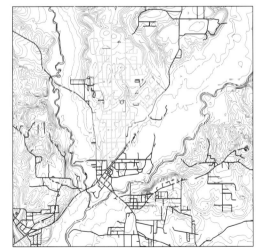

Brewton

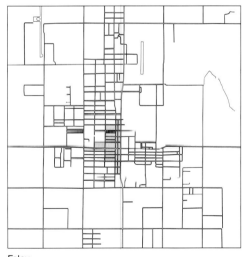

Foley

hydrology, grids can be regarded as a datum, a point of reference from which all subsequent deformations can be measured. Grids are distorted by every kind of local pressure, from terrain to transportation. Three examples from Alabama illustrate this deformation and accommodation. Ashland, Alabama, is a county seat on top of a hill with steep drops on all sides. Its grid clings to a small, flat area. Fort Payne, Alabama, squeezes between ridges of the Appalachians; and Brewton is situated at the confluence of two streams in the swampy lowlands of southern Alabama. At times the grid becomes so incomplete as to form a "ladder" rather than a gridiron pattern. A ladder is an urban splinter of two parallel streets with connecting "rungs" of cross streets. Eufaula, Demopolis, and Foley, Alabama, contain examples of this fragmentation. The grid can cease to be conceptualized as a weapon against environmental character and can become instead a measurement of responses to particular and diverse circumstances. The grids of the towns included in this study are crowded with accommodations and boundary irregularities that anchor them to the earth's surface. This comparison of urban form across a wide swath of North America illustrates many similarly fragmented grids, and in this consistency of singularity lies their beauty. The exigencies of site and place have acted upon them, and this adaptation to circumstances implies permanence.

The advantages of gridded town plans are several. A grid plan more easily relates to the larger county or state plan, and a grid is simple to lay out in the field. Only right angles are necessary, and these can be checked by measuring their diagonals. Pragmatism rather than design innovation was the predominant concern behind these simple town plans. The single greatest virtue of a grid is its acceptability as a generic organization for many disparate sites. If the immediate goal is the equitable and efficient distribution of property, hardly any other system is as efficacious. The grid can be extended indefinitely without altering the fundamental pattern or organic unity of a new town, and property can be apportioned in rectangular plots filling a neatly predetermined scheme of streets. The dimensions of lots within a town's grid may differ greatly from place to place, from the open, ordered squares of a town such as Demopolis, Alabama, to the dense, rectangular blocks of an industrial city like Bessemer, Alabama. Sometimes lots vary within a single town, allowing a wide variation in housing types and building sizes—a flexibility necessary in any speculative venture.

Imagine the complexity of establishing orderly private ownership of an area the size of a new state such as Alabama. Settlers poured in from Tennessee and Georgia; Native Americans were contesting the usurpation of their lands; and the entire state was wilderness, heavily forested mountains, numerous rivers, and extensive swamps. These difficulties were not unique to Alabama; all territories that became states after the American Revolution confronted similar challenges. The new government of the United States enacted the Land Ordinance of 1785, followed by the Northwest Ordinance of 1787, to deal with the rapid acquisition of all lands outside the original thirteen colonies. Because Thomas Jefferson promoted these ordinances, they are often referred to as the Jeffersonian Grids.

The organization was compellingly simple. A north–south meridian was drawn down the approximate middle of a state intersecting with an east–west parallel. Working north–south or east–west from these designated meridians, the state was divided into townships of thirty-six square miles. The term *township* did not refer to towns in any formal or incorporated sense; rather, it was a confusing name for a surveyed area. These squares are referred to as *ranges,* moving east or west from a meridian. Each township is further subdivided into thirty-six one-mile squares numbered sequentially from right to left, top to bottom. Each one-mile square, or *section,* could be easily subdivided again and again down to smaller and smaller squares. A square of forty acres, one-sixteenth of a square mile, was considered the minimal amount for a single family to purchase, clear, and cultivate.

On the larger scale, when a natural barrier such as a mountain ridge was encountered, the grid rolled relentlessly over it. A substantial river or wide bay required partial townships. In the open plains of the Midwest this system promoted an orderly if monotonous landscape stretching to the farthest horizon. In a state like Alabama, however, exigencies of topography, forest cover, or waterways swallowed up most visual regularity. Remnants of the grid survey remain obvious, however, in the straight roads and right-angle intersections around Foley, Ala-

bama, located in the flat outwash plains in the southern part of the region.

The new State of Alabama designated two meridians and three parallels. The Huntsville meridian ran south from the border of Tennessee to the mid-state parallel, and the St. Stephens meridian ran north from Mobile Bay. While these major organizing lines no longer serve any purpose and in fact never really existed except on paper, their "ghosts," or fragments, still form the actual boundaries of a few counties and form Alabama's boundaries with other states. The Tennessee-Alabama line runs along the thirty-fifth parallel, which is also the northern boundary of Mississippi and Georgia. A small town just north of Huntsville is still called Meridianville and connects to Huntsville along Meridian Street North. A ghost of the Huntsville meridian remains in a very short portion of the boundary between Morgan and Marshall counties where they join the northern line of Cullman County, and another ghost of the east–west line runs along the northern boundaries of Coosa, Tallapoosa, and Chambers counties. (See also the map of county boundaries in chapter 3.) The parallel that forms the southern limit of Alabama is, of course, the former boundary between Spanish West Florida and Alabama along the thirty-first parallel, now the northern edge of Florida's panhandle.

All this may seem rather abstract today, but it worked. As the state was settled, smaller and smaller land divisions could take place within the larger ordered grid. As land speculation was rampant in the nineteenth century, disputes could be adjudicated, settlements located, and,

**Demopolis, Alabama**

**Bessemer, Alabama**

**Range-and-township diagram with Foley, Alabama, located within a one-square-mile section**

| 6 | 5 | 4 | 3 | 2 | 1 |
| 7 | 8 | 9 | 10 | 11 | 12 |
| 18 | 17 | 16 | 15 | 14 | 13 |
| 19 | 20 | 21 | 22 | 23 | 24 |
| 30 | 29 | 28 | 27 | 26 | 25 |
| 31 | 32 | 33 | 34 | 35 | 36 |

sadly, Native Americans' lands confiscated and sold. The 1840 map of Alabama illustrates the rigid absorption of Native American lands into this cadastral grid. Interestingly, the boundaries of these earlier treaty cessions were delineated by natural features such as rivers, an indication of the clash between the two cultures and their differing views of ownership. When Native Americans made the original treaty boundaries, they used the physical features of the landscape.

Europeans and later settlers imposed a cadastral abstraction that ignored the realities of the earth's surface.

The easiest way to record the purchase of a new town, as opposed to a township, was in reference to the larger statewide grid. A section or several contiguous sections could be gridded off with streets and lots for sale, and these would orient to the cardinal coordinates of the compass. Many towns in Alabama and all across the

**Foley, Alabama**

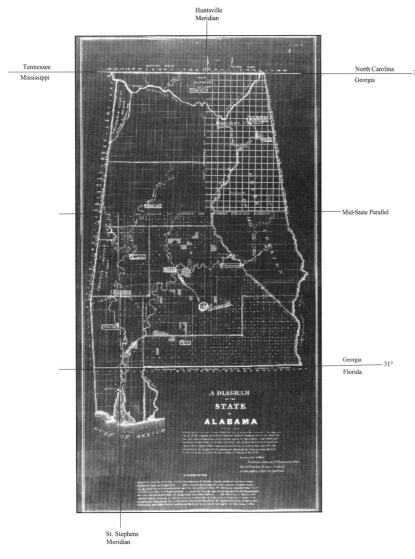

Huntsville
Meridian

Tennessee
Mississippi

North Carolina
Georgia                    35°

Mid-State Parallel

Georgia                    31°
Florida

St. Stephens
Meridian

**Alabama state survey of
1840. (Background map
courtesy of Special Collections, Auburn University
Libraries)**

United States run north–south, east–west. Their grids were simple, easy to lay out, and very pragmatic. What is delightful today is the infinite variety of these grids as they are realized in three dimensions as streets and squares.

Towns in Alabama that lie off true north–south usually responded to a natural feature such as a riverbank or a mountain ridge or a manmade obstacle such as a railroad. A comparison of Bessemer, Fort Payne, and Opelika shows that their street grids parallel the railroad tracks. Railroads needed to be as responsive to topography as did settlements.

Because there is almost no compass declination, or variation between true and magnetic north, in Alabama, these original survey lines orient true north–south or east–west. Since Alabama sits directly below the apparent location of magnetic north around Hudson Bay, Canada, true and magnetic north are the same. Field calculations that adjusted for magnetic declination during early surveys were not necessary, and the streets of most of Alabama's towns run true to the parallels and meridians inscribed on the globe's surface. Given the unreliability of early-nineteenth-century survey instruments and the difficulty of marking true lines through dense forest and uneven terrain, these fortuitous circumstances make many Alabama towns inadvertently "cosmic" in orientation, for their main streets run parallel to the celestial poles of the earth.

Within all of these Alabama towns, the beauty of their retail centers and the richness of their public streets can be traced back to the 1840 diagram for the entire state. What began in 1840 as abstract lines on a map or a piece of paper became, over time, the two sides of a street grid. With buildings defining their edges three dimensionally, the streets became spaces. For the discussions in the following chapters, it is important to visualize the space of streets as continuous and connected. A model of Selma, Alabama, renders the streets as solids to illustrate this continuity of the town's grid. The smallest architectural details reinforce this sense of continuity. Every downtown has examples of buildings with rounded corners that punctuate the intersection of two streets. These details acknowledge the public aspect of the street intersections and the private responsibility for shaping public space. As buildings were extruded along these spaces, around corners and onto other streets, town centers came into existence. A small town represents an uninterrupted process that results in tightly defined prisms of space and not a series of object buildings gathered together. The record of this process lies not only in the buildings; it is also embedded in the "voids," the streets.

Farther east 40 degrees along the Appalachians, steep ridges compressed the ordered grids of towns into rigid configurations unique to the regions of eastern Pennsylvania. Towns in the mountainous anthracite coal regions of Pennsylvania came into existence because of the mechanics of moving coal downhill to long waiting lines of railroad cars. Mine entrances were typically located partway up the slope of a folded ridge. The coal would be moved out of the tunnel to a vast structure called a breaker. The breaker crushed and sorted coal before dumping

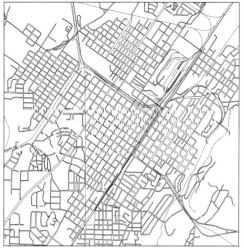

**Alabama railroad-town grids**

Bessemer

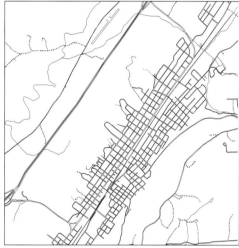

Fort Payne

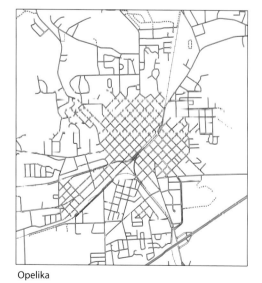

Opelika

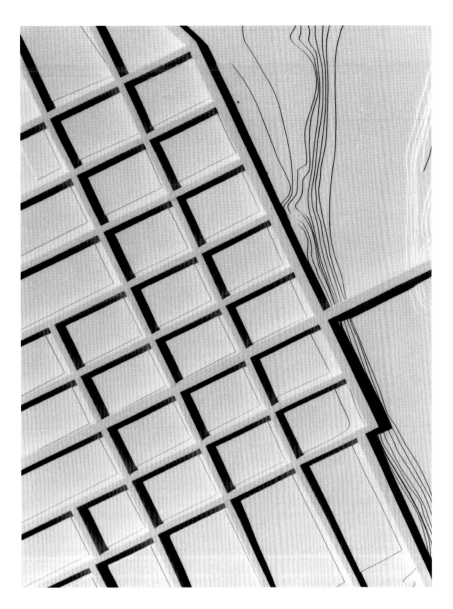

Model of Selma, Alabama,
with street voids rendered
as solids

it into open train cars that moved along tracks located at the lowest point in the topography, along streambeds. The tracks paralleled these watercourses and were able to thread through the mountains to faraway ports. All traffic in and out of these valleys was by train only, so mineworkers had to live within a short, straight walk of the mine and the breaker. Residential streets developed between the breakers in tight lines running parallel to the hilly contours and to the railroad tracks.

These severely constricted sites forced the towns into obdurate grids wedged within the valleys, much like slats on the bottom of a canoe. No concessions were made to public amenities such as in a courthouse square or a New England village green. The brutal pragmatism of the linear grid served but one purpose: to minimize the distance from home to work. As these unyielding lines were built upon and the spaces of public streets were shaped into a community, some remarkable extruded rows of worker housing emerged. Whole blocks, perhaps a mile in extent, are composed of similar simple structures. With the mines closed, the breakers destroyed, and the railroad tracks removed, these residential streets remain the only evidence of some of the most densely populated public spaces of any small towns in America.

Many of the long, linear towns encountered in these studies have been abandoned by their railroad. Their tracks have disappeared, and their main street has been bypassed by a modern highway, yet the towns still align along a forgotten transportation corridor. The survey that determined the track's or road's passage through the landscape firmly marked all futures for that particular settlement. The calipers of those earliest measurements may have been lost, but they refuse to loosen their tight hold upon the present. Each time one inhabits the space of a Main Street, each time one walks along a shadowed sidewalk or halts an automobile at an intersection, one participates in this past. One traverses still those extinguished survey lines that first established these places.

The last examples of cadastral influences on urban form are taken from settlements along the farther reaches of the Appalachians, on the Maine coast. Europeans established villages on the Maine seaboard 60 years earlier than in Alabama and 150 years earlier than the coal towns in the mountains of Pennsylvania or West Virginia. Consequently, these coastal villages arose from a different set of cadastral circumstances and from an interesting contrast to the regularity of later towns. One has only to look at early maps of Maine to see the apparent randomness of the boundaries of counties that lie next to the coast, compared with the north–south grids of those in the interior. Nevertheless, the founding circumstances of these coastal counties and towns remain equally embedded in their urban form today.

Originally these towns along the edges of the bays and rivers were approached only from the sea. There were no roads—nor would there be any for the first one hundred years of their existence. Water frontage was extremely important so that one could land a boat for transportation or fishing. Lots laid out in regular widths of 660 feet or multiples of this dimension paralleled the

**Building with rounded corner, Rockland, Maine**

**Anthracite coal towns of Pennsylvania**

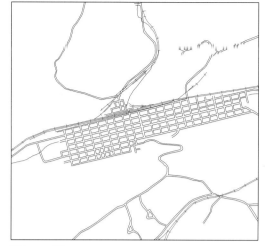

Mahanoy City

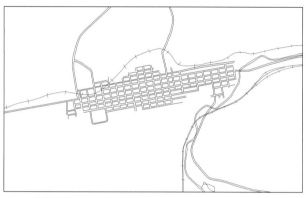

Ashland

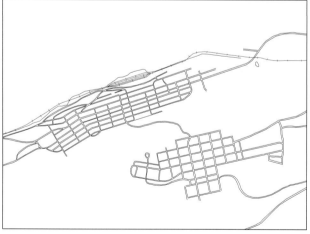

Lansford

shore and extended perpendicularly into the forest a distance ten times the width, or 6,600 feet. All properties had similar access to the water, and each owner could also be deeded several "back lots" for wood for fuel or, after clearing, for pasture. Any lots on streams with potential water power for future mills were treated as more valuable. Mill rights were complicated, as one dam could adversely affect another farther downstream. Mills were also among the first structures built in any burgeoning community.

The site of Bath, Maine, was laid out in the 1760s with a series of long narrow lots oriented east–west that sloped down to the Kennebec River. This allotment of property gave each owner a landing on the water, as well as higher ground for building that would remain safe from spring floods and the excessive tides of the Kennebec estuary. As explained in chapter 7, these waterfront areas of Bath became ideal locations for the shipyards that catapulted Bath into a major center of manufacturing of ocean-going vessels in the nineteenth century. High Street runs perpendicularly to the sloping lot lines—now streets—along the "high" ground of the inland ridge.

Farther east along the deeply indented coast of Maine, Rockland presents a similar pattern of long narrow lots aligned perpendicularly to the water's edge. The lot lines converge at an abstract point located in the harbor. As in Bath, these lines became streets that reached inland to intersect two arced roads that appear as segments of concentric circles. Rockland's unique radial form will be explained in chapter 7 in the discussion of coastal towns. A clue to its origins

lies in the name of the one prominent street—Lime Rock Street—which is not radial but rather wavers through the center of town.

Main Street, Belfast, Maine, records a different cadastral origin. The founding lots on the western shore of the Passagassawakea River ran east–west according to a compass bearing off by approximately 15 degrees from true north. As was usual, alternate lots had town rights of way between them. One of these became Main Street, which eventually extended overland all the way to Augusta, the state capital. This straight line did not terminate in the other direction at the most advantageous place on the water's edge, so an adjustment was made. The major commercial street of Belfast slants slightly northward to end at the "sandy beach" that was to become Belfast's important wharf district. The only clue remaining today of this shift in Belfast's central grid is the short block of Range Street. The acute angle between Main Street and Range Street is occupied by an oddly truncated bank building with a nine foot facade fronting on Customs House Square. (See the photograph of this space

**Property lines, Bath, Maine**

**(Opposite) Property lines, Rockland, Maine**

High Street

Kennebec River

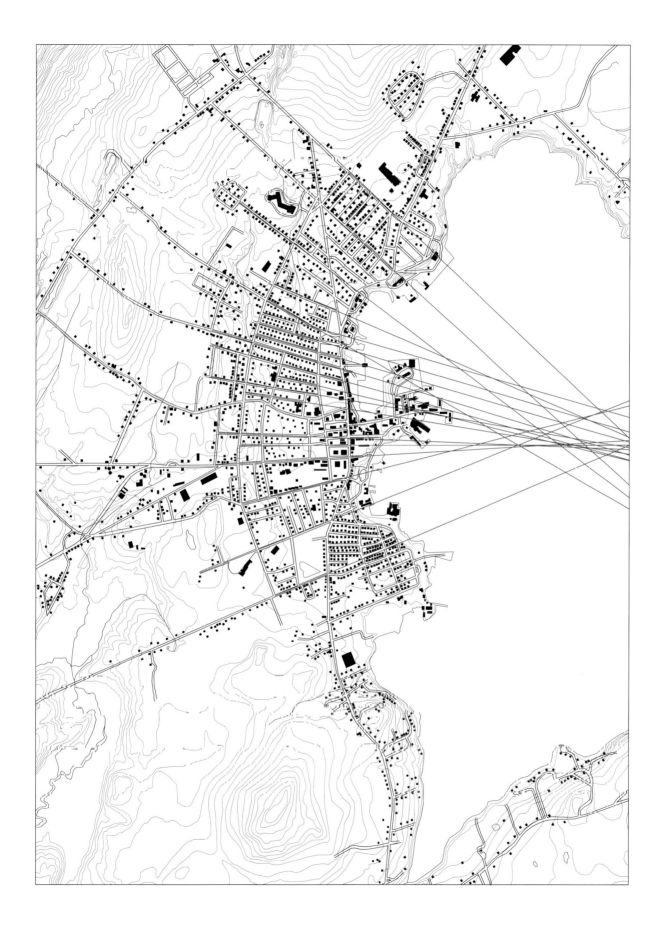

Property lines, Belfast, Maine. Adapted from the plat map of 1768 for the Waldo Patent, a subordinate land grant that the Plymouth Council portioned out to Maine in the seventeenth century.

True North

N
E
W
S

Variation 17° 30'

Salmon St.

Wright St.

Main Street to Augusta

on page 212; the bank facade is on the right.) It is entirely possible that Range Street refers to the original east–west range and township line that ran along the property boundary between the earliest lot lines.

These examples from different places along the Appalachian Mountains serve as reminders of our connections to a past hidden behind the scrim of time. In the chapters ahead there are many similar instances of survey lines whose influence remains long after their original intent disappeared. These cadastral marks persist, embedded in a town's form. From these first attempts to locate ourselves within a new terri-

tory derives a contemporary physical presence, be it an active main street, an entire downtown grid, or a somnolent courthouse square. The connection of these civic or public spaces to their originating survey lines anchors the towns to the past and to the earth's surface. The figure–ground analysis of three linear towns that will be studied in later chapters illustrates that similar forms may have different founding circumstances. Bath, Maine, runs along a river on the slope of a drowned valley flooded during periods of glaciation; Mahanoy City, Pennsylvania, sits in a valley between the entrances to two coal mines; Fort Payne, Alabama, clamps

Bath ME

Mahanoy City PA

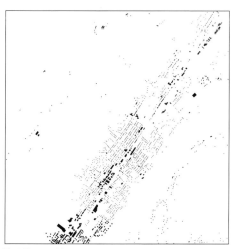

Fort Payne AL

**Three linear towns**

**(Right) Eufaula, Alabama**

onto a major railroad line that travels between two parallel ridges. These three studies are positioned on the page with north upwards so that their conformity with the twists and turns of the Appalachian Mountains can be compared. Bath orients north; Mahanoy City reflects the eastward bend of the Pennsylvania mountains; while Fort Payne tilts 40 degrees east of north, parallel to the folds of the southern Appalachians.

Each generation reinforces these marks by building structures, by forming spaces, by adding improvements. Even the simplest gestures of daily life, such as walking along a sidewalk, deepen the meaning of these first strokes upon the earth. These accumulated transactions over a town's history concentrate layer upon layer onto a street or other public space. If we consider a town's streets as being like repeated pencil marks on a blank white page, then each mark upon another blackens the sheet until a density of graphite appears almost etched into the multitude of strokes. With our inhabitation, we are the markers. Through our desires and designs we too etch a density upon the earth's surface and validate a place.

# 3

# Shared Realities

## Courthouse-Square Towns of Alabama

Records of those most common yet uniquely individual of human events—birth, marriage, death—are deposited within a county courthouse. Each county witnesses the passage of time with thousands of these occurrences, its people certified with untold births and deaths and licensed marriages. Without the institutionalized records of these events, the very fabric of our society would cease to exist, for we require both a place and a time to become members of a community. Until recently these events were recorded on parchment or paper. As handwritten documents they could not be easily dispersed, so they were collected and concentrated in places of public access. A county's or a town's records are priceless evidence of the diversity of ordinary passions through time; their archives are haunted rooms filled with clues that lead us into the rich labyrinth of human experience. Property rights too are inscribed within these walls. Even though land is mostly permanent, its ownership slips easily into the shadows of memory. Titles, deeds, and surveys are all required to prevent disputes. Courthouses gather these records of human aspirations and acquisitiveness into one place to avoid the transitory diffusion of agreements over time. And of course some people came to these same courthouses

to exercise that most basic of rights, the right to vote.

Tragically, racial differences were brutally segregated in southern towns, foreclosing any meaningful discourse between whites and blacks and depriving blacks access to those services and goods available within a community's center. Two parallel cultures were perniciously institutionalized until the civil-rights clashes of the 1960s. This injustice was the legacy of many of these towns, so poignantly told in Harper Lee's book *To Kill a Mocking Bird,* written in 1960. This story of prejudice and bigotry—and tolerance—is reenacted each year as a play on the courthouse square and in the exquisite second-floor courtroom of Monroeville, Alabama's historic center.

All these myriad legal transactions within a courthouse required an equal diversity of associated occupations, such as clerk, lawyer, and surveyor. Those taking advantage of the courts and records also required retail services such as hotels, restaurants, and livery stables. Traveling salesmen, land speculators, and landowners all jammed into the corridors and vestibules when the circuit court was in session. The streets and squares of the downtown were filled with people, wagons, cars, and produce. Advertise-

**Figure-grounds of court-house squares in Alabama showing a fifteen-minute walk radius centered on the courthouse**

Athens

Ashland

Scottsboro

Eutaw

Elba

Camden

Courthouse square,
Athens, Alabama
(Courtesy of Limestone
County Archives)

ments promoted goods and services, especially on the back streets, away from the major public spaces, where horses and wagons were once quartered. Later automobiles delivered clients and petitioners along the wide green space surrounding the courthouse. Passenger railroads placed stations a short distance from the square; hotels and restaurants clustered closely so that people could walk from one to the other and to the courthouse. Freight offices such as those of Railway Express and storage warehouses for baggage grouped nearby. Figure-ground studies of the six courthouse squares discussed in this chapter indicate a density of built form within the radius of a fifteen-minute walk centered on the courthouse. The pedestrian established the dimensions of the county seat, and that human scale remains embedded in their form.

A region's courthouses are a public landscape, the idea of democracy condensed into repeated formal episodes. J. B. Jackson wrote in *Discovering the Vernacular Landscape* that "landscape is a concrete, three dimensional shared reality."[1] Courthouses, courthouse squares, and counties, with their boundaries and connecting roads, constitute a uniquely American landscape, a web of relationships whose connective sinews tighten in regularly spaced knots of concise urban form. The wonderful episodic variations within the greater consistency of these knots of form scattered across regions constitute the basis for this chapter's comparisons.

County government is unique to regions where property ownership, especially land ownership, is paramount. This type of government is common in agricultural areas that were settled

1. Jackson, *Discovering the Vernacular Landscape*, 5.

rapidly outside the original thirteen colonies and also in most southern states whose societies included slaves as property. By contrast, in the more mercantile North, town-meeting government took precedence over county government as the smallest political unit, and the town hall or meeting house assumed greater presence. In the port cities and towns of the original colonies along the Atlantic seaboard, federal customs houses rather than courthouses became the most significant buildings in an urban setting. A shipping merchant in coastal Maine probably owned just the few acres around his residence; his real wealth was scattered across the globe in ships, whose cargoes were recorded in the customs house so that the federal government could collect duties.

In the South, the courthouse, along with the post office, was one of the first structures built before actual land division and ownership. Settlement required surveys and boundaries, and recorded deeds needed collection and repository lest disputes become too numerous and complicated to be adjudicated. Unimproved land was potential wealth and was quickly apportioned. To give an idea of the speed with which settlement took place, consider that Alabama's population increased from about 120,000 in 1819, at the beginning of statehood, to over a million just after the Civil War.[2] As the population exploded, records increased proportionally, so that the original simple courthouses were quickly replaced with larger and more elaborate structures. Often the building existing today is the fourth or fifth structure on the same site. As the population increased, the size of the counties

shrank to absorb the increased density of people and legal transactions and to allow equal access to the county seat.

A map of Alabama shows the county boundaries of 1839. A later map, of 1866, marks a significant number of land offices, built as the railroads began carving out their rights of way. This map also overlays the county boundaries on the range-and-township grid. The establishment of county boundaries was necessarily contentious as large landowners protested the arbitrary division of their particular landholdings between county jurisdictions. Since the county is the basic political unit for voting, electoral redistricting caused incredible disputes. Arguments about the courthouse's location were even more antagonistic, for the courthouse was a magnet for development. Settlers knew that while the courthouse and its immediate space would be public property, all surrounding parcels were ripe for speculation and development. Often an individual would donate the land for the courthouse knowing that profits would accrue from the sale of the inevitable commercial properties that would soon surround the government building. Competition at times became so intense that entire county records would be spirited away in the dead of night to a new location owned by another individual equally disposed to dubious gain.

Coupled with these speculative demands were several very real topographic constraints: the courthouse must be in the geographical center of the county, and it must be on high ground free from flooding. The court's main constituency could not be separated from the county

2. Richardson, *Alabama Encyclopedia*, 333. Alabama grew most rapidly in the years between statehood and the Civil War.

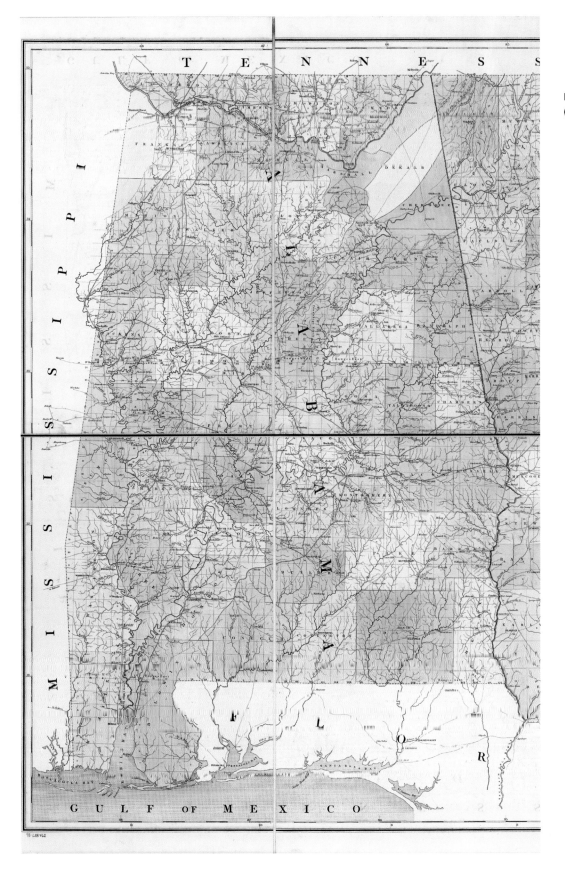

**Map of Alabama, 1839.**
(Library of Congress)

69

State of Alabama, 1866.
(Library of Congress)

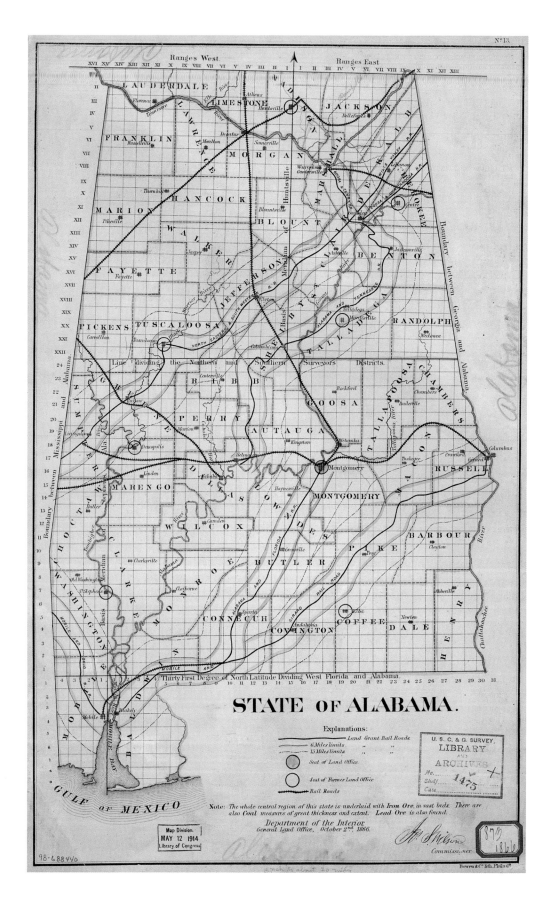

seat by a major watercourse. Initially in newly formed states, judges traveled from one county court to another on a regular circuit—hence the name *circuit court*—so the county seats had to be within a day's ride of each other to allow the circuit judges reasonable distances between sessions. To make these constraints more difficult, the number of counties in a new state were constantly increasing in numbers. Over a hundred-year period the number of counties in Alabama went from zero to sixty-seven. With each shift of boundaries, accommodations had to be made all over again to political, topographic, and ownership concerns. Yet over time all these influences were gradually negotiated or adjudicated until the counties and their seats were spread uniformly across the entire state in a clear example of a spatially constructed emergent form, a true shared landscape.

Not all courthouse squares are configured in the same way, and the seemingly subtle distinctions result in major differences in the spatial experience of a downtown. The most common arrangement is the block square, with one block of an otherwise consistently square grid plan reserved for the courthouse. The geometry of this plan forces all the town's blocks into squares as well—a shape less conducive to housing lots. This is why so many courthouse-square towns contain "ladders," incomplete grids that quickly dissolve into more random residential neighborhoods because of topographic constraints. These towns have a center grid only a few blocks in length. Eutaw, Alabama, is an example of what could be called a ladder configuration.

Much has been written about the origins

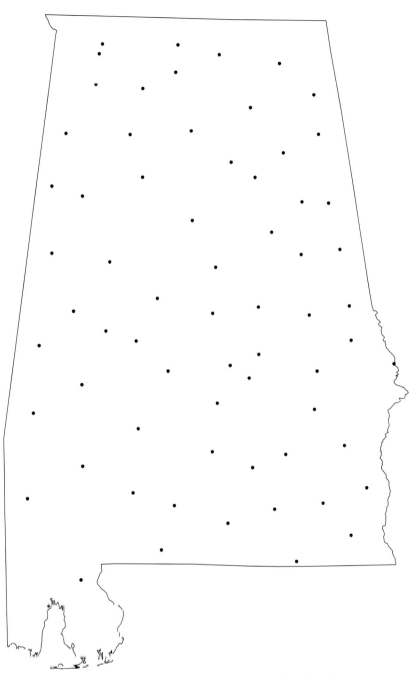

**Location of Alabama county seats, 2004**

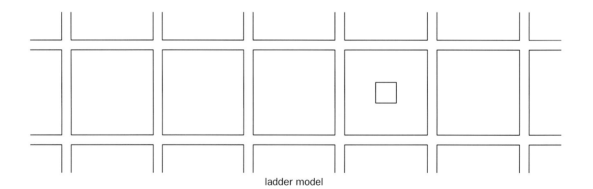

block-square model

Philadelphia model

combinations of Philadelphia and block-square models

ladder model

and spread of the particular urban form of the courthouse square from Europe to America and then across the new colonies. Philadelphia, with its centrally positioned city hall, seems to be one of the earliest antecedents in the American colonies, and because Philadelphia was the most important city in America in the eighteenth and early nineteenth centuries, its influence spread widely. Lancaster, Pennsylvania, and Shelbyville, Tennessee, are two early examples of courthouse squares built by settlers moving away from the Atlantic coast. From these examples, with an infinite variety of configurations, the courthouse square spread across the Midwest and into the Deep South.

The Philadelphia model is the most complex and least frequently repeated model. The streets enter midblock, affording dramatic axial views toward the courthouse or, in Philadelphia, the city hall. This configuration also forms four awkward reentry corners with no frontage, which makes retail development difficult. In Alabama only three out of sixty-seven county seats are arranged in this way. Another variation is the four-block plan found in many towns, with slightly different permutations. The framing blocks are divided in half, affording axial views of the courthouse, much like the Philadelphia plan without the awkward corners. The increased density of streets means more outside corners around the square and a reduced sense of enclosure, and it decreases the framing effect of the storefronts. While these differences may appear abstract, when elevated into building masses and enclosures of streets, the variations order and give character to an urban composi-

tion. For this study, it is instructive to see how the simplified type—the block plan—is used in vastly different topographic situations without losing its salient spatial attributes.

A public square uniformly enclosed by other structures has been common to most cultures since the beginning of settlements. The Roman agora was usually enclosed by an arcade that hid the irregularity of other buildings. Medieval monasteries also had ordered and arcaded cloisters set among the more random composition of the whole complex. Repetitive facades enclose the Place des Vosges in Paris, giving order to the very irregular urban fabric of the surrounding neighborhood. What is different from these European examples and unique to the courthouse square is the placement of a structure in the middle of its defining and ordered space. Development actually began with the courthouse; the square was built later. The courthouse was usually the first building erected in a new county, and it seemed reasonable to surround this structure with a buffered space to allow maximum flexibility in speculative land development. This buffered space was intended to protect the courthouse from fire, always a recurring problem in the eighteenth and nineteenth centuries since open flames were used for lighting where paper documents were stored. The great number and variety of courthouse squares across America reflects this pragmatism. Most later courthouses were constructed of masonry for additional fire protection. Some buildings, such as the Eutaw, Alabama, courthouse, also had steel shutters on the windows.

A study of county boundaries is the study

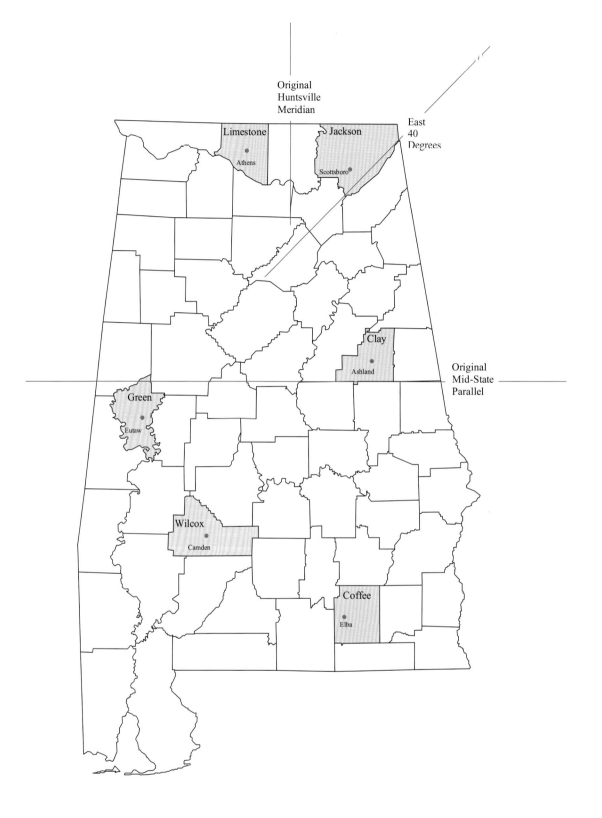

of a political ideal mapped upon the earth's surface and the accommodations of these cultural abstractions to the realities of topography. County boundaries are wonderful conceits upon the land. It is as though someone outlined topographic features such as mountains or rivers with a black pen and drew imaginary lines boldly along the ridges or upon the water surfaces. The lines are not there, of course, existing only as bold circumferences on our maps, yet the county is etched into our culture as a real place. The center is the focus, the hub, the county courthouse in its space. As Faulkner wrote in *Requiem for a Nun*, the courthouse is the "protector of the weak, judicate and curb of the passions and lusts, repository and guardian of the aspirations and hopes."[3] In the South especially, one comes from a county rather than a town. A person from Camden, Maine, comes from Camden, whereas a person from Camden, Alabama, comes from Wilcox County.

An examination of the county boundaries of Alabama reveals a combination of straight lines and highly irregular edges. The straight lines are those surveyed according to the original sectional lines of townships and ranges laid out when Alabama became a state in 1819. The irregular edges are watercourses that serve as boundaries. It was advantageous to keep as many streams and rivers as possible on the edges of counties so that travel to the county seat did not necessitate crossing one of these frequently flooding watercourses. Two counties whose seats are used as examples in this chapter illustrate these different edge conditions: Coffee County, in the wire-grass region of southern Alabama,

has four straight sides (with a small notch out of the northwest corner) running in the cardinal directions. By contrast, Greene County, in the more alluvial western part of the state, is defined on all boundaries by two rivers that join at the county's southern tip. Limestone County, in the north, is bounded by the Tennessee River; nearby, Jackson County's eastern boundary is a ridge line of the Appalachian Mountains that orients east 40 degrees.

The even geographical distribution across a region, coupled with the consistency of urban form within each county seat, is not unique to Alabama or to the Southeast. This same political landscape can be found all across the southern and midwestern United States. Texas, the largest state with county government, has 257 counties; Georgia, only slightly larger than Alabama in area, has 159, almost three times as many as Alabama—a very fine grain indeed of tiny urban centers.

To illustrate this universality, the courthouse-square towns in this chapter sample Alabama's topographic areas: Elba, in the flat south, is threatened constantly by the flooding of the Pea River. Ashland is in the rolling ridges that begin the Appalachians, and Eutaw is in the rich cotton-growing belt of the west. Athens sits in the fertile flood plain of the Tennessee River; and Scottsboro perches on the edge of the Cumberland Plateau, deep in the Appalachian Mountains. These selected examples from widely varied geographical regions tell much about the ability of a single building, the county courthouse, to order and shape urban space.

Elba sits precariously within a triangle of

3. Faulkner, *Requiem for a Nun*, 40.

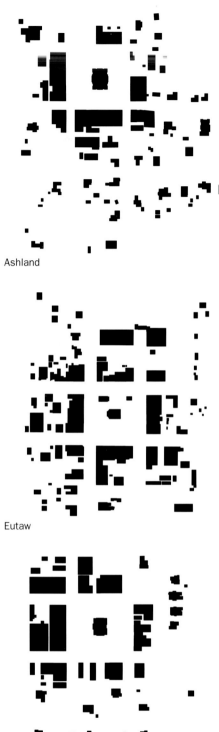

**Figure-grounds of Alabama courthouse squares**

Ashland

Eutaw

Elba

land at the confluence of two creeks and the Pea River. Flooding from these watercourses so frequently menaces Elba that a high red earthen levy surrounds the town. In Elba's case, water, not fire, has destroyed the county records multiple times throughout its history. Today the courthouse sits in a large flat square within the town's street grid, which, like the larger county boundaries, orients to the points of the compass. Dry cleaners, antique shops, hardware stores, and a new library enclose the square. Pearl's "World Famous" Deli offers both hearty southern breakfasts and quiet views of the square and its somber red brick courthouse. The old county jail sits empty, pushed back against the great mound of the levy.

The repeated and disastrous flooding of Elba has taken its toll on the surrounding residential neighborhoods. Many beautiful old homes have been abandoned, leaving the town center isolated within its fluvial landscape, not unlike its apocryphal namesake, the island of Elba, Napoleon's place of exile. A Sanborn map of 1930 labels numerous buildings as "flood ruins," attesting to the site's continued history of inundation. As a result, Coffee County uniquely has two competing county seats—Elba and Enterprise—both periodically submerged in this region of Alabama thickly laced with streams and creeks. Coffee County affords little high ground, and thus the federal government constantly restructures the levy and struggles to protect the original folly of Elba's placement within its alluvial landscape.

By contrast, the seat of Clay County, Ashland, sits in the gently rolling farmland of the lower reaches of the Appalachians. Its archetypal square and neoclassical courthouse rest on the crest of a ridge; its tall and distinctive dome is visible from all directions. Capped by a statue of a woman holding the scales of justice, the court-house presents a dramatic image of democracy made "concrete" within a distinctive landscape of small farms and modest properties.

Ashland's courthouse has four classical por-ticoes, facing the four cardinal points. Magnolia trees anchor the corners of the grassy plinth surrounding the structure. Single-story arcaded stores and municipal buildings frame the entire composition. The town hall, the police station, the county board of education's offices, all are just a short walk across the square; a beautiful old hardware store, a cleaners, and restaurants remain as authentic parts of a concise commer-cial core.

The naming of county seats and counties reflects the importance of history to their early inhabitants. Many of the county seats and their counties formed after the Civil War referred to other places. In 1866 the citizens of Clay County named their new seat, Ashland, after the estate of Senator Henry Clay in Kentucky. The county was named after the senator himself. Along with Daniel Webster and John C. Calhoun, Sen-ator Clay was fondly remembered for his efforts to hold the union together during the second quarter of the nineteenth century. Because of its hilly topography, Clay County was made up mostly of small landholdings with few slaves, and its representatives voted against Alabama's

Athens

Camden

Scottsboro

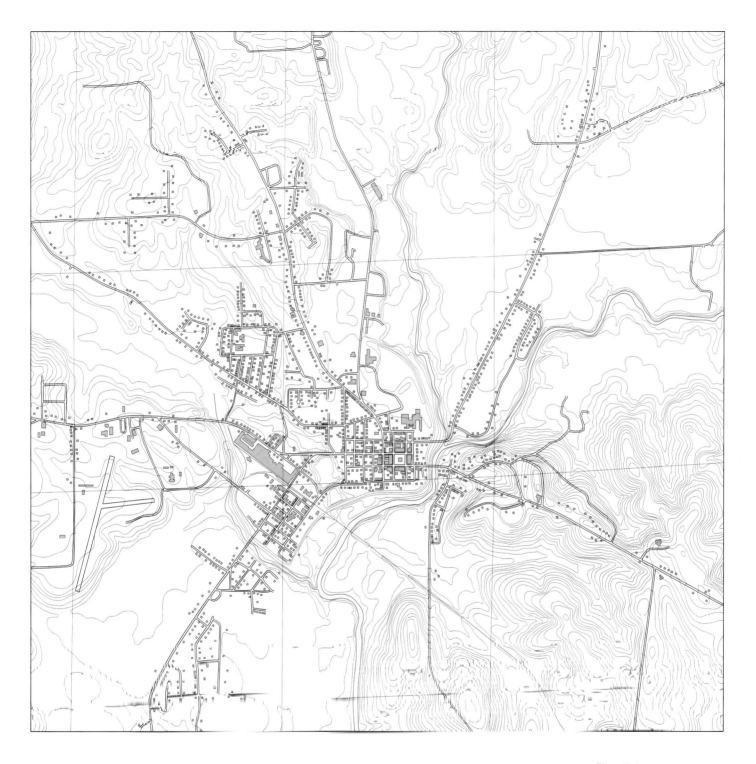

Elba, Alabama

(Opposite) Courthouse-
square towns of Alabama

**Courthouse, Ashland,
Alabama**

secession from the Union. Perhaps its name represents a revisionist history, a wistful alternative to the carnage of the Civil War.

Almost 150 miles west of Ashland, Eutaw, seat of Greene County, rests in a flat alluvial landscape crossed with creeks and rivers. Formed before the Civil War, the country was named for General Nathaniel Greene, a hero of the Revolutionary War. Eutaw was named after Eutaw Springs, South Carolina, the location of General Greene's defeat of the British in 1781. Five roads converge at the site of Eutaw, Alabama, coming together in a most unusual courthouse square. The roads come into town from Tuscaloosa and Mobile by way of Demopolis and connect to several river crossings on the Tombigbee and Black Warrior rivers. The court functions are housed in three structures: two small pavilions at opposite corners of the square and a large central building housing the courtroom. Located on the second floor, the courtroom was reached by a

grand stairway with wrought-iron balustrades. The two original ancillary structures contained the probate office and the grand jury room. A third pavilion is labeled "fire department" in a 1909 Sanborn map, and the fourth, now a fountain, was the city standpipe, a large cylinder to hold water with direct pipe access to the street water mains for fire protection. The separation of functions in different buildings was in response to the constant danger of fire.

Today Eutaw's quiet center belies its more hectic past as a thriving urban center. About 1855 its downtown contained the following: a courthouse, four dry-goods stores, one clothing store, a confectionary, a bookstore, several groceries, three hotels, several boarding houses, a carriage facility and harness maker, five churches, two newspaper offices, a Masonic lodge, and three schools. Clearly Eutaw once prospered.

Far to the north, Athens, the county seat of Limestone County, sits in the fertile flood plains of the Tennessee River. Athens marks a crossroads that collected produce from the surrounding farmlands and connected to an important ferry crossing. Later, when the railroad pushed south from Tennessee to Birmingham, James W. Sloss, a wealthy plantation owner and member of the board of directors of the Louisville & Nashville Railroad, made sure that the tracks ran through his hometown. The tracks continue straight south to the river, connect with the line coming east from Huntsville, cross at Decatur, and run southward through Cullman to Birmingham. Because the land around Athens is flat, the linear requirements of the railroad and the existing town grid were

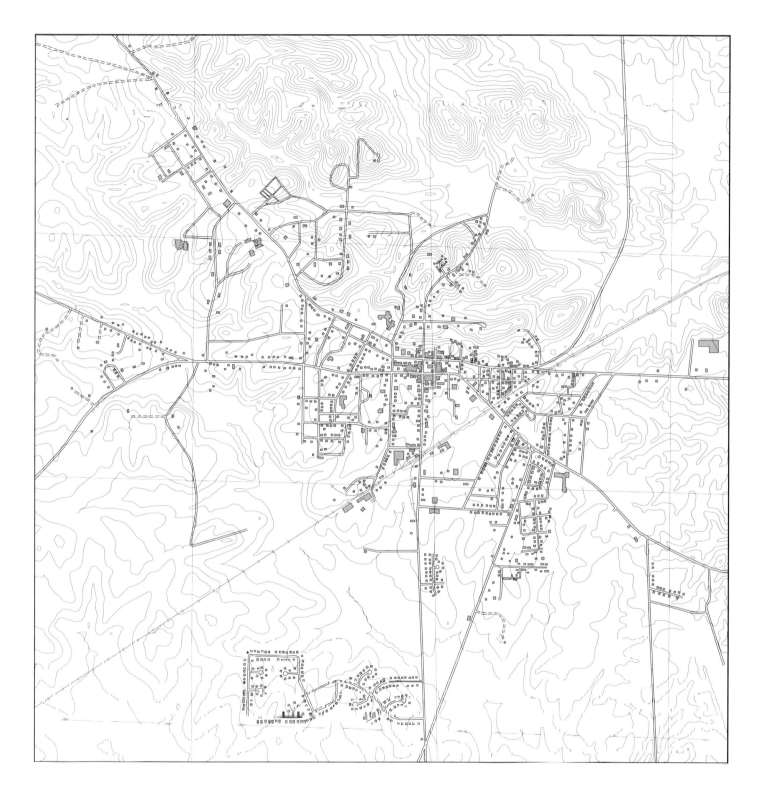

**Eutaw, Alabama**

**Courtroom entrance, Eutaw, Alabama**

easily resolved with no deflection in either. Roads, tracks, and topography all conspired to focus attention on the tranquil space of the courthouse square.

Not far to the east of Athens, Scottsboro sits on the important railroad line that follows the Tennessee River westward to Corinth and Memphis on the Mississippi River. Like the Tennessee River itself, this track follows a fault in the Appalachian Mountains southward and then turns abruptly west to wind through a series of valleys before coming out on the flat plains. It makes this turn at Scottsboro by bending around the two lobes of the Appalachian foothills called Tater Knobs. Scottsboro had no way to develop except southward, so it is asymmetrically placed along the tracks. The town illustrates a dramatic accommodation to topography, bringing together roads, railroads, and topographic features, all resolved elegantly in a tightly enclosed courthouse square.

History gives us many examples of the balancing of competing interests through order or ordering agreements. Laws and regulations admit to differences among individuals in a society yet allow agreed-upon methods for accommodating these differences in a common purpose. These agreements allow society to differentiate between public responsibilities and private ownership. The same is true of most urban compositions, although the agreements are less codified. Throughout the history of settlements certain status and privileges and restrictions have been given to the most public spaces so that the more private spaces could be utilized to suit the individual owner's concerns.

The many small courthouse-square towns of Alabama offer instructive lessons in urban design. Order prevails; the courthouse sits in the middle of a landscaped space; the commercial structures all defer and frame this space both through a regularity of height and a consistency of setbacks. Sidewalks and arcades reinforce the overriding order of the total composition. Urban form encompasses space as well as building solids. The streets and open spaces of these courthouse squares constitute the primary public network. Sometimes the streets bend around the courthouse to make a square within a larger grid. There is a hierarchy of streets, a main square, side and back alleys. There are service streets that face the railroad tracks and heavily traveled streets that lead to other towns.

These squares act as public meeting rooms with a series of ordering agreements. First, all buildings line up along the enclosing sides of the square. None shift back or protrude forward; no blank spaces or "missing teeth" occur in the fabric. Public street intersections are recognized by private buildings with rounded cornices, terminating turrets, or bow windows at corners. Today, whenever a building is torn down or a drive-through bank teller or gas station is inserted, enclosure is reduced and the drama of the space dissolves. The second agreement is uniformity of height. Almost always the dome of the county courthouse is the highest structure. With few exceptions these squares do not have buildings more than three stories high. Individual cornice lines may vary, but there is a sense of meeting the sky with a substantial parapet or cornice.

Store entrances that invite and display windows that come to within a foot of the sidewalk

(Left) Athens, Alabama. (Right) Scottsboro, Alabama. (Aerial Experts)

EAST SIDE OF SQUARE.
ATHENS. ALA.

**East side of courthouse square, Athens, Alabama. (Courtesy of Limestone County Archives)**

recognize the importance of the pedestrian. Overhangs and arcades protect from sun and rain and unify disparate facades. The surfaces of buildings are broken up with windows and well-scaled materials such as stone lintels and metal cornices. All these agreements are met with restraint, yet with no sacrifice of individuality. Every decision, every detail, every sign respects the continuity of the street composition. The whole becomes greater than the parts—the essence of true urban form.

To understand the extent of the respect given to the public spaces of the courthouse square, one need only look behind the enclosing buildings to the hidden back alleys and service drives.

These represent the chaos that results from individual necessity. Loading bays, trash receptacles, and utility lines all fill these rear spaces. Yet these alleys are intrinsic to the form of the complete town. All those messy service functions that take place here, without which a commercial endeavor could not exist, protect the agreements of the public facades. Alleys represent a decision to allow the building front to enclose a civic space that belongs to the community and to relegate individual needs to a secondary but no less important rear space.

Successful urban form requires not only order but a hierarchy of order that leads from the surrounding agricultural landscape into the

Classical details from courthouses in Ashland (left) and Athens (right), Alabama

town's center or that moves from the openness of the residential areas to the closed service alleys and side streets to the main space of the courthouse square. The courthouse sits within a very ordered frame, and it is no accident that the architecture of courthouses, the preeminent example of both urban and societal order, is most often classical in style—the most hierarchical architectural order of Western culture.

When people are brought together into a desired density, their myriad interactions provide a surplus of benefits and amenities. Clustering buildings together creates a compositional unity and pleasure that none can give separately. An individual building may be a work of architec-

ture, but many buildings together bring forth another kind of art. A courthouse without its square does not offer the same beauty that the entire composition of the courthouse and its square offers. Compositions of buildings allow the creation of other kinds of spaces. A public realm is created that all share: streets are formed, corners turned, longer perspectives open down an avenue or across a tree-shaded square. Space between buildings has a proportion and quality of its own beyond the structures that create it. Successful urban form takes all the elements that make our environment—buildings, sidewalks, signs, traffic—and weaves them together with dramatic results. For a small

Trade Day, 1924, court-house square, Athens, Alabama. (Courtesy of Limestone County Archives)

town is truly a dramatic event in the larger agrarian landscape.

As these chapters travel east 40 degrees to study other, similar places, they pose questions about the decline of many of these towns, including courthouse squares. The proliferation of newer spatial settlement patterns such as malls and linear strip developments privatizes and even trivializes our need for places that encourage concentrations of differences. Do we still respect our public realms, or do we no longer care to walk upon the stages of Main Street and courthouse squares? As these public stages disappear, the drama of our lives will diminish.

# 4

# *Urbis* Alabama

## River, Wagon, and Railroad Towns

*U*rbis, from the Latin root *urbanus,* refers
to the form or physical artifact of a city or
town. The form of a town is distinguished from
the inhabitants and their collective actions, the
*civitas.* For the ancient Romans the town, or
*urbis,* was a place to dwell and a place to come
together to exchange ideas, goods, or produce.
Historically, all settlement patterns serve this
purpose through a concentration of form rang-
ing from several structures to vast cities with
millions of inhabitants. Today *urban* generally connotes these larger groupings, especially
enormous centers such as New York City or Los
Angeles, including their larger metropolitan and
regional surroundings.

Alabama, by contrast, has traditionally been
viewed as the most rural of states, with its great
fields of cotton depicted in antebellum literature
and dirt-poor farmers described in Depression
writings, a region left behind by mainstream
development. In the title of this chapter two apparently disparate words are joined—*urbis* and
*Alabama*—and this chapter argues a radical position: that Alabama is settled town urban, not
rural, in character and settlement. Alabama's
settlement pattern consists of tight, distinct
groupings of structures spread evenly across an
agricultural landscape. Of course, neither towns

nor agriculture exist separately: towns need
farmland for sustenance, and farms need towns
to distribute their produce. At the confluence
of these two needs arise settlements, along with
their necessary connections to a wider transportation network, be it river, road, railroad, or sea.
This chapter focuses on the influence of Alabama's natural features upon transportation and
the effect, in turn, of both transportation and
geography upon urban form. These dependencies upon earlier infrastructures may have lost
their original significance, leaving behind towns
no longer tied to geography, yet the physical
form, the artifact of the *urbis,* endures as vivid
evidence of humans' ability to construct towns
and cities collectively.

The narratives of the individual towns of
Alabama begin before the arrival of Europeans,
with the rich but tragic history of Native American settlements. Always located in the most
advantageous locations, these earlier societies
lived in large, permanent villages safe from the
region's constant flooding. Cleared land was especially valuable in such a heavily forested area
as Alabama, so European settlers usurped these
sites for their own towns. There are many examples of this expropriation, for almost every town
in the state sits on a former Native American

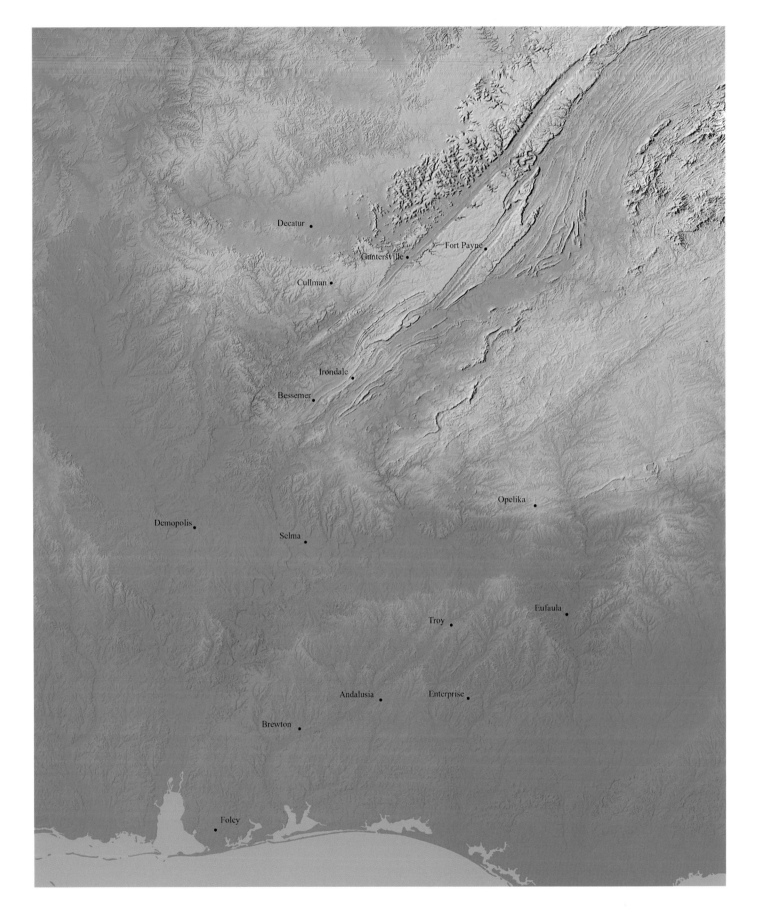

site. Etched into the vowels of so many Alabama place names are the spectral images of these forgotten cultures; their eradication is made all the more haunting by the tenacity of their words within our own contemporary world. Names like Coosa, Tallapoosa, Wetumpka, even Alabama, form enduring and fitting memorials to the vanished nations of the Creek, the Cherokee, and the Choctaw.

Abundant moisture falls across Alabama from the southernmost folds of the Appalachian Mountains in the north to the swamps and bayous of the Gulf coast. Rain in the north gathers in the Tennessee River as it flows west across the state before turning sharply north to join the Ohio River and then the Mississippi River for a thousand-mile journey to the Gulf of Mexico beyond New Orleans. The segment of the Tennessee River that crosses Alabama drains some of the richest farmland in the southeast. This area also had the decided advantage that cotton grown in this valley could be floated downstream to New Orleans on flatboat barges or steamboats.

In the lower half of Alabama, hundreds of small creeks drain off the Appalachians and fill rivers like the Coosa, the Tombigbee, the Cahaba, or the Tallapoosa, which are all gathered by the Alabama River to flow southwesterly into the vastness of the Mobile-Tensaw Delta and eventually into Mobile Bay. The deep swamps and secret bayous of this delta remain one of the largest unspoiled areas in the state and at one time presented an impenetrable barrier to overland travel. These two separate drainage systems, the Tennessee River basin and the Alabama River basin, touch only as tiny rivulets along the ridges of the Appalachians and made it impossible to travel by water from north to south in Alabama. (The Tombigbee Waterway, a series of locks and dams, now connects the Tennessee River with the Alabama River and Mobile Bay.)

The many navigable waterways that funnel southward into Mobile Bay compensate for this lack of continuity in north–south river travel. Other than the straight Chattahoochee, which defines the boundary between Alabama and Georgia, and a few smaller streams that flow into Pensacola Bay, all these Alabama rivers skirt the western end of the Florida Panhandle and collect at Mobile. A beautiful map from the late seventeenth century illustrates the confluence of Alabama's rivers at Mobile Bay. This accident of geography was fortunate since Florida, all the way west to Pensacola along the thirty-first parallel, belonged to Spain and then England in the early days of Alabama's statehood.

Although Alabama has little coastline, its rivers afforded access to the fertile agricultural lands of the interior. The low gradient, lazy currents, and sweeping bends of these rivers provided plantations with maximum frontage to their banks along their entire course. By comparing the lower river courses with the rich arc of the Black Belt agricultural soils, one sees the fortuitous circumstances that promoted cotton growing. The best soil in the state has the most water access (see the frontispiece). Given this funnel-like drainage pattern of the cotton growing area, Mobile's development as a port city was inevitable, as water drained to its bay and cotton arrived at its docks.

With a flat gradient, a watercourse sweeps back and forth within its soft alluvial flood plain, forms oxbows, meanders, and of course floods across the shorter distances between bends. Three river towns discussed in this chapter—Selma, Demopolis, and Eufaula—sit on bluffs on the outside or farthest swing of riverbanks high above flood level and away from the hydraulic forces of meandering. (The Chattahoochee River at Eufaula has been dammed, and the resulting lake has submerged the original riverbanks.) The erratic seasonal flow of Alabama's rivers and creeks, which remain dry and shallow in the summer and are full and flowing in the winter and spring, created equally unpredictable boat traffic. River steamers tied up at the banks without benefit of wharfs or structured landings. A town's access to the water was often a great mud slide down a steep bluff.

Demopolis on the Tombigbee, Eufaula on the Chattahoochee, and Selma on the Alabama River all developed as major river ports because they were safely above high water. Produce, mainly cotton, from some of the richest agricultural counties in the region came to these towns on their protected bluffs to be loaded and carried downstream to the Gulf. Frederick Law Olmsted, in his compelling book *The Cotton Kingdom* (1850), provides a detailed description of the loading of cotton bales, each weighing more than five hundred pounds, onto a steamboat bound for the Gulf:

There was something truly Western in the direct, reckless way in which the boat was loaded. A strong gang-plank being placed at right angles to the slide-way, a bale of cotton was let slide from the top, and, coming down with fearful velocity, on striking the gang-plank, it would rebound up and out on to the boat, against a barrier of bales previously arranged to receive it. The moment it struck this barricade, it would be dashed at by two or three men, and jerked out of the way, and others would roll it to its place for the voyage, on the tiers aft. The mate, standing near the bottom of the slide, as soon as the men had removed one bale to what he thought a safe distance, would shout to those aloft, and down would come another. Not unfrequently, a bale would not strike fairly on its end, and would rebound off, diagonally, overboard; or would be thrown up with such force as to go over the barricade, breaking stanchions and railings, and scattering the passengers on the berth deck.[1]

Olmsted could have been describing the chalk bluffs at Demopolis. Demopolis rests against the outside of a deep hairpin bend in the Tombigbee River just below its confluence with the Black Warrior River. Demopolis's main street once terminated at an indentation in this bluff, giving access to the river below. No longer tied to the water, this street reaches back along an open square to the town's commercial center. Demopolis is unique in having square blocks (rather than rectangular ones) that move evenly out from the center until stopped by the surrounding wetlands. The tightness of its site made it impossible for the town to expand.

1. Olmsted, *Cotton Kingdom,* 214.

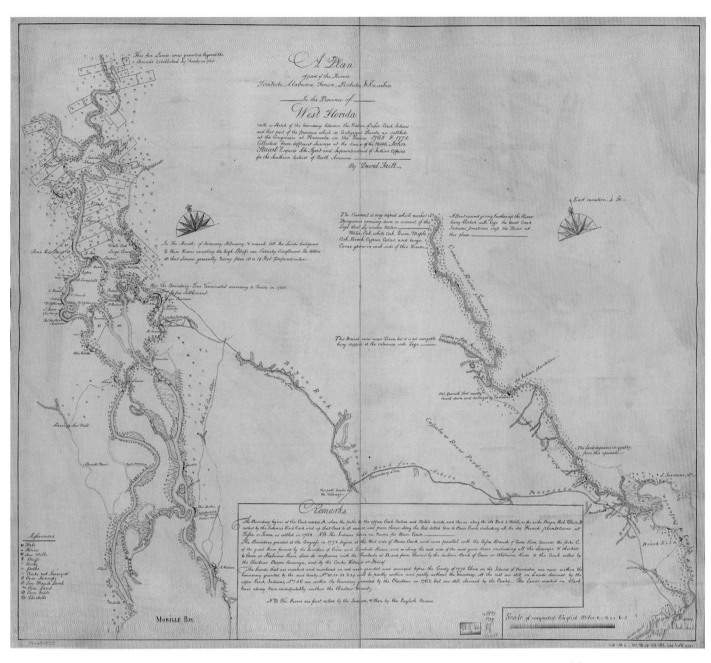

A Plan of part of the Rivers Tombeebe, Alabama, Tensa, Perdido & Scambia in the Province of West Florida, on. 1771. (Library of Congress)

**Topography of three**
**Alabama river towns**

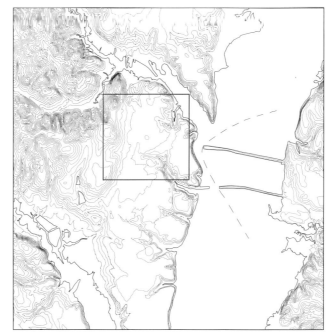

Eufaula

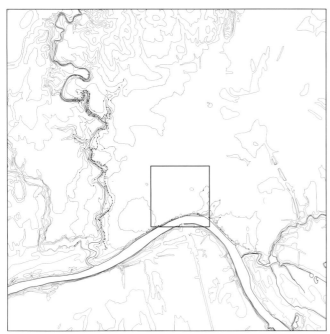

Selma

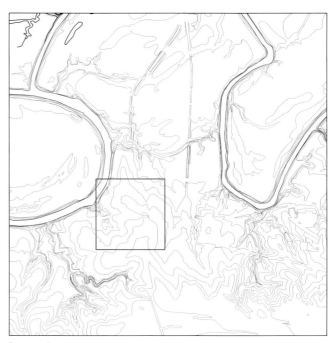

Demopolis

Demopolis, whose name means "city of the people" in Greek, was settled in 1817 by aristocratic refugees known as the Vine and Olive Colony from Napoleon's France. With little experience in agriculture, they tried unsuccessfully to grow grapes and olives in the acid soil of the Black Belt. Within a few years they were forced to relinquish their town to nearby American settlers because they had erroneously built on land not included in their original claim. The French vacated their site, retreated to New Orleans, and eventually returned to France.

Like Demopolis above the Tombigbee, Eufaula, whose name is from the Creek name Yufala, sits upon a high bluff above the Chattahoochee River. Like most rivers in Alabama, the Chattahoochee is now dammed into a lake, but early maps show a convex bend at Eufaula that remains outlined in the part of the bank still visible above the new shoreline. Eufaula's main street once led to the steamboat landing far below the current water level. A forgotten line of street trees remains as a ghost of this former connection. An important north–south road from Columbus to Fort Gaines passed through Eufaula, so its center became a crossroads. The east–west axis leads from the river through the main intersection, up a hill, and into the rich farmland beyond. When the railroad replaced river travel, the depot was also placed as a terminus on the same axis. Eufaula is a simple diagram of spaces once drawn together and connected to a river through a dense urban intersection.

Selma has had a series of descriptive names emphasizing its advantageous location: Bien

**Cotton warehouse, Selma, Alabama**

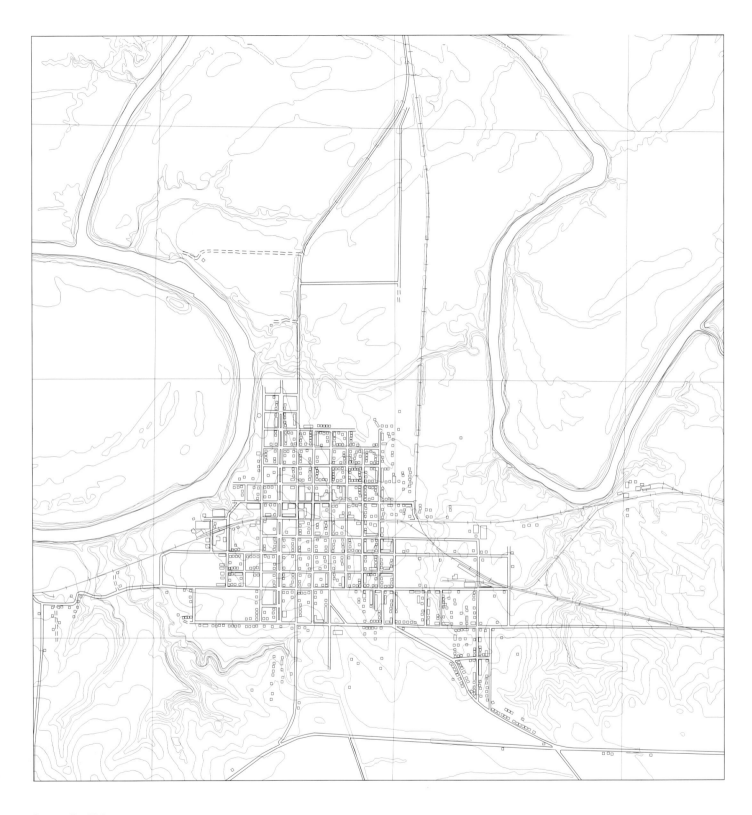

**Demopolis, Alabama**

ville's Bluff, High Soap Stone Bluff, and Moores's Bluff. William Rufus King, of the speculative Selma Land Company, borrowed the name Selma from *The Poems of Ossian,* by James MacPherson, and renamed the town in 1819.[2] In one of history's strange twists, another man named King, Dr. Martin Luther King Jr., put Selma firmly on the world stage in 1960 as he began the march on Montgomery in Selma's public spaces. Like Demopolis and Eufaula, Selma too orients its main street perpendicularly to the Alabama River, but the river landing is now the Edmund Pettus Bridge to Montgomery. Along this main street sits the commercial and retail center; to the west the grid continues into beautiful tree-lined residential streets. During the Civil War, Selma became one of the South's important industrial and munitions centers, with extensive rail connections. However, the railroad shifted the grid away from the river as it traveled west. A seam of a different texture is apparent between the two grids; the earlier one orients to the river, while the later one conforms to the tracks.

Unlike the previous three towns, Decatur and Wetumpka are "portage towns." Taken from the French word *porter,* "to carry," *portage* is the term for a place in a river where navigation is not possible because of rapids or rocks. Boats and cargo had to be unloaded and carried around the obstacles and reloaded on the other side. Decatur, named after Stephen Decatur (1779–1820), a hero of the battle of Tripoli in 1804 and a commodore in the United States Navy during the War of 1812, sits on the Tennessee River. The Tennessee River was navigable up-

Coca-Cola sign, Demopolis, Alabama

stream from its junction with the Ohio River in Kentucky all the way to Florence, Alabama, and from Decatur, Alabama, to Knoxville, Tennessee. Between Florence and Decatur were thirty-seven miles of impenetrable rapids known as Muscle Shoals. (These formidable obstacles now lie submerged beneath the lake impounded by the Wilson Dam, constructed in 1924.) Attempts were made to circumvent the rapids by canals and aqueducts. Decatur, on the high bluffs of the original southern bank of the Tennessee, became a portage town where cargo was unloaded from boats and loaded into wagons for the overland journey around these obstacles. Decatur's main street runs perpendicular to this long, straight stretch of the river and connects its commercial

2. Foscue, *Place Names in Alabama,* 125. Selma was the palace of Fingal, father of Ossian, the hero of the Ossianic cycle of poems.

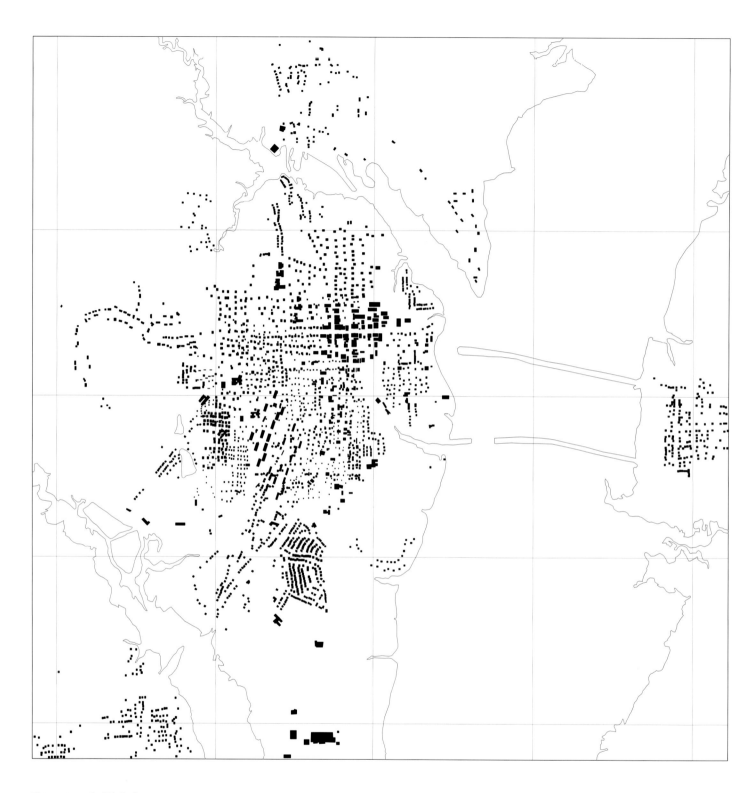

**Figure-ground of Eufaula,**
**Alabama**

PERSPECTIVE MAP OF
SELMA, ALA.
COUNTY SEAT OF DALLAS COUNTY.
1887

center to two distinctly different residential neighborhoods. In the mid-nineteenth century the expanding Louisville & Nashville Railroad extended southward to Birmingham, crossed the Tennessee River at Decatur, bifurcated the town physically and racially, and installed a major repair facility in its midst.

Like Decatur, Wetumpka is also a portage town. As one moves upstream along any of Alabama's rivers, one eventually encounters the hard rock of the Piedmont Plateau in the form of rapids or waterfalls. Shallower, smaller craft with as little as twelve to eighteen inches of draft could continue beyond this point, but their cargo had to be unloaded and carried around

the falls or rapids and reloaded for the longer trip upriver. At this fall line on the Coosa River, Wetumpka came into existence very early in the nineteenth century. The name Wetumpka, meaning "tumbling water," comes from the Creek words *wi,* "water," and *tanka,* "sound,"[3] so Wetumpka endures as a euphonious legacy of a vanished culture and a submerged landscape. The original course of the Coosa River lies beneath a series of dammed lakes, and Wetumpka's commercial core lies on one side of the river, opposite its residential section on the other.

Before impoundments behind the dams of the Tennessee Valley Authority submerged entire landscapes, the Tennessee River had three

*Perspective Map of Selma, Ala.,* 1887. (Library of Congress)

3. Ibid., 147.

**L & N Railroad caboose, Decatur, Alabama**

important crossings in Alabama. One of these, at Guntersville, sits on a high ridge on the southern bank at the easternmost ford, where the river makes its dramatic turn out of the Appalachian foothills into the broad valley to the west. A large Cherokee settlement was established at this strategic location. As early as 1818 it was a preferred river crossing for settlers from the north, with a ferry service run by Edward Gunter. The original banks of the Tennessee disappeared under the present impoundment behind the Guntersville Dam in 1939, but the town remains on the northern end of Dividing Ridge, now the terminus of an artificially created peninsula. A major overland route northward out of Alabama travels up Big Spring Valley onto this ridge and is carried steplike across what is now a series of islands. Highway 421/231 follows this path through the center of Guntersville and over a long bridge northward. Earlier this road, named the Dixie Highway or Florida Short Route, brought people in automobiles south from Chicago to the Gulf coast on the roads that follow

the ancient trading ways of Native Americans. Guntersville developed as a linear town along an important trading route on high ground safe from floods. Today a drowned landscape surrounds the town, while ridges and islands dot the water, hinting at thousands of years of history submerged beneath its surface.

Our comparative examples of river towns include the port towns Selma, Demopolis, and Eufaula; the portage towns Decatur and Wetumpka; and the river crossing or ferry town Guntersville. An examination of their comparative topographies proves the soundness of the original Native American choices for settlements at the six locations. All are situated on flat sites high above the water that allowed, except in the case of Demopolis, the one chosen by Europeans, wide expansion away from the river's edge. A comparison of four representative street grids—of Selma, Demopolis, Decatur, and Eufaula—reveals that the grids are typically parallel to a tangent along an outside bend and that none of the grids deflect in response to the curved bank. In these four towns the main core of retail is gathered away from the embankment into a tight knot of buildings that makes a definite urban space. In each town this intensive grouping of buildings forms a street that once extended over a bluff to the river below. With the almost yearly catastrophic flooding against this bluff, there was little incentive to build permanent structures any closer to the river.

What is remarkable is how a single street with a minimum number of structures can ground a community to its original reason for existence. The space of the street emphasized

Decatur, Alabama

Wetumpka, Alabama

100

Guntersville, Alabama

101

Selma

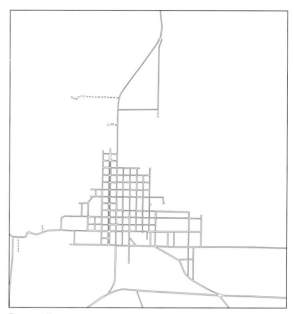
Demopolis

**Street grids of Alabama river towns**

4. Bartram, *Travels, and other Writings,* 357.

by the buildings leads inevitably to the river. The diagram remains simple and powerful as a way of binding settlement to an important natural feature. This relationship is all the more remarkable for its persistence through many changes. The rivers have disappeared beneath dams; railroads and highways have subsumed the importance of water transportation, yet the urban form remains, marking the significance of waterways as openings into our histories.

In contrast to river towns, wagon towns were anchored to trading routes and overland trails, and their urban form reflects these founding circumstances. Five main Native American tribes or federations gathered in permanent villages and towns on advantageous sites across Alabama, Georgia, and Mississippi. These large groups were the Creek, the Choctaw, the Cherokee, the Chickasaw, and the Seminole. Smaller groups migrated seasonally north and south across the area for better hunting and for trade.

Trade routes crisscrossed the region in many directions as different groups bartered for goods that came from as far away as the Great Lakes and Mexico. These were not casual commercial encounters but a way of existence that spanned many generations and took advantage of products and crafts unavailable locally. William Bartram, in his *Travels, and Other Writings,* written in the late 1790s about Alabama, describes a Native American trading company he met on his way north from Mobile to the Alabama and Tallapoosa rivers: "About the middle of the afternoon, we were joyfully surprised at the distant prospect of the trading company coming up, and we soon met, saluting each other several times with a general Indian whoop or shout of friendship, then each company came to camp within a few paces of each other."[4] William Bartram was a keen observer and explorer who admired the Native Americans. While the arrival of other European traders and trappers opened additional

Decatur

Eufaula

opportunities for successful exchanges with the different tribes, the long-term consequences were disastrous for the Native Americans.

Overland trails connected established Native American villages and reached considerable distances into the interior of Alabama. These paths took advantage of topographic features such as ridges, valleys, and river crossings. As each generation wore its mark into the earth, these trails became entrenched ways, constantly maintained and widely known and used. Bartram, an intrepid traveler, journeyed throughout the South mostly on horseback. He writes of paths, trails, and forks, of winding up and over hills and into valleys and coming to streams at fording places. His journal tells of traveling twenty miles and sometimes as many as forty miles per day. These distances could only be realized on established trails. A broad path through dense forest gave invaluable advantage to early European explorers like Bartram.

Wagons and stagecoaches soon moved along these trails as thousands of settlers flooded into the new state, demanding ever-increasing accessibility. These early-nineteenth-century immigrations mandated the need for a highway across southern Alabama to reliably deliver mail from Washington, DC, to New Orleans, then the major port at the mouth of the Mississippi and the center of commerce in the newly purchased Louisiana Territory. A mobile military presence was required during these years of constant hostilities with Native Americans as the settlers took more and more of their lands. Begun during the first administration of Thomas Jefferson and maintained and expanded during the eight-year presidency of Andrew Jackson, the Federal Road sliced across the upper Atlantic Piedmont, skirted the lower Appalachians, touched at Mobile, and continued on to New Orleans. The Federal Road entered Alabama by crossing the Chattahoochee around Columbus, Georgia,

**Sign advertising Snowdrift shortening, Three Notch Street, Andalusia, Alabama**

continued west to Montgomery, where an alternative route by riverboat was an option, and then dropped southwesterly to access the upper reaches of the Mobile-Tensaw Delta. The most common route, and the easiest, continued by sea along the Gulf coast to New Orleans. A letter from Washington, DC, to New Orleans took five to seven days under ideal conditions, an amazing feat considering the methods of travel and the physical obstacles to be overcome.

Another early trail weaved its way across the ridges and creeks of southern Alabama. Named the Three Notch Road, referring to the original surveyors' method of marking a trail through the forest with three blazes, or cuts of an axe, upon a tree, it ran parallel to the Federal Road but stretched farther south through wagon towns like Andalusia and Troy. The Three Notch Road quickly became a military road used by General Jackson during his invasion of Spanish Florida in pursuit of hostile Creek Indians. Both Andalusia and Troy have streets bearing the name North Three Notch Street and South

Three Notch Street. By following the current paved highway (Route 15/29) between these two towns one gets a sense of how this earlier road lay upon the landscape.

The Three Notch Road crossed the Conecuh River at a place named River Falls. Native Americans and early settlers could, if the water was high, float down the Conecuh to the Gulf. In fact, a flood in 1841 forced the abandonment of Montezuma, a major Spanish settlement near River Falls. The town was subsequently relocated on higher ground at the conjunction of the Three Notch Road and another Native American trail, the old Salt Road to the coast. Betraying the Spanish history of this area, the new settlement named Andalusia replaced both the earlier towns, but the Three Notch Road still goes through its unique courthouse square, placed high upon a ridge.

At another terminus along the Three Notch Road, the town of Troy sits upon a ridge and astride an older Native American trail going north into the richer hunting grounds of the hardwood forests of the Tallapoosa and Coosa watersheds. When Troy became the county seat in 1837, the Three Notch Road traveled through its courthouse square as well, a wonderful accommodation between a tiny gridded town and the demands of a road that must conform to the exigencies of topography by following the line of least resistance. The ridges at Troy and Andalusia leave little space for an expansive grid, so these towns act centripetally to gather disparate lines of movement across the landscape into their symbolic and actual seats of government.

Two wagon roads spawned a settlement at

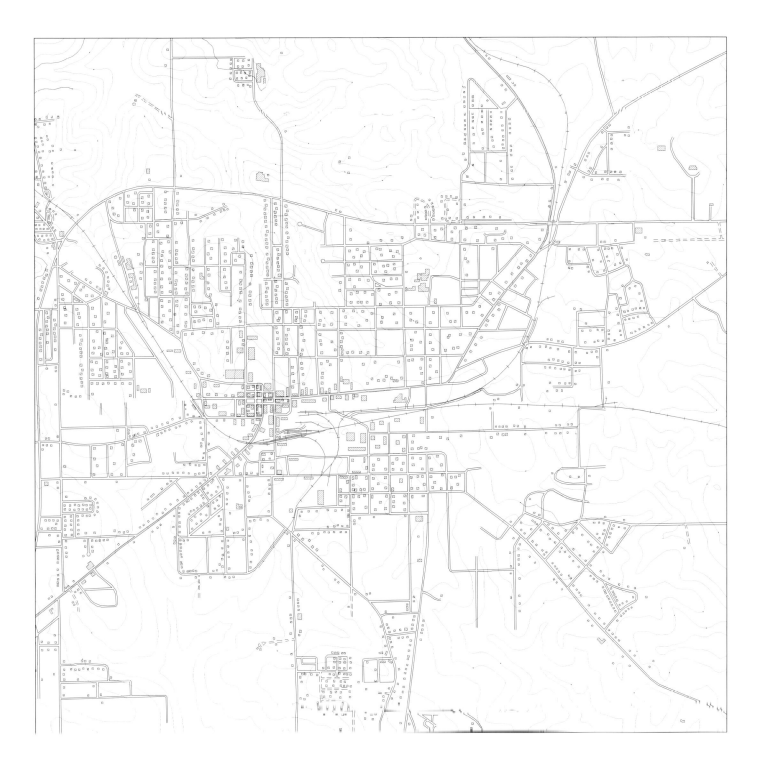

Andalusia, Alabama

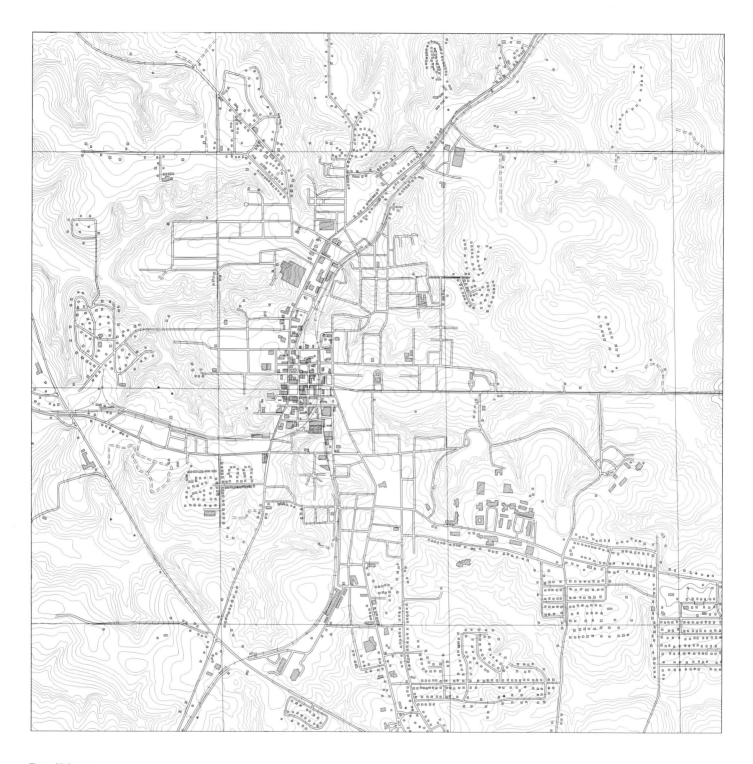

**Troy, Alabama**

106

Cotton gin, Troy, Alabama

Main Street, Enterprise, Alabama, 1926. (Courtesy of the Pea River Historical and Genealogical Society)

**Valve on caboose, Foley, Alabama**

the eventual location of Enterprise, Alabama, in 1881. Enterprise sits upon a broad, flat ridge between the Pea River on the west and the Choctawhatchee to the south. Enterprise became a center first for the timber industry; then, as the land was cleared, for cotton; and then, after the famous boll weevil epidemic in 1915, for peanuts. Its first street was paved in 1919, allowing traffic from the Lone Star Trail from Florida to Texas to pass through its downtown. As can be seen from the photograph of its Main Street, Enterprise in 1926 contained all the necessary requirements for auto touring: gas, auto repairs, restaurants, and an elegant hotel.

Farther to the south, the town of Foley began as a small farming community (see chapter 2 for a plan of Foley). As tourism increased, es-

pecially to the beaches of the Gulf, afforded by the freedom of automobile travel, Foley became the gateway to Alabama's resort areas. Because of the flatness of the surrounding terrain, Foley exemplifies the quintessential grid town based upon section lines from the township and range surveys of the early nineteenth century discussed in chapter 2. The grid extends out into the landscape in regular squares. The main street deflects slightly to accommodate the railroad and then returns to the section line to run straight south to the Gulf resorts. This shift results in a reorientation of the downtown blocks and gives Foley the sense of being Alabama's entrance to the Gulf beaches.

In the mountains of northern Alabama a different set of topographic circumstances resulted in a settlement pattern opposite to that of the south. Settlements occurred in the valleys rather than on the ridges. People came into Alabama from the northeast by floating down the Tennessee River from Knoxville and Chattanooga in flatboats, unloaded their possessions at Guntersville or Decatur, and then headed southwest along the thin valleys of the ragged ends of the Appalachian Mountains. Older Native American traces became roads under the enormous pressure of thousands of settlers. Because of the difficulties involved in traversing perpendicular to this distinctive ridge and valley topography, few roads cross the grain of this landscape. Where they do, however, their valley junctures inevitably became settlements, such as Fort Payne or Scottsboro.

As towns and cities prospered during the later nineteenth century, roads were improved and widened; stagecoach stops and taverns profited, and overland travel became much less hazardous and even faster than travel by riverboat. After the Civil War, railroads usurped the place of river steamers for long-distance travel, only to be eclipsed again by cars as roads gained ascendancy with the mass production of automobiles in the 1920s and 1930s. Downtown streets and old wagon ways were paved as Americans rushed to embrace automobile travel. Many of these towns experienced a sequence of transportation shifts: river and wagons, then railroads, followed by

automobiles. A hundred years apart, wagons and then automobiles used the same routes to cross the landscape.

The years after the First World War saw the introduction of auto touring, with magazines extolling favorable routes within a state or region or even across the country. Routes were named or marked over long distances. As the Rand McNally map of 1922 shows, Alabama had its share of these named routes with very romantic sounding titles, such as the Old Spanish Trail. This interest in touring grew in popular-

**Mule teams and wagons, Athens, Alabama. (Courtesy of Limestone County Archives)**

Gas pump, Demopolis, Alabama

(Opposite) *Rand McNally Main Highway Map of Alabama,* 1922. (Courtesy of Special Collections, Auburn University Libraries)

ity through the Second World War, until it was overshadowed by the vast construction of the interstate highways in the fifties and sixties. Today it is hard to imagine traveling by car in the early days of its manufacture. Cars could safely maintain speeds of only thirty to forty miles per hour; routes went from town to town; there were no bypasses or belt loops; one drove straight down Main Street. Gas stations, restaurants, and overnight accommodations were all located in the town centers. Guidebooks extolled the history of the towns traveled through and recommended points of interest. It must have been an unhurried exploration; one drove into a small town for lunch at a restaurant serving home-cooked food and spent the night at a hotel rather than at an interstate motel. Today, greater speed

allows us now to experience the grosser grain of landscapes, yet it removes us from the intimacy and richness of regional cultures.

Railroads radically altered the urban character of Alabama. Besides serving established communities, they created new ones; they reshaped existing towns and gave distinctive form to the state's largest city, Birmingham. No discussion of railroads in the South can be complete without recalling the phenomenal development of Birmingham in the last quarter of the nineteenth century. Coal to fire blast furnaces and ore to smelt into iron lay in the hills and mountains of northern Alabama. Railroads were needed to haul both resources, and so from 1876 onwards track was laid to mines and furnaces on an unprecedented scale.

Before the Civil War, Alabama, along with much of the South, was railroad "poor," with little track mileage, disparate track widths or gauges, and few continuous or connected lines. One line ran from Montgomery to Mobile; another ran along the northern part of the state, parallel to the Tennessee River. There was no north–south connection between the two lines, nor was there reason for one. Cotton, the major produce, could be shipped more cheaply by river. The ravages of war further depleted rolling stock and motive power and destroyed much usable track. And yet by the early twentieth century, Alabama ranked seventeenth among all states in track mileage.[5] Large or small communities across the state were served by regular passenger and freight trains. A 1938 map of Alabama shows more than thirty-five railroads crossing the state in a dense network of track. The rapid

5. Stover, *American Railroads,* 204, table 8.2.

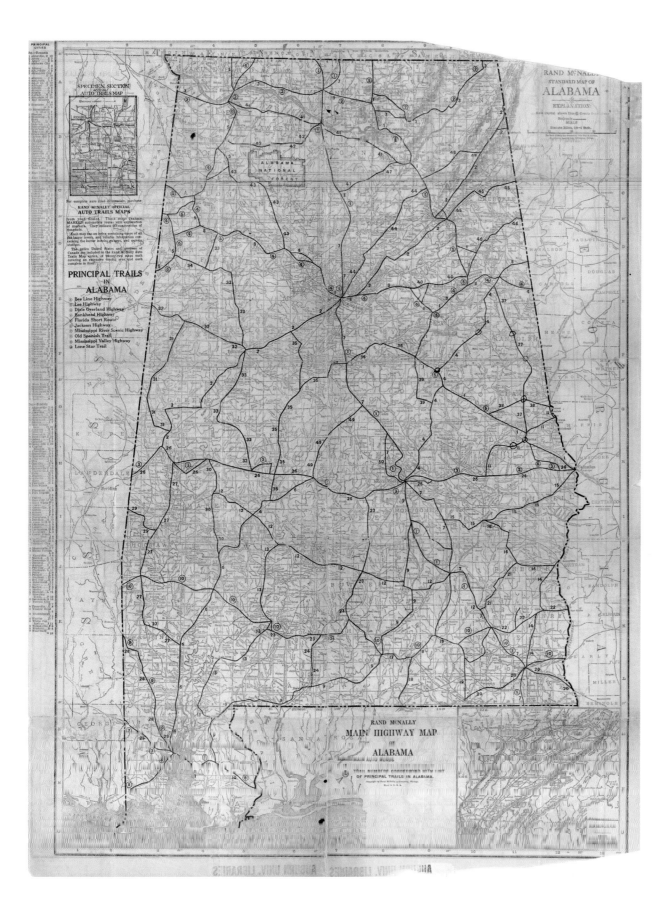

RAND McNALLY
STANDARD MAP OF
ALABAMA

EXPLANATION

PRINCIPAL TRAILS
IN
ALABAMA

Bee Line Highway
Lee Highway
Dixie Overland Highway
Bankhead Highway
Florida Short Route
Jackson Highway
Mississippi River Scenic Highway
Old Spanish Trail
Mississippi Valley Highway
Lone Star Trail

SPECIMEN SECTION
of the
AUTO TRAILS MAP

RAND McNALLY
MAIN HIGHWAY MAP
OF
ALABAMA
MAIN AUTO ROADS

TRAIL NUMBERS CORRESPOND WITH LIST
OF PRINCIPAL TRAILS IN ALABAMA.

Starkey Motor
Company, Athens,
Alabama. (Courtesy
of Limestone County
Archives)

(Below) Gas station,
Athens, Alabama.
(Courtesy of Limestone
County Archives)

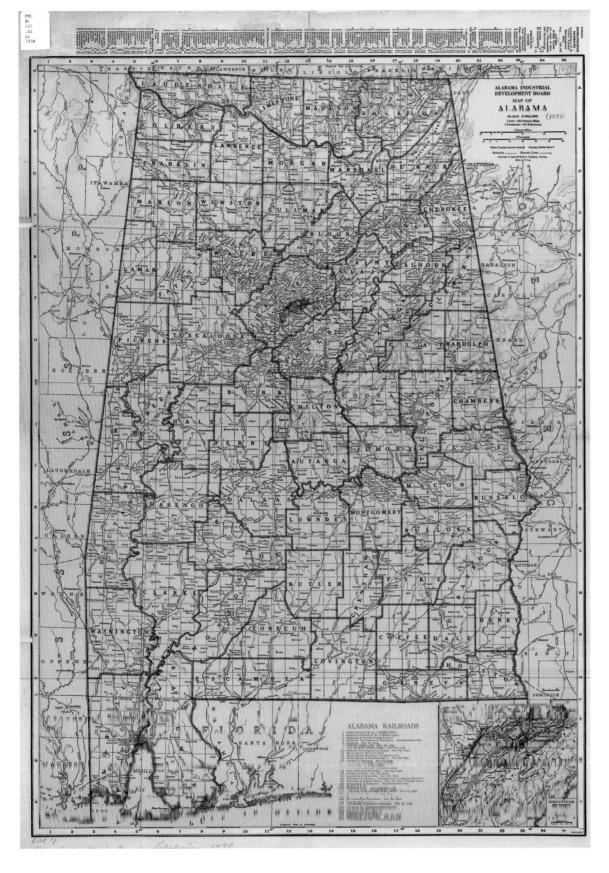

*Alabama Industrial Development Board Map of Alabama,* 1938, showing Alabama railroads. (Courtesy of Special Collections, Auburn University Libraries)

development of the mineral resources of the lower Appalachian Mountains explains much of this dramatic growth, but rail also quickly replaced the less reliable river transportation of the cotton industry. In the thirty years before and after the turn of the century—the golden age of railroads—Alabama's towns were created, shaped, and supplied by some of the most reliable trains in America.

By 1916 the United States had an all-time high of 254,037 miles of track. Railroads carried 98 percent of intercity passenger business.[6] This dramatic growth connected two edges of a vast continent, funneled the produce of the Midwest to the markets of the East, and built cities like Chicago, St. Louis, and Kansas City. The history of railroad expansion in America is also one of greed, corruption, and financial manipulation

on a scale equal to that of its growth, and Alabama was no exception.

Building railroads is an expensive, capital-intensive, very risky business. Government subsidies for land acquisition and construction of major infrastructure were necessary. The most common subsidy was additional land. A railroad corporation was given both its rights of way and extra properties along its entire length. These alternate sections could be used for future speculative real-estate development or as collateral for mortgages used to finance construction. Often they were used for both simultaneously. This public underwriting of rail development made a ready recipe for all kinds of chicanery, graft, and political influence peddling. Location on a right of way greatly enhanced a town's economic viability, so competition was intense and bribery of

6. Stover, *Routledge Historical Atlas of the American Railroads*, 52.

Bessemer

Cullman

Fort Payne

Irondale

Brewton

Opelika

**Street grids of Alabama railroad towns**

public officials rampant. After lines were completed, rate manipulation could ruin a competing town's economy. Opelika, one of the railroad towns discussed in this chapter, was bankrupted when the Western Railway of Alabama raised its rates prohibitively for travel into and out of the town. Conversely, the history of railroads is also the history of the regulatory powers of government, both state and federal. Courts and legislatures eventually required the railroads to serve fairly their entire constituencies, even those remote communities at the end of a spur line, and to eliminate monopolies and price fixing.

The building of a railroad requires precise engineering of grade and curved radii. The maximum grade should be less than 6 percent; a reasonable radius is 850 feet. A long, straight run of track is best. Where the negotiation of difficult terrain requires it, costly bridges and tunnels must be constructed. Especially in the rugged Appalachians of northern Alabama, these topographic constraints left little flexibility in the choice of rights of way, as both Scottsboro and Fort Payne illustrate. Trains need marshaling yards, "ladders" of track or multiple sidings to store and sort freight cars to be made into

**Cullman, Alabama**

larger, long-distance trains. Sidings are needed next to, but separate from, the main through tracks to facilitate loading and unloading of freight. Passenger trains need station platforms for shelter and safety. All these require large expanses of flat land and straight runs of track. The pragmatics of rail construction generally took precedence over other concerns, including the planning of towns.

A diagram for a typical settlement served predominantly by train illustrates these constraints: first the through track is built, followed by the sidings, with as much track as possible constructed parallel to the main track and to long rows of warehouses. Freight could be easily moved directly from boxcars into covered storage. On the other side of the warehouses are streets for loading wagons or trucks for distribution of rail cargo. This street is essentially the bulk or wholesale district of the town. The next street contains the retail center, the hardware store, the bank, and the hotel. The residential streets move farther away from the main street and the railroad. The diagram can be realized on one side of the tracks or can occur symmetrically on both sides, as in Opelika. It should be clear that the railroad determines the town's order, and not the reverse. Towns already in existence, such as Selma, modified their pattern to conform to the tracks. In either case, there is a clear and functional movement of goods and people from train to station to town. The station is the pedestrian entrance or gateway into the town or its portal to the larger world. The architecture lavished upon even the smallest stations reflects their importance.

Two railroads entered Alabama from the north, both heading for Birmingham. The Louisville & Nashville ran straight south from Nashville to Birmingham. The railroad town of Cullman sits on the L & N's main line between these two points. The Southern Railway's main line threads its way southward down valleys in the Cumberland Plateau from Chattanooga parallel to the Tennessee River and connects to another railroad town, Fort Payne.

Cullman came into existence solely because of the railroad. In 1872 an energetic German immigrant, John S. Cullman contracted with the L & N to locate several hundred fellow German settlers at a point fifty-three miles north of Birmingham. On empty land he founded the town that bears his name. Eventually more than five hundred families settled there, and the town flourished, becoming the county seat and thereafter contributing considerable revenue to the railroad. Cullman provides the classic diagram of a railroad town clamped on both sides of the tracks. For part of the way the rail lines are in a cut, so that traffic passes above the tracks on bridges, making grade crossings unnecessary. The rails swing slightly southeast, taking the whole commercial center with them. The Bee Line Highway, the direct route to Florida, follows the tracks on its way south and runs down the town's main commercial street. All this activity made downtown Cullman a vibrant and lively place, and it remains so today. The beautiful residential streets move away from the tracks and shift the grid back to north–south and the original survey section lines of 1820.

The long fingers of the Appalachian Moun-

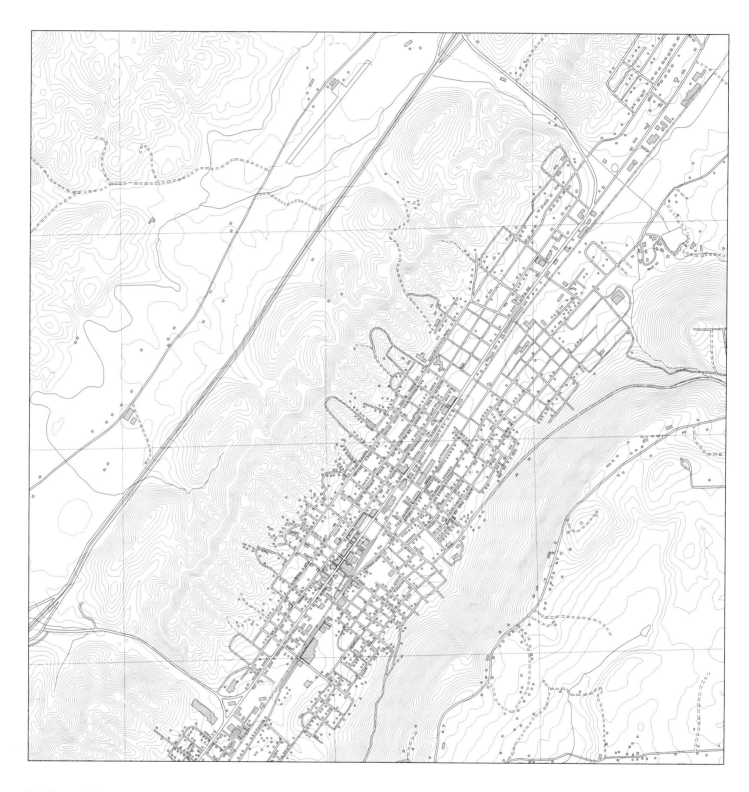

**Fort Payne, Alabama**

tains stretching southward from the Cumberland Plateau into Alabama afforded but one way for the Southern Railway line to enter the state from Chattanooga. Settlement followed the same route, resulting in the unique linear form of Fort Payne. Jammed between two ridges in the Big Wills Valley, Fort Payne accommodates topography, railroad, and road by organizing its commercial downtown in a long straight line. The main commercial street is one block over from the tracks, while the residential areas climb the slopes of the valley.

Opelika was a major railhead and today is a center of textile mills. Tracks, formerly with many sidings and warehouses, run straight through Opelika, connecting Atlanta to Birmingham and Columbus, Georgia, to Montgomery. These two lines cross in the center of Opelika at right angles, necessitating a most unusual casting, or "frog," for the tracks. This intersection evokes a sense of connection to the larger world, for trains of the old Central Georgia Line, from Chicago to Miami, and those of the Western Railway of Alabama, running from New York to New Orleans, passed over this point. The diagram of the typical railroad town fits perfectly upon Opelika's downtown. The gridded streets are symmetrically placed around the tracks; the street grid rotates 45 degrees, and all are accommodated on level ground on top of a long ridge between lowlands and swamps. Heavily laden freight trains still rumble through Opelika at any time of day or night, contemporary reminders that this small, somnolent town was once at the crossroads of a much larger world.

Brewton is named after its first station-

master, an example of a name change that fit the latest mode of transportation. The earliest railroads in Alabama connected Montgomery to Mobile as a way of moving cotton more reliably to the Gulf port. This part of the state is crisscrossed with creeks and swamps, making overland travel difficult and the construction of bridges and embankments necessary. Brewton, on this route, was originally called Crossroads because two roads intersected there. It was later named Newport because of a landing at the confluence of two streams. It is an unusual site at the intersection of two creeks with their extensive wetlands, a kind of peninsula facing southwest in the direction of travel. The railroad follows the level bank along one stream and runs straight down the middle of town. Two differently oriented grids meet at the tracks, much like fabrics meeting at a seam, giving Brewton its distinctive form. The main street is, in fact, the railroad, with the sidings and yards located outside the town's core. It is a most unusual site, with railroad, topography, and town resulting in a remarkable urban space

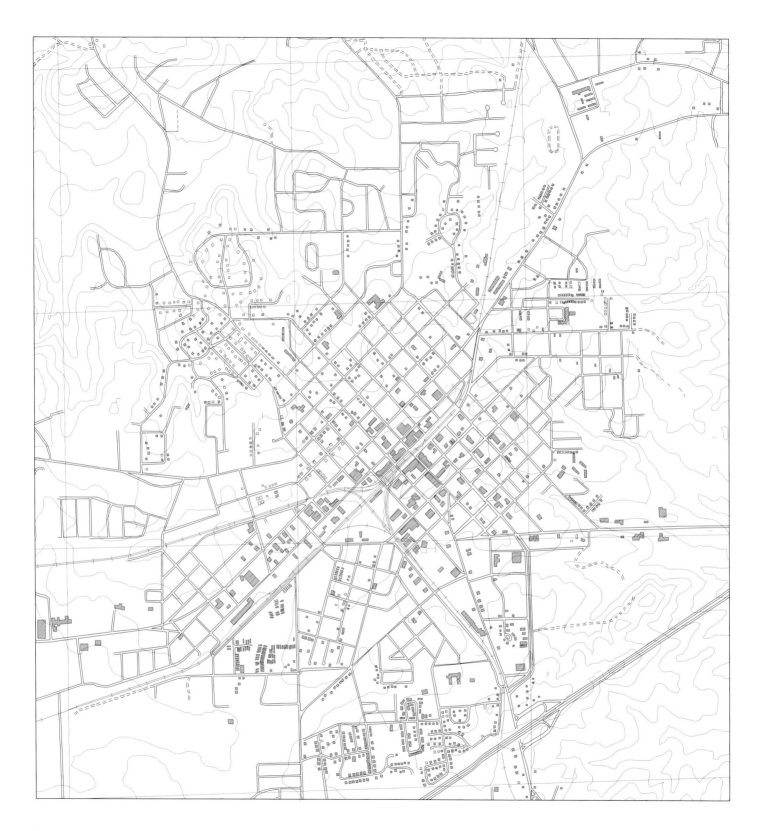

**Opelika, Alabama**

During the first years of the twentieth century, railroads in the United States accounted for most passenger service and carried well over three-quarters of all freight. There were few alternatives, and certainly only horse and carriage over short hauls. As these examples illustrate, the monopoly of transportation lent a certain character to settlement patterns because of two salient aspects of train travel. Trains stopped at fixed locations—stations—and on a regular time schedule. People and freight moved from town to town, city to city, point to point, at prescribed times. From these points people and goods disbursed by wagon or by foot. So railroads concentrated functions, structures, and, by extension, urban form.

Arriving by train in a small town such as Cullman or Opelika in the early 1900s, one had little choice but to continue on by foot. Merchandise and services were placed within a reasonable walk of the railway depot. This is why, surprisingly, so many small towns had hotels. One traveled on the railroad's schedule, and if this meant arriving late at night or necessitated an overnight stay before the next train, then accommodations were readily available.

Spatially all towns served by railroads were dense. Land around the depot was valuable, and merchants built right up to the property line. Those streets contiguous to the tracks were tightly enclosed by buildings with retail below and offices or housing above. All these railroad towns had within short blocks of the tracks an urban core containing most services and goods necessary to sustain a transient guest or permanent residents.

**Railroad warehouse, Opelika, Alabama**

The final two towns discussed in this chapter were brought into existence by railroads and exemplify the connection between resource development and transportation. Irondale serves as a mountain-grade crossing, while Bessemer was planned as a company town next to the furnaces and iron mills surrounding the gritty industrial complex of Birmingham. A beautiful 1890 geological map of the Cahaba Coal Field shows both Irondale and Bessemer, as well as Birmingham, in their very earliest stages of growth.

Irondale exists because of an accident in topography. Red Mountain separates Birmingham from the valleys to the east. A gap, or dip, in Red Mountain, called Red Gap allows railroads to cross over with an acceptable grade and gain access to the valleys of the Appalachians. Paths, trails, and roads also originally slipped across at this same location; today the main interstate from Birmingham to Atlanta travels this route. Four railroads squeezed through Red Gap, turned abruptly west, and ran downhill to Birmingham's smelting furnaces. Cars of the

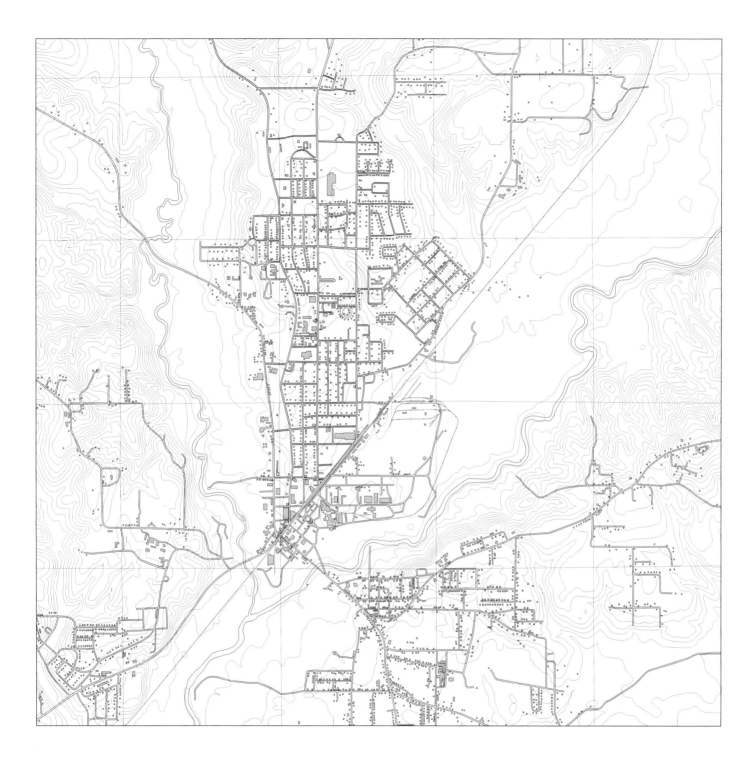

**Brewton, Alabama**

(Right) *Map of the Cahaba Coal Fields and Adjacent Regions,* 1890.
(Courtesy of Special Collections, Auburn University Libraries)

122

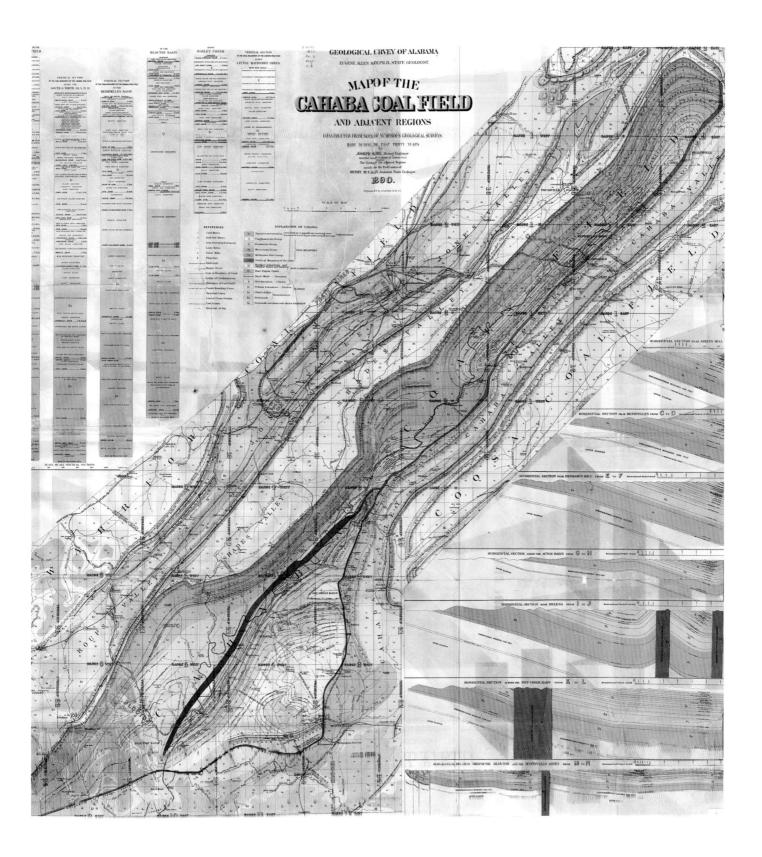

GEOLOGICAL SURVEY OF ALABAMA

EUGENE ALLEN SMITH, STATE GEOLOGIST.

# MAP OF THE
# CAHABA COAL FIELD
### AND ADJACENT REGIONS

CONSTRUCTED FROM NOTES OF NUMEROUS GEOLOGICAL SURVEYS

MADE DURING THE PAST THIRTY YEARS

by

JOSEPH SQUIRE, Mining Engineer

The Geology of the adjacent regions
mainly for the field notes of
HENRY McCALLEY, Assistant State Geologist.

1890.

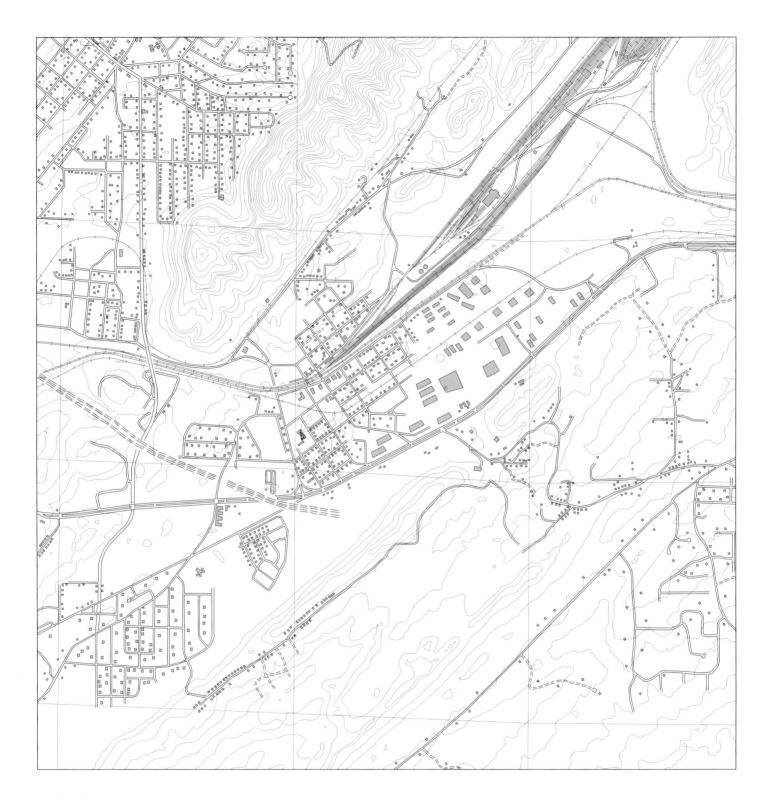

**Irondale, Alabama**

former Southern Railway bound for Atlanta and the eastern seaboard were stored and sorted in vast switching yards east of Red Gap. To either side of the main tracks through Irondale are two avenues. On the north side, directly facing the tracks, is a single block of retail buildings. Brake- and switchmen and other workers in the marshaling yards could climb off their locomotives and walk home. Today one can sit in the small pavilion in Irondale next to the tracks and watch the continuous lines of freight trains moving through the gap in both directions.

The great iron and coal tycoon Henry B. DeBardeleben formed the Bessemer Land and Improvement Company in the early 1880s to buy up acres of land around what was to become Bessemer and laid out an extensive gridded town next to the DeBardeleben Coal and Iron Furnace. Speculation was rampant and rapid; lots that sold for ten to twenty-five dollars in 1886 sold for eighteen thousand dollars one year later.[7] This incredible profit gives one a sense of the fortunes to be won (and lost) as the iron industry expanded. Bessemer grew so quickly and dramatically that it had trouble attracting enough people to work in the iron and steel mills. The local newspaper, the *Bessemer #63*, advertised on Saturday, 11 August 1888: "It is a new city; a growing and developing city. One with such resources awaiting utilization; such facilities for manufacture and conversion; such immense territory for market; such superb system of transportation and distribution; such a salubrious and attractive climate, and such a grand and beautiful country in and surrounding it, that it presents unusual inducements to the immigrant."[8]

Bessemer contains perhaps the most completely preserved collection of late-nineteenth-century buildings in the South. These structures enclose contiguous streets, making an expansive uninterrupted fabric of many blocks. The relationship of streets to the mills, to the topography, and to the railroads is wonderful in its clarity and pragmatism. Bessemer sits surrounded by a mountain of iron ore and on top of an extensive seam of coal. It is a pure resource town, a boom town that sprang into existence in ten years. Even today, though the ore and coal are no longer mined, Bessemer maintains a decidedly symbiotic relationship to the railroads, topography, and manufacturing and industrial complexes intertwined with its straightforward urban grid.

It was an accident of geology that gave Irondale its distinctive form along the tracks. Bessemer arose at the confluence of two minerals: coal and iron. Its extensive rail network gathered and redistributed both raw materials and finished products. Both towns can be classified

**Railroad flatcar, Irondale, Alabama**

7. Jubilee Historical Book Committee, *From the Rough*, 33.

8. Barefield, *Bessemer*, 26.

**Bessemer, Alabama**

126

as railroad towns, but for different reasons. Resource extraction once brought the railroads to these locations, yet the towns evolved their structures in response to the tracks. Today trains have disappeared as the preferred method of transportation. Tracks, sidings, and warehouses have been removed, leaving large open spaces, ghosts of former times and functions. Because passenger stations such as Cullman's or Fort Payne's are so beautiful, they remain, mute testimony in abandoned railroad yards to the gathering influence of transportation on concise urban form.

Both the uniqueness and the complexity of the origin of each town discussed in this chapter illustrate the tenuousness of the categories of river, wagon, and railroad towns. The influences upon the development and form of each town cannot be so easily isolated as these groupings would suggest. River towns succumbed to the advantages of the railroad's reliability; rail towns to the convenience of roads. Each town was reinvented many times, first by geography and geology, then by transportation and economic factors such as the price of a bale of cotton, of a board of long-leaf pine, or of a ton of coal. Yet their wonderfully diverse urban patterns remained through all these vicissitudes.

Before journeying east 40 degrees into Kentucky, Virginia, and West Virginia in the next chapter, it seems wise to reflect upon this wealth of urban form within Alabama. Against the preponderance of distinctive examples of settlement patterns, this study casts into sharp contrast the contemporary homogenized landscapes that replace this layered past. Hidden among the ridges and folds of the Appalachians are town after town, discrete and singular, small concentrations of differences, places that encouraged the breadth of human experience—places that nurtured other kinds of histories, other ethnic groups, other kinds of people. These numerous, diverse stages are necessary to the dramas of ordinary life. The more concentrated these dramas, the more frequently they transpire, the more we all benefit. Our culture has given us these towns as our many theaters; we should not give them up lightly.

# 5

# Volatile Matter

Towns of the Bituminous Coal Fields

The towns of the southern Appalachian bituminous coal fields exist in shadows, the deep purple shadows cast by their enclosing mountains and the somber shadows of darkened streets and blackened windows. These two layers of shadows hide two histories—geological history, measured in epochs of millions of years, and another history measured in the short decades of human toil and industry. This chapter explores the intersection of these two continuities where events that occurred millions of years ago give shape to modern settlements that dwell precariously in the most fragile of places, crescent-shaped alluvial shelves formed by the twists and bends of creeks and streams that are constantly threatened by flooding. These places fill with the twilight of a culture that once fueled momentous changes in the larger world. The eight towns of this segment of the journey east 40 degrees flourished for barely fifty years. Like the highly flammable volatile matter encased in the shinny nuggets of bituminous coal, they could not sustain themselves or their culture.

Six hundred million years ago a shallow inland sea covered what was much later to become the southern Appalachians. Green ferns and spreading trees filled these swampy waters with dense vegetation. As the plants died and

decayed, bogs of peat formed hundreds of feet thick. Over millions of years these layers were covered with soil and mineral deposits from eroding mountains that further compressed the vegetative matter into beds of thick black coal. Locked into these veins of bituminous coal was the sun's energy—to be released millions of years later to fuel the furnaces of America's industry.

The inland sea drained and dried up, forming a flat plain. Across its surface lazy streams meandered. Distinctive graceful curves of water moved slowly across a level area, while many hundreds of feet below the surface lay the seams of coal. Approximately 400 million years ago the impending continents of Africa and Europe pushed against North America, forcing the ascension of the braided Appalachians. To the west of these mountains, this flat plain squeezed upward as a great block hundreds of miles long. As it slowly rose over millions of years, its streams and rivers continued to cut down through its surface, much like a saw through a piece of plywood, exposing layers formerly hidden deep within the earth. The buried coal now appeared high along mountain slopes displaced by the plateau's uplift.

This enormous flat block of the earth rose as

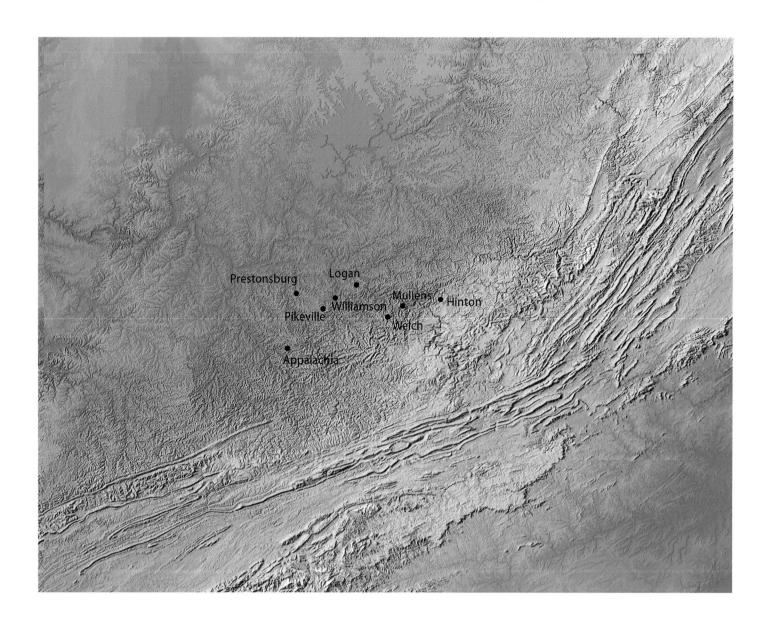

**Southern Appalachians**

a level plain, carrying with it the sinuous curves and slack currents of its streams and rivers, which became ever more sharply etched into the earth's surface, forming deep valleys and steep mountains. Today known as the Appalachian Plateau, this area stretches southward from New York and Pennsylvania across most of West Virginia, parts of Kentucky and Tennessee, and into Alabama. It is a landscape dissected by streams, resulting in a rugged and inaccessible terrain of relatively low elevations. Some of the thickest and most extensive beds of bituminous coal in the world layer among the many horizontal strata of sedimentary sandstones and shales. These deposits, exposed along valley walls, were discovered by those few intrepid explorers and settlers who ventured into this forested fastness and were bold and rapacious enough to find a

way to transport the coal to the quickening furnaces of industry waiting in the world outside.

Boone County, West Virginia, is in the very
heart of the southern Appalachian coal deposits.
A detail from a soil map of Boone County in 1913
illustrates the clearly defined dense dendritic
pattern of rivers, streams, and creeks typical of
the entire region. The crescent-shaped brown
and tan colors with letters delineate alluvial
deposits along the river edges. These became
the locations for the towns. The dotted black
lines running along the faintly drawn contour
lines represent ridge tops and further emphasize
that this area is formed of deeply indented valleys carved out by water over millions of years.
A 1905 map of this plateau, bounded by the
Kanawha, New, and Guyandotte rivers, shows
the extent of coal deposits. The green color represents areas of visible coal already under some
kind of ownership or mineral rights. The complete map encompasses about three thousand
square miles of mountainous terrain. Charleston, the capital of West Virginia, is at the top
right; Logan, West Virginia, is in the southwest,
just east of the bulge of the United States Coal
and Oil Company's landholdings.

In the late nineteenth century the railroads
came; long thin rails threading their way
through this labyrinth of mountains along the
delicate streams and creeks. The elegant radii
and gentle gradients of their tracks paralleled
the watercourses inscribed into the plateau millions of years earlier. The stream banks afforded
the best routes from the east or west, and soon
the sides of most waterways were locked in an
iron vise of rails and ties, of locomotives and

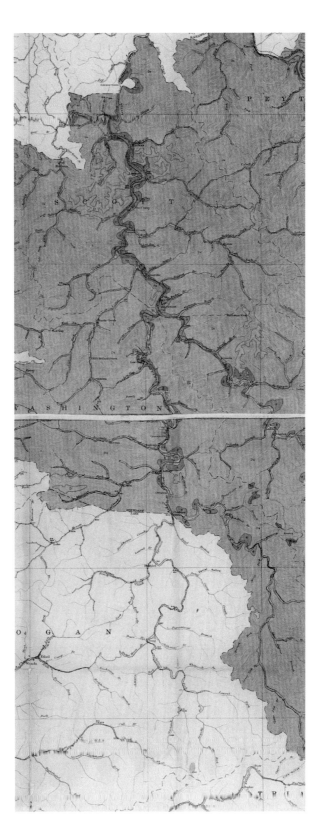

Detail of soil map,
Boone County, West
Virginia, 1913.
(Library of Congress)

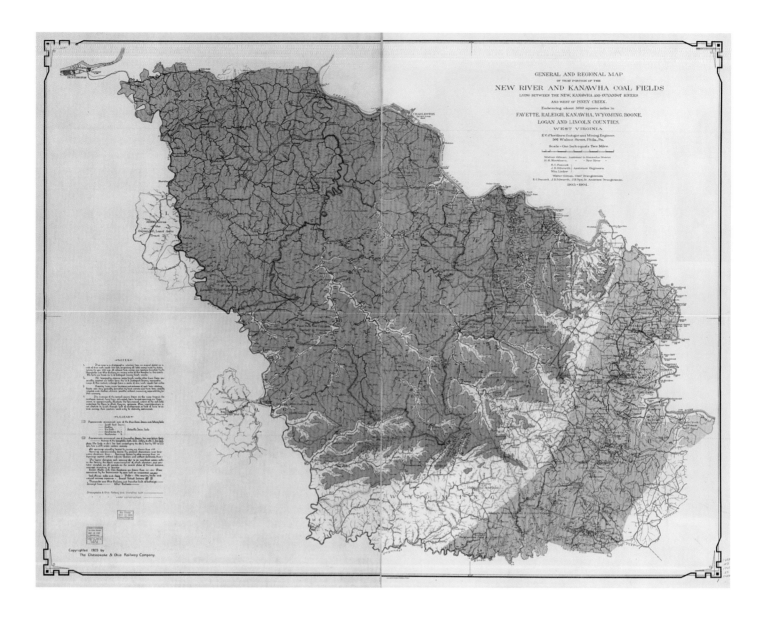

**General and Regional Map
of That Portion of the New
River and Kanawha Coal
Fields Lying between the
New, Kanawha and Guyan-
dot Rivers and West
of Piney Creek,** 1905.
(Library of Congress)

**(Opposite) Route of the
New River Railroad,** 1880s.
(Library of Congress)

lengthening rivers of coal cars moving west to
the steel mills of the Great Lakes and east to the
port cities of the Atlantic.

Two detailed maps of railroads drawn by the
"Engineer Office of Jed. Hotchkiss, Staunton
Va.," in the 1880s provide wonderful illustrations of the manner in which railroads pushed
into this rough terrain along stream banks. The
first, labeled "Route of the New River Railroad,"

shows the proposed tracks following the New
River from Central, Virginia, through the cut in
Peter's Mountain up to Hinton, West Virginia.
(Central, Virginia, is now Radford, and most of
this route along the New River lies beneath the
impoundment of Bluestone Lake.) The second
map, dated May 1881, delineates the preliminary
line of the East River Railroad. These tracks
leave the New River not far from present-day

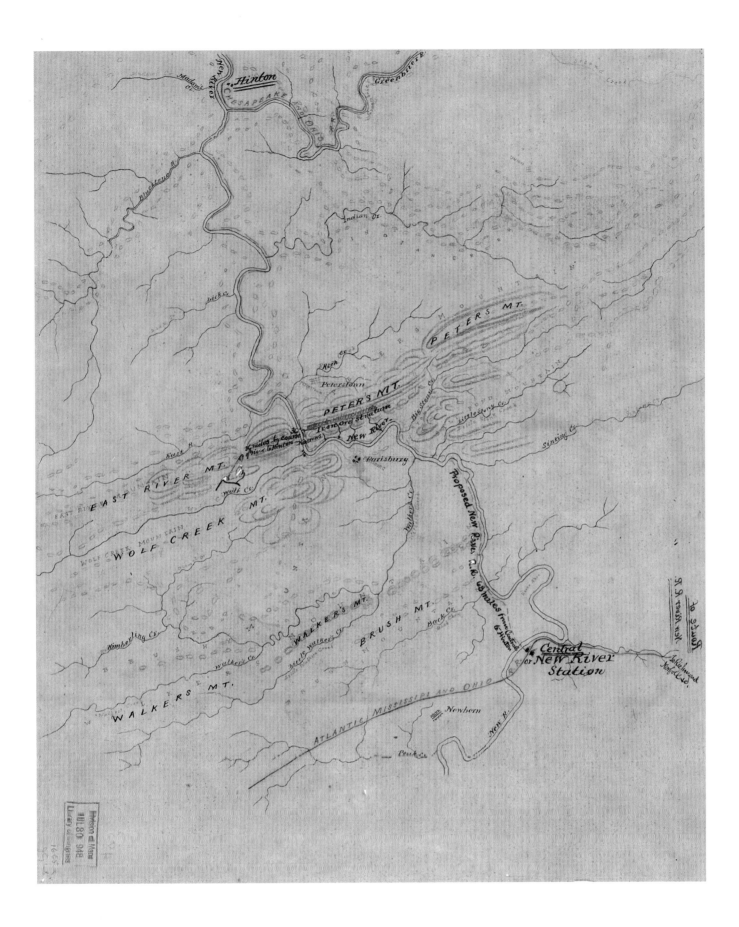

"Hinton

New River

CHESAPEAKE AND OHIO R.R.

Madams Cr.

Greenbrier R.

Bluestone R.

Indian Cr.

Lick Cr.

Rich Cr.

PETER'S MT.

Peterstown

PETERS MT.

PETERS MOUNTAIN

Bluestone Cr.

Little Stony Cr.

Sinking Cr.

Tramore station

30 miles by course

9 miles to Hinton

Narrows

New River

Rush R.

EAST RIVER MT.

EAST RIVER MOUNTAIN

Parisbury

Wolf Cr.

WOLF CREEK MT.

WOLF CREEK MOUNTAIN

Walkers Cr.

Proposed New River R.R. 68 miles from Central to Hinton

Little Walkers Cr.

WALKERS MT.

WALKERS MT.

BRUSH MT.

Back Cr.

Kimberling Cr.

Walkers Cr.

Little Walkers Cr.

Reed Creek

Central or New River Station

to Richmond Norfolk &c.

Route of R.R.

WALKERS MT.

ATLANTIC MISSISSIPPI AND OHIO

Newbern

New R.

Peak Cr.

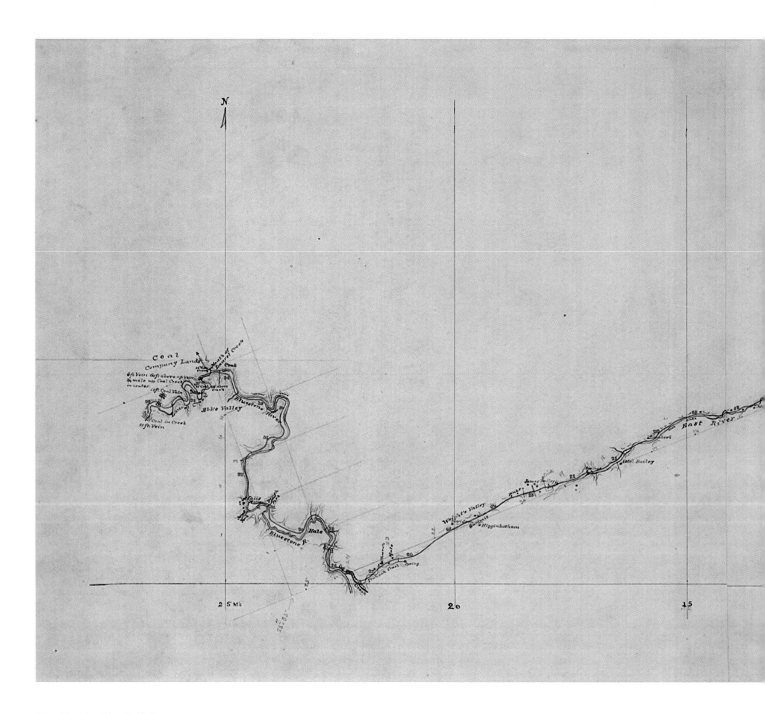

*Map Showing the Preliminary
Line of the East River Railroad,
May 1881.* (Library of Congress)

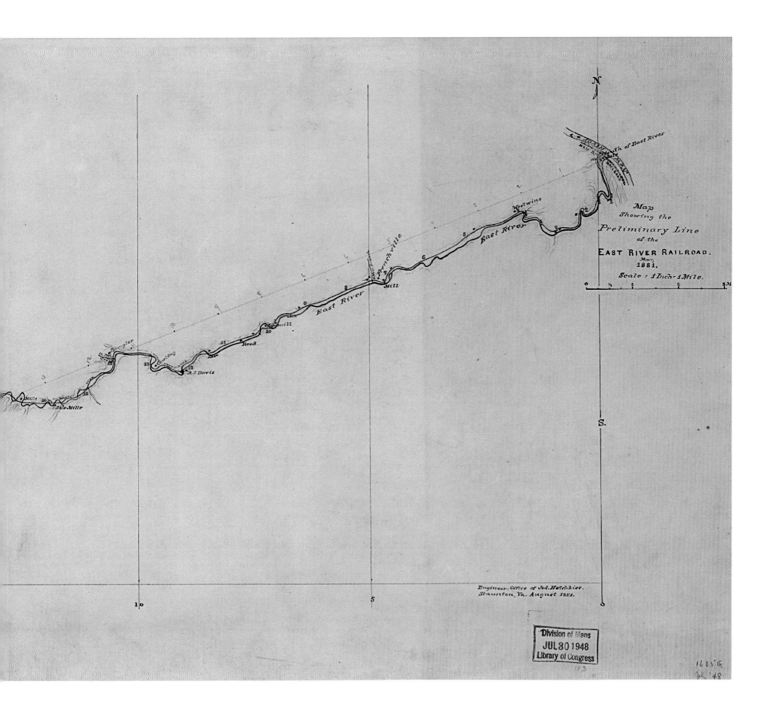

Map
Showing the
Preliminary Line
of the
EAST RIVER RAILROAD.
May,
1881.
Scale : 1 Inch = 1 Mile.

Engineer Office of Jed. Hotchkiss.
Staunton, Va., August 1881.

135

Rail yard, Williamson, West Virginia, 1935. (Library of Congress)

Glen Lyn, West Virginia, and wind up the valley over to the Bluestone River near Bluefield, West Virginia. (Route 112 follows this valley, and the Norfolk Southern tracks are still in existence along the East River.)

Like so many others, Jed Hotchkiss returned to this area of West Virginia after the Civil War to survey coal deposits and to entice financial investors in railroads to construct ways into this mountainous region.[1] The engineering and construction of these railroads required capital and risks beyond the means of all but the largest of investors. Financial backing came from people outside the region, who were interested only in the potentially huge profits; they had no interest in any long-term investment in the local economies. This disparity between outside capitalists and local labor established the basis for a future in which little remained except misery and poverty once the coal boom dissipated. Remarkably, coal mining in this part of the southern Appalachians flourished for very few years—roughly from 1890 to 1940—yet these years witnessed the rapid construction of many new towns to serve both the mines and the railroads. The towns remained even after all else disappeared, haunted places in spectacular settings, remote, inaccessible, tiny, and yet complete urban complexes with dense centers of compelling architectural beauty. Their built form, often abandoned,

1. Shifflet, *Coal Towns*, 29.

crumbles with neglect, the result of a culture's losing gamble in the ruthless sweepstakes of the industrialization of America.

After a productive coal seam was located and mapped in a remote valley, the rail lines pushed through to transport the mined material. A company town would be built close to the mine entrance to provide permanent housing for the miners. Often prefabricated wood frame structures, these buildings were shipped in by rail and erected quickly in uniform rows along the tracks. Since these company towns were accessible only by rail, the coal company owned everything—the land, houses, schools, the "company store"—and it controlled all supplies in and out of town. An insidious paternalism occurred that would later foster labor strife with disastrous consequences for the entire industry.

At the mine entrance, coal was loaded into waiting hopper cars through an elevated structure called a tipple. These loaded cars were pulled to the nearest marshaling yards to be sorted and coupled into longer train sets of more than one hundred cars for the haul to distant destinations by powerful locomotives. Two photographs taken in the Williamson rail yards, probably the largest such facility in the world at the time, capture the magnitude of these operations. In the foreground of the first image are hopper cars filled with different sizes and

kinds of coal, and lines of cabooses in the background. Another view of the same yards looks down upon seemingly limitless rows of hoppers stretching into a smoke-obscured distance. Today it is hard to imagine the immensity of the operations shown in these photographs. Long trains of coal moved out every hour, twenty-four hours a day, to supply the insatiable demands of steel mills and power plants. This is especially sobering when one considers that the initial extraction of coal at the seam face deep in the earth was done by hand, each piece of coal cut and loaded by individual laborers.

Such an enormous transportation infrastructure required whole towns of engineers, switchmen, brakemen, and maintenance workers to keep the rolling stock moving smoothly and regularly. A remarkable photograph taken in 1939 shows a yard brakeman oiling an enormous steam engine. The huge driving wheels dwarf him completely. These powerful machines required constant care to run efficiently and consistently throughout these deep valleys and up the long, twisting gradients. The maintenance yards were also built on the only available flat lands in the region, narrow shelves along the stream courses. Next to the rail yards grew the towns to house the myriad laborers that served both the trains and the more remote and dispersed company towns farther up the line.

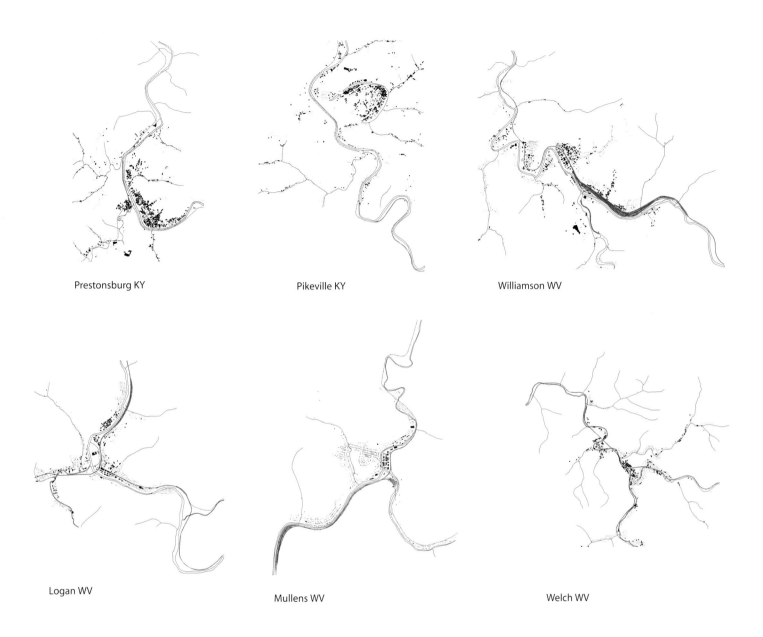

Prestonsburg KY

Pikeville KY

Williamson WV

Logan WV

Mullens WV

Welch WV

**Figure-grounds of six Kentucky and West Virginia towns with rivers and railroads**

**Figure-grounds of eight
Kentucky, West Virginia,
and Virginia towns**

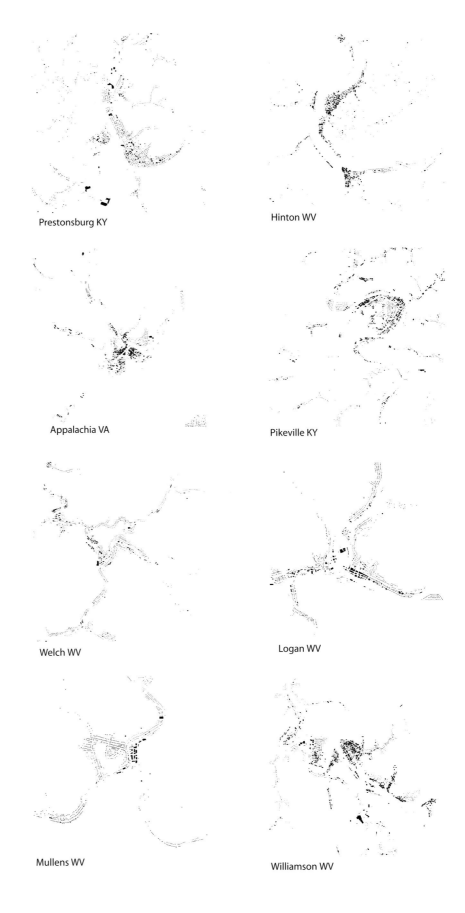

Prestonsburg KY

Hinton WV

Appalachia VA

Pikeville KY

Welch WV

Logan WV

Mullens WV

Williamson WV

These alluvial shelves too accommodated these
burgeoning settlements and gave form to a pattern of development unique to these remote
mountains.

A sequence of partial figure-ground studies of six of the eight towns included in this
chapter illustrates the sweeping curves of river,
railroad, and urban form. If all eight towns
are analyzed on the basis of their built form as
figure-grounds, they appear as swirling stel-
lar constellations with many tentacles reaching
up into the surrounding small valleys. If one
compares these drawings with the soil map of
Boone County and imagines the brown- and
tan-colored outlines of alluvial deposits as urban form, one can grasp the contiguity of towns
formed by the same processes as the earth.
Towns paralleled the fluvial dendritic curves of

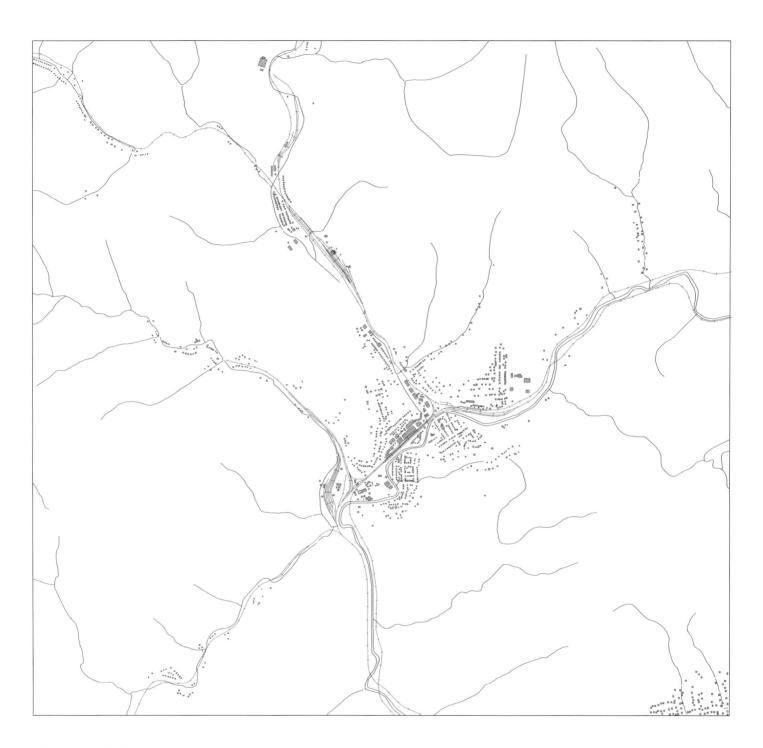

Settlement patterns of
the area around Appala-
chia, Virginia, with rivers,
streams, and railroads

142

**Figure-ground of West Main Street, Appalachia, Virginia**

143

(Top) Railroad coupling,
Appalachia, Virginia

(Bottom) Post Office,
Pikeville, Kentucky

the streams and creeks and located on narrow crescent-shaped places that ran beside bulging tracks. At times the tracks became the town's main street, as a 1938 photograph of Davey, West Virginia, dramatically illustrates. (Davey was a small satellite community of Welch, West Virginia, on the same watershed, the Tug Fork. Little remains of the row of buildings in the photograph, although the tracks are still in use.) An initial grid within each town's original dense core struggled to remain against this organic shape as buildings strung out along the ever-narrowing stream bank. The distant geological past remains embedded in the form of these towns, their configuration fixed by the languid curves and bends of rivers that millions of years ago coursed over a broad, sunlit plain. In their obsession with coal's extraction Americans built the most transient of communities, which bound them unequivocally to the natural processes that shaped this region. The chimerical illusion of industrial progress hides the deeper passage of time that allows these places to touch the earth with such meaning.

There are two kinds of settlement patterns within these deep valleys and along the hidden river courses. Appalachia, Virginia, and its satellite settlements offer examples of each. Appalachia is a small trading center for the Wise Coal Fields, which stretch out into the surrounding mountains. It sits beside the Powell River, where three major tributaries branch off and wind their way back up into smaller valleys. Coal was mined in these valleys, so the railroad followed. Wide sweeps of railroad tracks formerly reached out from marshaling yards up along the valley

**Pikeville, Kentucky**

145

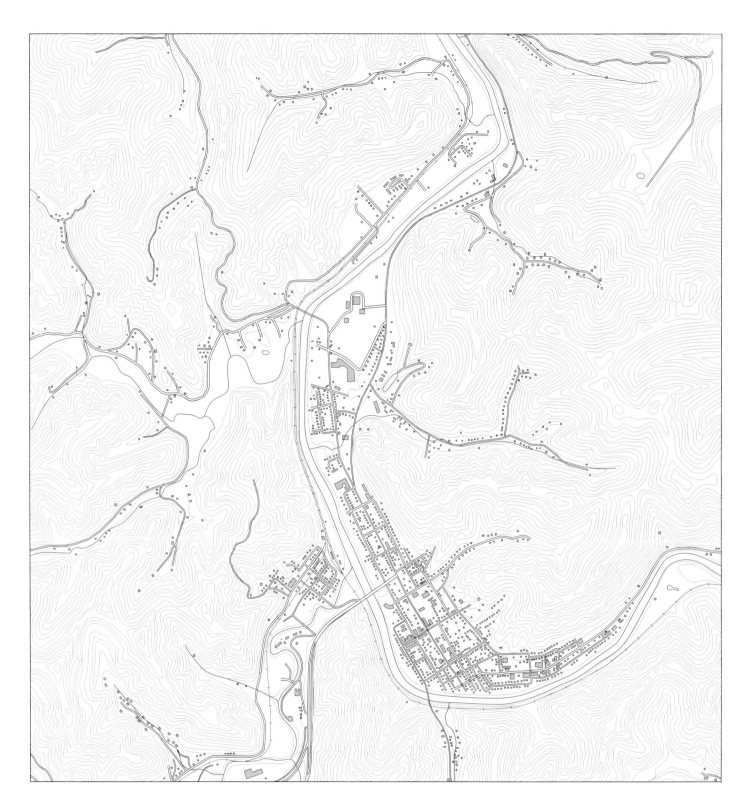

**Prestonsburg, Kentucky**

Williamson, West Virginia

147

"Saturday afternoon, 24 August 1946, Welch, West Virginia," Russell Lee, photographer. (National Archives)

(Opposite) Rail yard, Williamson, West Virginia, 1930s. (Norfolk Southern Historical Photograph Collection Ms88-120, Digital Library and Archives, University Libraries, Virginia Polytechnic Institute and State University)

streams. The smaller residential camps were closer to the mines, where the confined streambeds widened to provide enough level ground for structures. As the mines developed, these camps grew into tiny hamlets of uniform rows of prefabricated dwellings. Even today, with the mines and tracks dismantled, the worker houses remain identifiable by their straight rows and identical forms. Layers of renovations cannot hide their uniformity. Numerous other towns, such as Imboden, Exeter, Inman, Andover, Stonega, Osaka, and Roda, existed as residential satellites "up the tracks" from Appalachia. (The naming of towns in the coal region is fascinat-

ing. Relatives, wives, mistresses, and Native American places all served as referents.) The forking pattern of the watershed held these tiny hamlets on the only available flat land, while the branching order of the railroad tracks connected them back to the hub of Appalachia.

Appalachia proper was built around two railroads that approached the Powell River from opposite directions. Tracks were everywhere, leaving little room for structures. The primary commercial street, West Main, rests upon a high narrow shelf of land parallel to the large track sidings below. Stores, restaurants, the Houston Hotel, two banks, two movie houses, the post

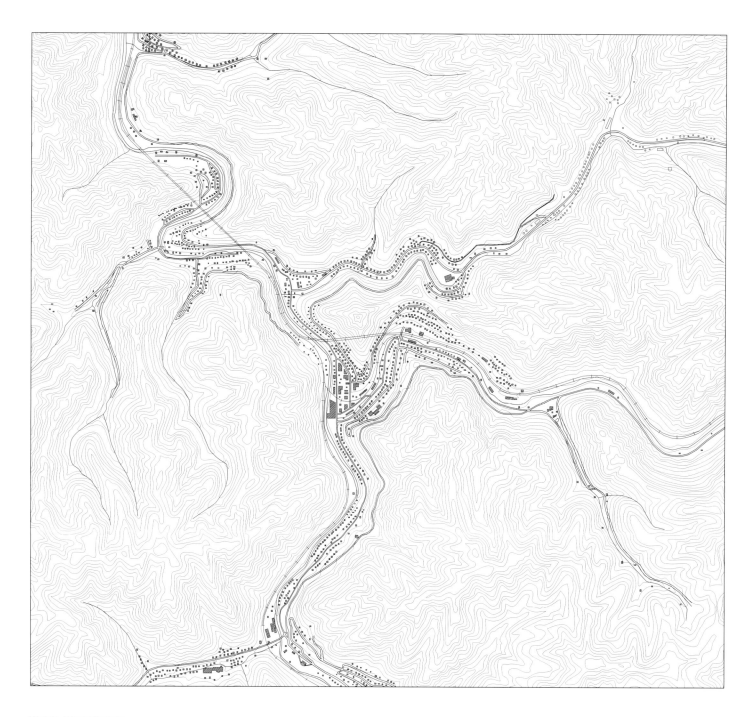

**Welch, West Virginia**

150

office, and the Methodist church enclosed this street with a tight grouping of brick structures. Residences climbed the steep hillside behind, while tracks and modest houses covered the riverbank below. The passenger stations of the L & N sat on the east end of town, and the maintenance and repair shops of the Southern Railway were to the west.

Appalachia is a remarkable example of a concise commercial core that served widely scattered and remote mountain settlements through a dendritic pattern of tracks, streams, and topography. Today's twisting roads follow the same streams, reminders of a culture's changing history, which remains etched upon a geological landscape. Such sinuous congruity and the utilitarian logic of coupling transportation with fluvial erosion makes a system of inhabitation unlike any other. Only in the farthest and highest valleys does one discover the cost of such in-

frastructure in the scarred earth and blackened hills.

The settlement patterns also grouped around watersheds because the railroads had to follow the beds of streams and creeks to maintain reasonable grades into these remote areas. Several well-known rivers of this region of the southern Appalachians gather abundant moisture and rain from the hills and carry their drainage northwest to the Ohio River, which forms the western boundary of West Virginia. Coal deposits and mine complexes were often identified by access river systems. The names of the Kanawha, New, Guyandotte, and Big Sandy rivers are associated with railroads and coal districts. The names of many rivers in this region contain the word *fork*, such as Tug Fork or Levisa Fork. To call a stream a "fork" of another watercourse recognizes it as part of a branching system that moves away from the

Mullens, West Virginia

152

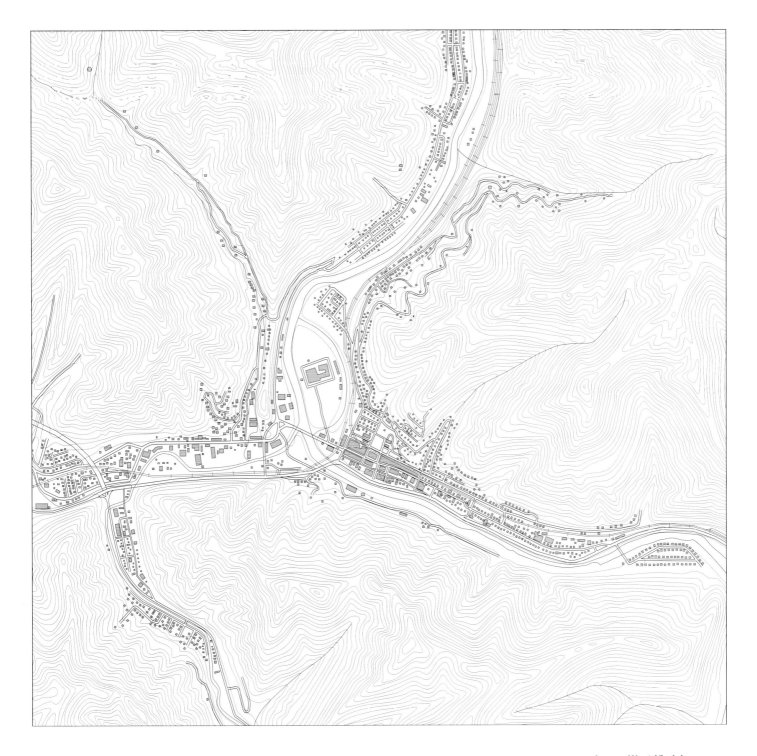

Logan, West Virginia

direction of travel and can be followed up-stream, which is how the railroads penetrated these hills and mountains.

Pikeville and Prestonsburg, Kentucky, are located on the Levisa Fork of the Big Sandy River. Pikeville, the county seat for Pike County, Kentucky, sits within a most unusual turn in the Levisa. The river formerly made a sharp bend around a series of hilly knobs to form a flat area on the inside of the curve. The tiny grid of Pikeville rests precariously on this alluvial shelf. The railroad once followed the same curve, with a passenger station and freight depot against the steep hillside. Grouped in a tight knot along Main Street were the county courthouse, two large hotels, the post office, the U.S. courthouse, and all other necessary businesses associated with a remote county seat. Today the hotels are gone, but the lovely county courthouse remains, as does the beautiful post office with its fine terra-cotta details. When the new state highway cut through the mountains across the short-est end of the river bend, a channel was also made for the Levisa Fork. Within a few years humans accomplished what eons of erosion could not, and today the town faces a dry, empty streambed used mainly for parking. The town's crescent-shaped urban form responds only to a ghost of past geological forces.

Prestonsburg too rests on a small alluvial plain along the Levisa Fork. Like Pikeville, it is a county seat—of Floyd County, Kentucky. Two twisting creeks thread their way from Prestons-burg up into the surrounding mountains. Today the automobile Route 114, rather than rail lines, follows Middle Creek over to Salyersville and the

Mountain Parkway, which takes one straight to Lexington, Kentucky. In contrast to the Pikeville bypass, many of the contemporary highways of the southern Appalachians inscribe the same valleys and waterways that the railroads did one hundred years ago.

Downtown Prestonsburg has a small grid of streets laid out upon the widest part of the only available level ground, securely wedged between the river and the steep mountains. Its concise commercial core runs from Front Street, on the river, by way of Court Street to the courthouse, the post office, and other municipal buildings. Two financial institutions anchor the corners of Front Street and Court Street. The greatly fore-shortened wall of trees and steep hillsides termi-nates the view down the space of Court Street. The slanting orange light of a late November sun brightens the storefronts and the Masonic hall, while the street lamps opposite glow in the lengthening gloom of late afternoon shadows cast by the omnipresent mountains.

Following the Tug Fork, another tributary of the Big Sandy River upstream, one arrives first at Williamson and then at Welch, West Virginia. Williamson's tightly gridded center nestles on a broad plain formed by the Tug Fork. Streaming southeast out of Williamson for miles along the riverbank are the remnants of the huge mar-shaling yards and maintenance facilities of the Norfolk & Western Railway. Vast strings of coal cars were gathered in these yards before the long haul west to the Ohio River and the Midwest. These extensive rail yards stretched around river bends and hills into the far distance. The tracks cut straight through the center of Williamson on an elevated structure before sweeping around the sharply turning Tug Fork. The tracks extrude southward, drawn through the center of town like threads through the eye of a shuttle to expand outward in long lines that curve and recurve around the topography. It is as though the town spun gossamer threads of steel that provided the weft to its urban fabric's warp. The operations of these yards required great numbers of people, and Williamson grew to accommodate the extensive services necessary to support them. Its downtown contained just about every service imaginable: the Mingo County Court House, the federal court, and the post office provided government offices. Hotels, restaurants, and commercial and retail stores furnished all the things required for visitors and business people. The streets of Williamson are lined still with uniformly dense brick buildings, old hotels, and empty storefronts, punctuated by the Mingo County Court House and the post office.

On a crisp April morning a coal train so long that neither end is visible waits on the tracks in the center of Williamson. With a jerk it comes alive like a beast roused from sleep, activated by locomotives far ahead around the river's curve, and slowly, silently moves away. Williamson exists because of the railroad, and its concise urban form still clings tightly to the tracks that now simply allow trains to pass through.

A very narrow area at the confluence of the Tug Fork and Elkhorn Creek holds the tiny settlement of Welch, West Virginia. The Norfolk & Western tracks slip down both watercourses to join at Welch before running through Davey

**Abandoned building, Logan,
West Virginia**

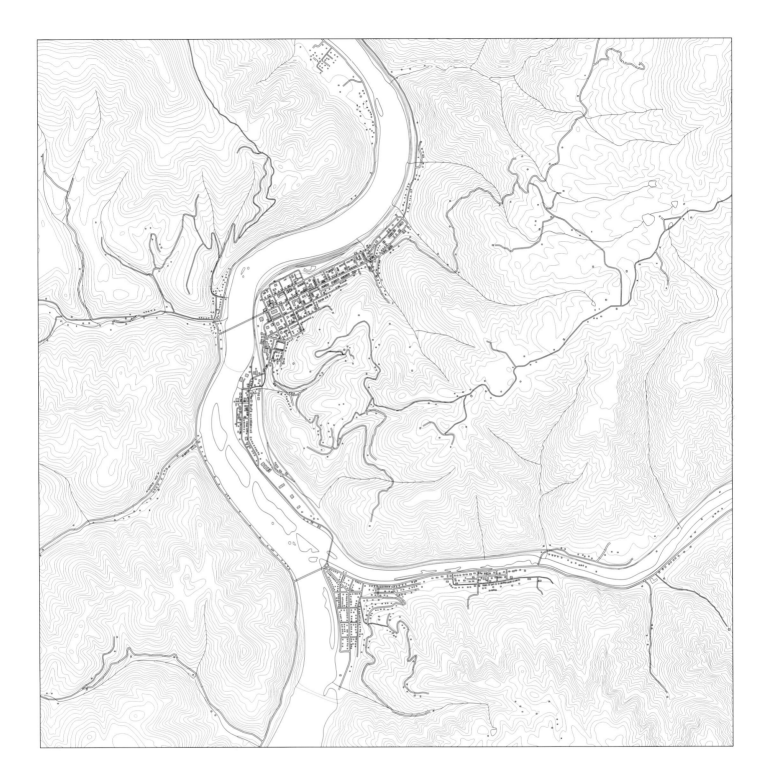

**Hinton, West Virginia**

156

to Williamson. The tracks could just make the radius turn by cutting through the downtown. A later tunnel shortened the diagonal of the bend and allowed trains to avoid the slow, tight curve and downtown traffic. The placement of Welch is so constrained by the two rivers that buildings hang out over the water. A long residential block lines the Elkhorn Creek with beautiful wooden balconies overhanging the stream. A remarkable photograph taken in 1946 shows Welch's main thoroughfare festooned with signs and cluttered with cars, the cars foreshadowing their agency of the town's demise. Downtown Welch was so congested that in 1941 the town built a parking structure to hold 425 cars. The parking deck remains mostly empty now, as newer parking lots have assumed most of the open space formerly occupied by the tracks and freight and passenger stations. A new theater is being built on the empty site of the tracks, and a new composition of civic structures replaced the passenger station. These new structures do not define the street edges as Welch's gridded urban form did when it oriented around the magnificent McDowell County Court House. When hotels, theaters, and other retail structures clustered together in this dramatic composition of water, mountains, rail lines, and buildings, Welch was the ultimate example of concise urban form.

Over the mountains on the parallel watershed of the Guyandotte River, the town of Mullens sits, like Welch, at the confluence of two rivers, the Slab Fork and the Guyandotte, and at the confluence of two branches of the Norfolk & Western Railroad. As in Williamson, but not as extensive, a long marshaling yard extrudes

downstream along the Guyandotte for miles. Mullens's retail core occupies a tiny flat area between the tracks and the Slab Fork, while its residential neighborhoods wrap around behind a protruding hill. The grid of only eight blocks had two hotels, the Wyoming and the Guyandotte, as well as two movie theaters. Sadly, the entire block that held the Guyandotte Hotel, opposite the former passenger station, has been demolished, as have two other blocks. Few buildings of Mullens remain occupied, although the Norfolk & Western (formerly the Virginia Rail Road) still schedules coal trains through its immense yards across the river. The remaining brick and stone buildings of Mullens comprise a wonderful complex—a tiny gem of urban form locked away in distant mountains.

Logan, West Virginia, is located farther downstream on the Guyandotte River at its confluence with Island Creek. Logan is really a sequence of settlements strung along the alluvial shelves of the Guyandotte River: McConnell, Stollings, West Logan, Black Bottom, and Mount Gay all blend together as they face one another across the water. As the county seat, Logan, however, is the hub of these disparate towns. The Logan County Court House commands the center of town, placed in a separate square surrounded on all sides by well-scaled architecture. Hotels and banks reinforced the continuity of the urban fabric, even though on-grade railroad tracks separate the retail blocks from the residential neighborhoods that climb the hills away from the river. Logan is a long, linear urban pattern barely two blocks wide that parallels the tracks along the Guyandotte River. It expands

**Figure-ground of Hinton, West Virginia**

to three blocks to incorporate the courthouse square. Island Creek forms an island—hence its name—as it intersects with the Guyandotte River. The Hatsfield Regional High School sits on this island like a castle, surrounded by a moat accessible by a single bridge.

The last town we shall look at in these bituminous coal fields is Hinton, West Virginia, on the New River. Actually very old geologically, the New River has become a major recreation destination with a long segment designated as a national river administered by the National Park Service. Not far downstream from Hinton the New River slices through the deep and dramatic New River Gorge, a popular whitewater-rafting destination. This increased activity benefits Hinton, with rafting outfitters and camping sites located in the nearby beautiful Bluestone State Park and Wildlife Management Area along the water impounded behind Bluestone Lake Dam.

Hinton is a classic alluvial town that rests on a broad shelf at a smooth bend in the New River. The Chesapeake & Ohio tracks follow this same curve along the riverbank. Hinton's C & O locomotive-maintenance shops were formerly located between the town and the river; an enormous roundhouse and turntable could accommodate seventeen engines at once. Of these extensive facilities only isolated water towers that once serviced the steam locomotives remain.

Hinton is a wonderful example of the tension between a regularized street grid and the sweeping curves of topography and water. Streets end abruptly at the river's edge, the rail lines, or, in the opposite direction, at the hillside. A figure-

ground of Hinton shows the shifts in its street grid. At Union Street, next to the civic complex of the Summers County Court House and the post office, the grid rotates 45 degrees to conform to the sweeping bend in the New River. A statue of a Confederate soldier stands on the tiny triangle of grass formed by this transition in front of the Baptist church, marking both a rift

in the urban grid and a fracture in West Virginia's perception of itself as a northern state.

Downtown Hinton contains a well-preserved fabric of commercial and retail establishments that retain much of their vitality because of the seasonal influx of whitewater rafters. Second and Third avenues and Temple Street have kept the elegant facades that enclose the public spaces

**Hinton, West Virginia, early twentieth century. (Library of Congress)**

of the streets. Always these spaces frame views across the empty land of the former railroad yards to the broader river beyond. An early black-and-white photograph captures the topographic constraints of Hinton's placement. The railroad curves along the river, and the town sits on flat land enclosed tightly by mountains.

Deep shadows of sadness cannot hide the once rich and vital past of these towns in the bituminous coal region of the southern Appalachians. Even though many of the buildings in the town centers are vacant, these structures still contribute to urban compositions that are unmatched in America. These are places of urban form whose content left with the last train, places whose resolute beauty derives from a past in which form, content, and topography all conspired to create towns unique to the region and to the world. Were Mullens or Welch anywhere else—accessible to greater centers of population or, like Hinton, near recreational amenities— they would be the quintessentially preserved small towns with handsome buildings pragmatically arranged within spectacular natural settings. But they are not near such places, so they slowly dissolve as individual buildings weather and collapse or are demolished through neglect. It seems impossible to imagine any economically viable future for them.

Others, like Logan or Williamson, hang on as remnants of the once overwhelming presence of the railroad. New centers of commerce—malls made accessible by the same roads built to bring economic growth—flourish at great distances from the old historic downtowns. Ironically, these new developments sprout upon similar alluvial plains along state and interstate highways. Often these shopping malls reuse the vacant land of the discontinued railroad marshaling yards that once brimmed with waiting coal hoppers. The larger regional population hubs continue to grow and to attract more and more sprawl in the seemingly inevitable cycle of more highway infrastructure and more undifferentiated communities. The shift from concise urban settlements to these loosely joined conglomerates of sprawl appears equally inevitable.

Towns like these in West Virginia, Virginia, and Kentucky tell complex narratives of greed and exploitation. They also speak of our ability to imagine places whose form and connecting rail infrastructure were wedded to the larger natural context. The processes that began millions of years ago gave these towns the reasons for their brief existence as they, like the coal, glowed brightly for a millisecond within the larger span of time, only to softly fade from our landscapes and our memories.

# 6

# Harvesting Sunbeams

## Towns of the Anthracite Coal Valleys of Pennsylvania

The Alleghenian orogeny continuously crushed the eastern edge of the North American plate more than 200 million years ago and deformed the flat layers of sedimented shale, limestone, and coal into steep folds, much like a tablecloth wrinkling along a tabletop. Tectonic compression not only formed the highest mountains but changed the direction of a segment of the Appalachians in Pennsylvania from northeastward to eastward for almost three hundred miles. Beyond this location, the Appalachians swing again 40 degrees east to continue into New York State and New England. These tremendous geological forces, with whole continents contending, applied ever so gradually and constantly over millions of years, subjected the enormous thickness of mineral deposits to additional pressures—pressures intense enough to bend an entire mountain range and far greater than those that compressed the seams of bituminous coal to the south. This folding and faulting formed four fields of anthracite coal across a small area of the now steeply rolling hills of northeast Pennsylvania. This area became known in the nineteenth century as the anthracite region. These tightly twisted beds of coal are pushed together at times, so that they are almost

vertical, and have sharp dips that make mining expensive and difficult.

Geological history dealt these hills and mountains a single hand in which the winners would take all as players in one of the most brutal extractive moves imaginable. Anthracite coal's apogee as a preferred fuel lasted barely one hundred years, yet vast fortunes were won by a lucky few. For the thousands of others there remain only discarded towns, cast aside in a losing gamble, places of resolute beauty with names like Mahanoy City, Tamaqua, Ashland, and Lansford. This study turns now to the context of these wonderful and unique examples of urban form with a discussion of the particularities of anthracite coal and its extraction.

Unlike bituminous coal, anthracite coal is hard to ignite, but once burning, it is almost smokeless and is relatively clean and efficient. It was ideal for residential use, especially in the rapidly growing dense metropolitan areas of the East Coast, such as Philadelphia and New York. Fortuitously, these coal fields are less than one hundred miles from either city. In spite of the difficulties of mining anthracite coal, cheap transportation and contiguous markets fostered its extraction fifty years earlier than that of

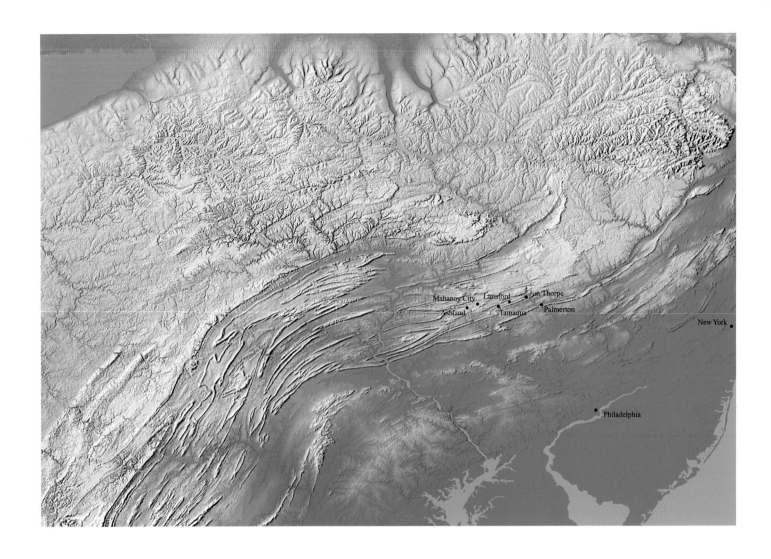

Mahanoy City  Lansford  Jim Thorpe
Ashland  Tamaqua  Palmerton

New York

Philadelphia

**Appalachian Mountains in Pennsylvania**

bituminous coal in the more distant fields of Kentucky, West Virginia, and Virginia.

These crushed and folded coal beds lie in a landscape of equally contorted ridges that spread in steep waves toward the Allegheny Plateau of western Pennsylvania. Once covered with forests of hemlock and hardwoods, the slopes now bear the black scars of the recent rapacious past. There is a beauty here still, but it is the bleak beauty of scars and stuntedness. Little is left except the heaping culm mounds of what was a swamp millions of years ago. It is a

landscape forever harrowed by humans that will require thousands of years to recover. Its beauty suggests something unmentionable—an earth devoid of life. It is a landscape turned black. Towns came into existence in these narrow valleys along creeks and rivers, connected by railroads, overlooked by mines and piles of debris. Tenaciously, these towns remain locked within a topography rendered in the grey palette of coal dust.

Native Americans and the earliest European settlers knew from the many surface outcroppings that there was coal in America. Coal had already been used as fuel in England, and its combustible qualities were well understood. While the bituminous seams in western Virginia were also known, transportation through the mountains to the eastern seaboard was difficult in the eighteenth century, so the colonies actually imported coal from England. The American Revolution and the War of 1812 changed all this and brought into focus the vast markets of the growing cities of the Northeast, from Baltimore to Boston. Anthracite, or "stone coal," was first regarded with suspicion by most because of the difficulty in lighting and burning it. However, blacksmiths in the anthracite region were aware of its higher combustion temperature and therefore used and transported it in very small quantities. Experiments with both induced and forced drafts to blow air through the anthracite coal to speed combustion soon confirmed its adaptability, and demand grew rapidly.

Coal was useless without bulk transportation to potential markets, and even the distances to Philadelphia and New York were too great for early-nineteenth-century wagons. Roads were dirt tracks, muddy and wet in the warm months, frozen solid into wheel-breaking ruts in the winter. In a classic example of market-transportation-resource development, methods of bulk transportation were expanded. First came flatboats—known as "arks"—on rivers such as the Susquehanna, the Lehigh, and the Schuylkill. But as in the South, these rivers were unreliable, with torrents in the spring, then dry in summer. Unlike rivers in the South, these rivers froze in the winter, the period of greatest

demand. The next effort during the early quarter of the nineteenth century was to improve these natural waterways with a series of canals, locks, and dams to provide a more reliable system of distribution. An amazing network of canals was built connecting the anthracite coal fields to Philadelphia, New York, and the cities of New England. A map from 1856 illustrates the various means of available transportation to New York City. Coal could be moved by flatboat or barge to a seaport, then by coastal schooner to northern cities. Canals, however, had the same problems as the rivers. They still depended upon water, and worse, containing "flat water," they froze regularly. The British blockade of American ports during the War of 1812 squeezed the market for coal and made overland demand even greater. In the second quarter of the nineteenth century this demand brought into existence railroads, steam locomotives, and extensive coal mines, which were so interdependent as to form one history. Coal without railroads would have been unavailable; railroads without coal for fuel would not run, but railroads also needed vast quantities of freight to pay their way. Steel, iron, coal, steam power, and rail systems all came together in the great industrial explosion of the second half of the nineteenth century. To put this industrial expansion into perspective, in 1890 Pennsylvania provided more than half of the steel and iron manufactured in the United States on a rail system that had more miles of track than that of any other state.[1] And nowhere did this powerful partnership gain more influence or more capitol than in the anthracite fields of Pennsylvania. As the long trains

1. Stover, *Routledge Historical Atlas of the American Railroads*, 129.

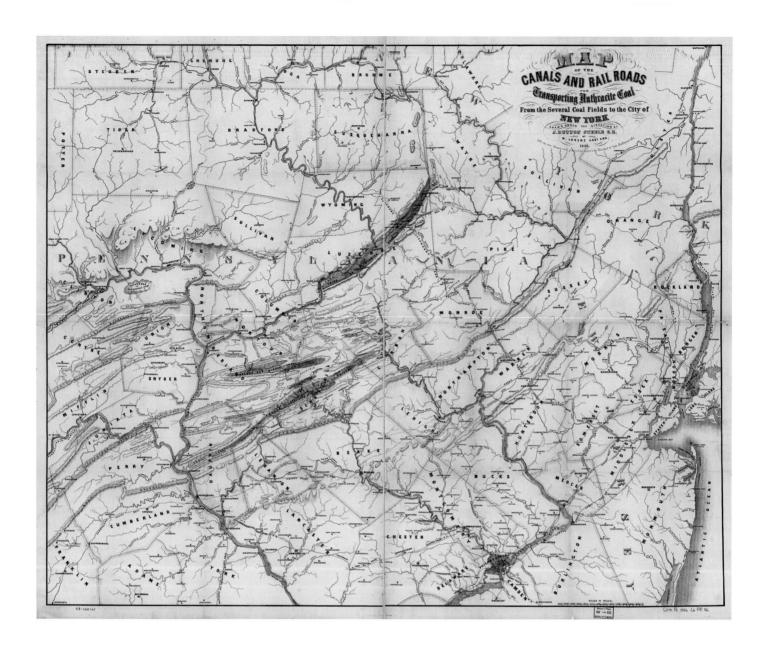

*Map of the Canals and Rail Roads for Transporting Anthracite Coal from the Several Coal Fields to the City of New York,* 1856. (Library of Congress)

of brimming black coal wound their way out of the valleys and mountains of this region, towns and settlements grew to house the mineworkers, the laborers in the collieries, and to service the dense network of railroads that moved their heavy cargo of "black diamonds." Through once pristine valleys and along river courses that would soon be polluted beyond recovery,

tracks stretched from the eastern cities into the mountains.

The location of the coal seams in the ridges and valleys determined the mine entrances, and the mine entrances determined the placement of towns. Without any other means of transportation, laborers and miners walked in the gray early morning light to the mines, so distances from lodging to work needed to be short. Later, as the valleys filled with towns and smaller residential "patches," trolley lines strung the settlements together like beads along a string connecting people to more distant collieries. Rail lines and watersheds connected the towns of this chapter in pairs. Lansford and Tamaqua are located in the Panther Valley, which is drained by Panther Creek and the Little Schuylkill and flows into the Schuylkill River to Philadelphia. Ashland and Mahanoy City rest in valleys drained by Mahanoy Creek, a creek that runs all the way west to the great Susquehanna. The town of Jim Thorpe came into existence because of its site on the Lehigh River, while downstream Palmerton sits on a broad flood plain at the intersection of the Aquashicola and the Lehigh. These smaller creeks were not navigable, but the Lehigh, Schuylkill, and Susquehanna rivers were, and all three figured prominently in the early nineteenth century for barge and canal transportation. It is significant that these towns sat beside watercourses because later in the century, as railroads became synonymous with coal, their tracks could extend into these remote valleys along the flat land beside these same streams. On a map from 1873 the Philadelphia & Reading Railroad threads its way up the Schuylkill River from Philadelphia. Coal moved from the mines downhill by gravity through breakers, to be fed into long waiting lines of black hopper coal cars. Topography, drainage, and settlement patterns came together in a carefully orchestrated choreography of coal veins, mine entrances, slope, and town placement—a dance begun millions of years ago when verdant

swamps covered these areas and began the process of coal formation.

The operation of a colliery for processing coal at a mine's entrance influenced a town's structure far more than did a tipple in the bituminous regions. A colliery comprised the entire structure of the mine, the mine entrance, loading facilities for railroad cars, and the breaker. The breakers were huge. Their great ominous structures dominated the grey landscape of these valleys and became the anchors that gathered towns, railroad trackage, and vast piles of waste. Coal from within the mine was conveyed to the top of the breaker by belt, then moved downward by gravity and crushed into different sizes or grades. This process removed impurities such as slate or rock. The mining of coal is not a bucolic enterprise, yet, ironically, agriculture provided the names, with *buckwheat coal, pea coal,* and *rice coal* indicating the grade of the coal. The coal was washed to remove dust and fine particles and then chuted into waiting coal cars at the very bottom of the breaker. It was a noisy, dirty process, full of grinding machinery and moving belts. In the nineteenth and early twentieth centuries boys as young as ten or twelve worked in the breakers ten hour a day, six days a week, sorting coal with hands rubbed raw by their exhausting work. Later the process became more mechanized, but it was no less dangerous. There were many breakers grouped along the valleys and scattered up the mountainsides. Only a few remain, isolated looming structures dark against the sky, empty except for the black coal dust that veneers every surface. Long attenuated towns such as Lansford, Ashland, and

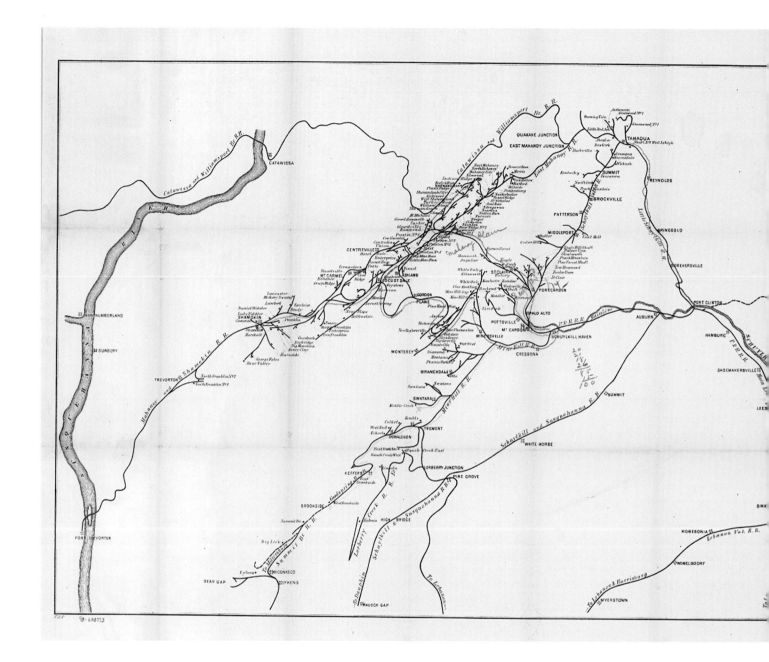

*Sketch Map of the Phila.
& Readg. Rail Road and
Its Branches, May 1873.*
(Library of Congress)

166

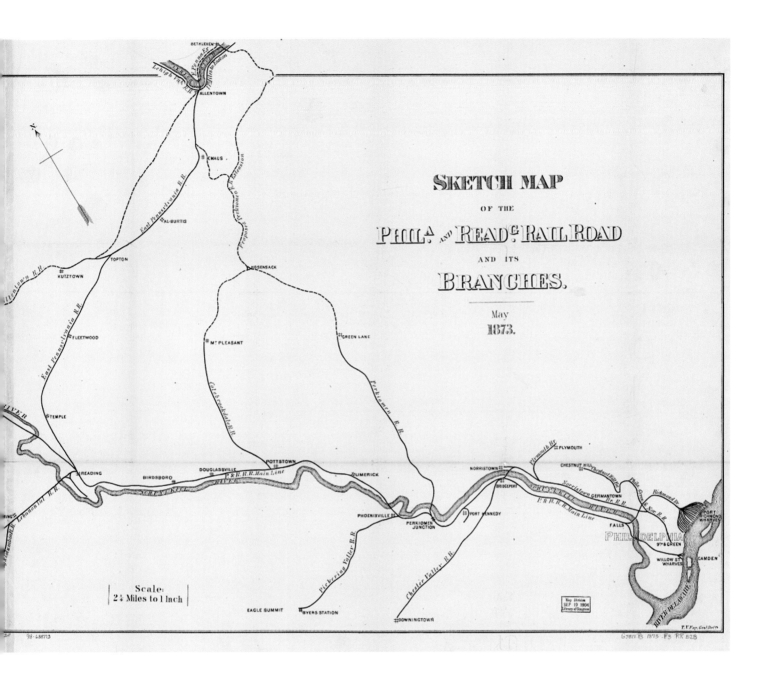

# SKETCH MAP

OF THE

## PHILA. AND READ'G RAIL ROAD

AND ITS

## BRANCHES.

May
1873.

Scale:
2¼ Miles to 1 Inch

**Detail of abandoned
breaker**

**Lehigh Navigation Coal
Company, Lansford Colliery,
1940. (Library of Congress)**

Mahanoy City grew between the collieries, as did the compact railroad-maintenance and iron-manufacturing centers like Tamaqua.

The town of Jim Thorpe—formerly Mauch Chunk—on the Lehigh River provides an ideal introduction to the earliest history of the region. The town sits at the eastern end of a long ridge of the Appalachians where the Lehigh River slices through on its way to the Delaware River and Philadelphia. Early in the nineteenth century, coal was discovered exposed near the surface along the top of this ridge, part of the vast Mammoth Bed, which continental pressures had caused to fold back upon itself millions of years earlier. An open quarry mine exploited this readily available coal, and a gravity railroad was constructed to carry it several miles to the Lehigh River, where it was loaded onto barges for the journey to Philadelphia. The railroad ran along the top of the ridge on a gently sloping gradient and then slid steeply down a natural drainage ravine to the river. First mules and then fixed steam power pulled the empty cars back up to run on a parallel "switchback" track to the mine. There were no moving steam engines involved, even though these were being developed on competing sites. Jim Thorpe was a river port where coal gathered from the mountain above was loaded into barges on the river. The barges were eventually superseded by railroads, but

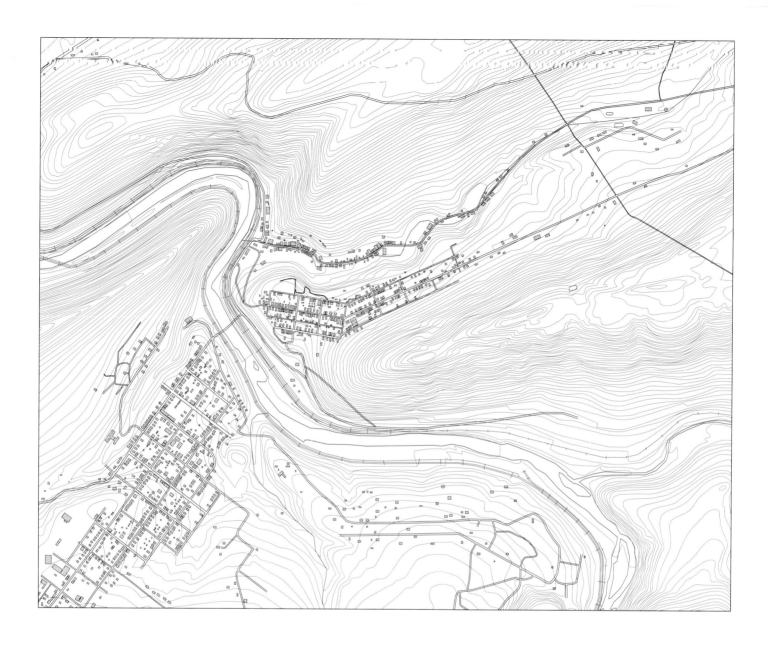

**Jim Thorpe, Pennsylvania. Broadway Street is rendered in yellow.**

the tracks paralleled the riverbanks. Because of the great engineering and technical aspects of this switchback, people traveled from considerable distances to view and ride this marvel of ingenuity and industrial prowess. The plane of tracks upward through the town eventually disappeared, but an urban grouping remained that cascades down the ravine to a tiny plaza at the railroad station. The site and the extraordinary architecture of Jim Thorpe—the Carbon County Court House, the Lehigh Navigation and Coal Company Building, the Opera House, the Inn at Jim Thorpe, the several beautiful churches—make this town a scenic composition unlike any in the region. From its beginning, the switchback railroad made Jim Thorpe a tourist destination. Today it remains a thriving resort community filled with shops and restaurants tucked dramatically into the Poconos Mountains.

Jim Thorpe is really three settlements spread across the topography on both sides of the river and on different plateaus. East Jim Thorpe is a gridded residential community on the opposite side of the Lehigh River. Upper Jim Thorpe is a small grid on a flat area above and overlooking the commercial core. The dramatic topography forced this tripart division and segregated the commercial from the residential areas. These different layers of settlements give Jim Thorpe a picturesque quality within its tight valley that still attracts many visitors.

The commercial core of Jim Thorpe winds up the little stream between the two lobes of the mountains behind. The ravine was cut by a stream that subjected the town to severe flooding until it was dammed above the town. This crease in the topography became the logical and easiest route for the coal cars to descend to the riverbank. Later this track formed the central street, twisting and weaving its way upward, with structures scattered along the sides like random blocks fitted into the hillside. The stream and then the rail cars incised their marks repeatedly upon this cleft in the landscape until the settlement pattern became more suggestive of a hill town than a former industrial river port.

Jim Thorpe encapsulates the history of coal extraction and reveals the inseparable connection between the development of bulk transportation and the success of mining. Transported first by canals and barges and then by railroads, coal as a resource was valueless without the means to get it to markets. Technological innovation combined with economic incentive gave this region an incredible boost in the early nineteenth century and allowed it to become a center for industrialization for the entire country. Tourists flocked to Jim Thorpe to witness this growth and industrial mastery. They flock still to this tiny town locked both in its topography and in its past. For other towns, more single-

**Broadway Street, Jim Thorpe, Pennsylvania. (Library of Congress)**

minded and even ruthless in their pursuit of
industrial capitalism, time has been less forgiv-
ing. Located several miles downstream from Jim
Thorpe, Palmerton offers a cautionary contrast.

Palmerton was named after Stephen Squires
Palmerton, head of a plant for mining and processing zinc from 1892 to 1912. Palmerton was
a company town built in 1899 to service what
became the giant zinc-manufacturing conglomerate of the New Jersey Zinc Company. Zinc is
used in galvanizing steel and iron for protection
against rust and as zinc oxide in paint and many
other applications. Unfortunately, the manufacturing of zinc produces several highly toxic by-
products, such as cadmium, which have polluted
these sites beyond salvation.

Palmerton was built from the ground up between the two great plants that were situated like
bookends at opposite ends of the town. It sits on
a flood plain of the Aquashicola Creek and the
Lehigh River. More importantly, the tracks of
the Lehigh & Susquehanna Railroad, part of
the New Jersey Central System, ran along the
site and made the shipping of ore and finished
products convenient. The great anthracite
coal mines nearby provided the energy for the
sprawling zinc industry. At its zenith, the New
Jersey Zinc Company employed three thousand
workers in its two plants at Palmerton, so it
could afford to built an entire community to
serve the factories. Palmerton's simple urban
form is reinforced by long rows of wonderfully

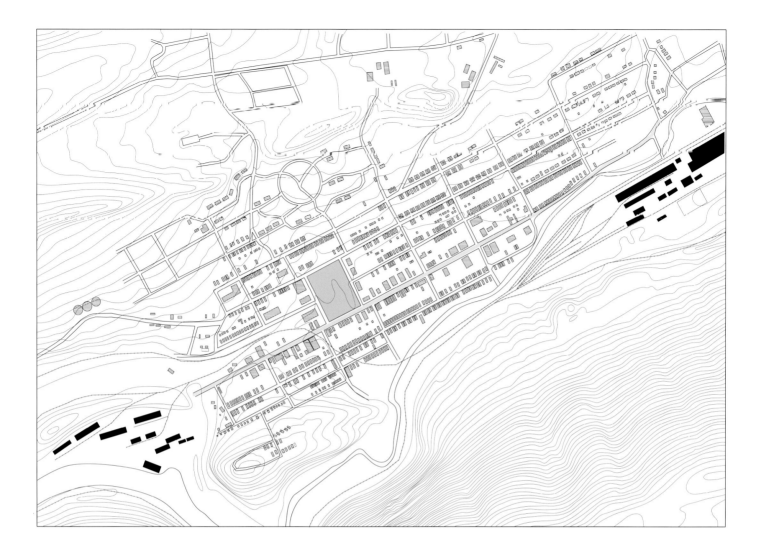

scaled modest worker housing. Its main thoroughfare, Delaware Avenue, is a wide commercial street bordered by a lovely park surrounded by civic structures such as schools, churches, and the headquarters of the New Jersey Zinc Company of Pennsylvania.

The wide swath of Delaware Avenue sweeps through the town from west to east parallel to the river and connects the two industrial areas; its public space is enclosed by a continuous wall of retail facades. A beautiful shaded municipal park stands at the center of Delaware Avenue

and connects the downtown with the area uphill where the more elegant homes of the plant managers are located. The large park, interrupting at least four blocks, today is filled with greenery and provides a respite, an oasis of grace midway between the sites of one abandoned and one still functioning zinc plant. Palmerton is one of the few towns in this region with such an amenity; the dark shade of the park focuses the grid and the strong linear vista of Delaware Avenue. Sadly, it hardly seems compensation for the bare, sterile ground that brackets Palmerton at either

**Palmerton, Pennsylvania**

end as evidence of the zinc-manufacturing processes of the past.

In valleys to the west, Lansford, Mahanoy City, and Ashland are three similar towns whose long narrow linear forms arise from their similar conformance to topography and their origins between breakers within the coal fields of the southern anthracite beds. They are not the only towns along these valleys, but because they share many characteristics they can be discussed together as a trilogy. A diagram for each distills several salient attributes that identify all three as enlarged variations of the typical "patch" towns found throughout the anthracite region. Today the collieries and breakers have gone, the rail tracks have been sold for scrap, and the mountains of coal and debris are hidden under a thin

veil of struggling birch and sumac. These towns, as wreckage left from one of the highest tides of industrial expansion, tell of the travails and triumphs of the human spirit.

Mine entrances determined a town's placement, and these entrances were driven deep into the earth to advantageously intersect as many coal seams as possible. The distance of these veins beneath a ridge, the inclined angle of the vein in relation to the nearest surface, and the necessity of water drainage all determined the shaft's opening. Mine entrances were scattered across the blackened landscape, but because of the steeply varied terrain, they most often occurred on the side of a slope. A moving belt conveyed the coal directly from the mine entrance to the top of a breaker, where it began a down-

ward journey to the waiting coal cars at the bottom. The tracks for these cars and their numerous attendant sidings ran along the inevitable stream and creek bottom lands that afforded the level ground and gentle gradients necessary for railroads. The workers' towns grew between and within walking distance of these looming breakers and the mountains of slate, rock, and culm piles. The towns typically paralleled the railroad tracks and filled the bottom areas of a valley bracketed between two or more breakers. Mining, or, more specifically, the workings of a colliery, required additional labor beyond that produced by the highly skilled men toiling deep within the earth at the coal face. Some men moved the coal from within the mine to the surface, others sorted and graded the coal inside

the breaker, and many serviced the machinery of hoists, crushers, and railroad operations. The long continuous lines of coal-hopper rail cars required steam engines and all the personnel of a railroad to keep the coal moving from the anthracite fields to distant markets. These myriad workers needed housing both for themselves and for their families. They also needed communal infrastructures, so these towns built churches, retail centers, schools, and the various other components of a community. As these towns extruded along the landscape between collieries, the larger ones, such as Ashland, Lansford, and Mahanoy City, grew into remarkably concise examples of persistent urban form.

Subsidiaries of the coal companies still own the land just outside these towns' boundaries.

**Figure-grounds of three
Pennsylvania towns**

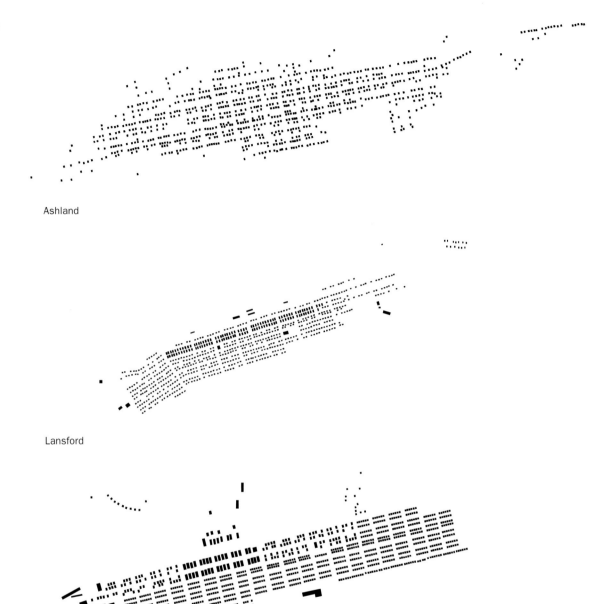

Ashland

Lansford

Mahanoy City

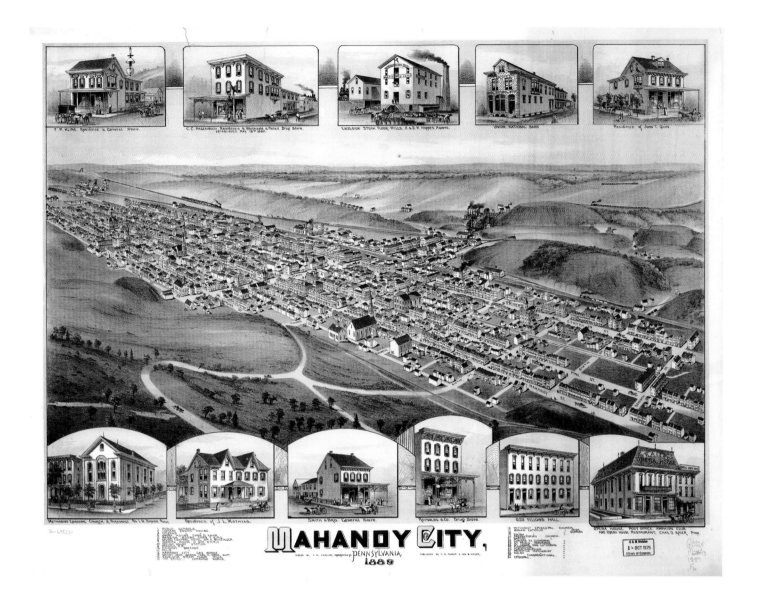

Consequently, unlike most settlements, these can have no sprawl, and their downtown retail cores remain viable. One enters these towns abruptly from the surrounding woods and is carried through their wide main streets and out the other side into forest. Across their short axes topography too restricts expansion. While each town may be several miles long, they can be only a few blocks wide because the steep banks of mining debris, now covered with vegetation,

or the shear wall of the enclosing ridge contains them laterally. Often the vista across the narrow dimension of blocks ends dramatically with a foreshortened wall of green that covers the disturbed earth.

Most housing in these towns was originally either financed or leased by the coal company for workers in the collieries. Lines of modest dwellings extrude from end to end of the entire settlement. Generally, several variations of a

**Bird's-eye view of Mahanoy City, Pennsylvania, 1889. (Library of Congress)**

simple type of house are repeated either as tight row housing or as unassuming single-family units defined by narrow alleys. These types began as carbon copies that had identical details of fenestration and trim, yet over time their turned wood railings have been replaced with stock wrought iron, and their cornices and window frames have been covered with grossly rendered vinyl siding. The wonderful perversity of human individuality expresses itself in the history of each residence. Today no two are exactly alike, yet a careful study of any street reveals the consistency of the original form beneath all the incrustations and improvements. Each dwelling has a shallow porch fronting directly onto the narrow sidewalk that provides a deeply shaded transition from the public street to the private interior. These porches are also individualized with hanging plants, porch chairs, children's toys, national flags and bunting, or religious icons. Pride of ownership, modest and humble, and the perception of security and openness give these streets a sense of community unique in America. Ironically, as this same sense of public and shared streets slips away from so much of contemporary suburban development, Ashland, Lansford, and Mahanoy City retain

their civility and serve as models of strong communal loyalty.

The two- and three-story repetitive dwellings maintain the human scale of these extended streets within the mountainous landscape with a continuous enclosure of the public space and a consistency of elements such as porches and cornices. Multiple blocks of similar housing assemble together into an urban fabric that maintains its integrity across the entire town. This fabric successfully preserves the precarious balance between public streets and private ownership so essential to urban form. The many churches that punctuate every residential neighborhood reinforce this equilibrium. The churches—and what churches they are, with tall, soaring steeples of stone and fully rendered golden onion domes—sit tightly within the housing blocks with little or no space around them. Their steeples and domes hover over their flock and give focus to each neighborhood, testimony to both the faith and the rich ethnicity of the community. The number of churches in all three towns is astounding. With average populations of four to five thousand, each community contains more than a dozen churches. Each church represents successive waves of immigrants that came to

**Drawing of typical worker housing in a Pennsylvania mining town**

the anthracite region as the first step toward realizing their American Dream. First came the German (Pennsylvania Dutch) and English settlers with their Protestant denominations. Skilled Scottish and Welsh miners soon followed to become supervisors and engineers. During the potato famines of the 1840s Irish Catholics fled Ireland for employment in the mines and brought with them their religion. Soon Italian Catholics joined the Irish in an uneasy mix as they competed for jobs. Late in the nineteenth century waves of eastern Europeans settled in these valleys to labor in all trades. At the center of their communities rose the beautiful Orthodox churches of eastern Catholicism. The various ethnic groups left these magnificent edifices as reminders of their faith and courage during times of adversity and suffering. The structures of Ashland, Lansford, and Mahanoy City express an indomitable aspect of the human character in physical form and suggest that the more arduous a community's past, the stronger its ability to sustain itself.

The retail centers of these three towns are modest given the limited means of many of their original inhabitants. Stores and other services coalesce around an intersection, as in Mahanoy City, or group along a principal thoroughfare, as in Lansford. Ashland has an amazingly broad vista down its gently sloping main street, which measures almost two miles in length. Gone are the hotels, the variety stores, and the opera houses. Only the banks with their Roman-temple fronts persist—always among the grandest structures in any town. Gone too are the other industries besides coal—the breweries, the

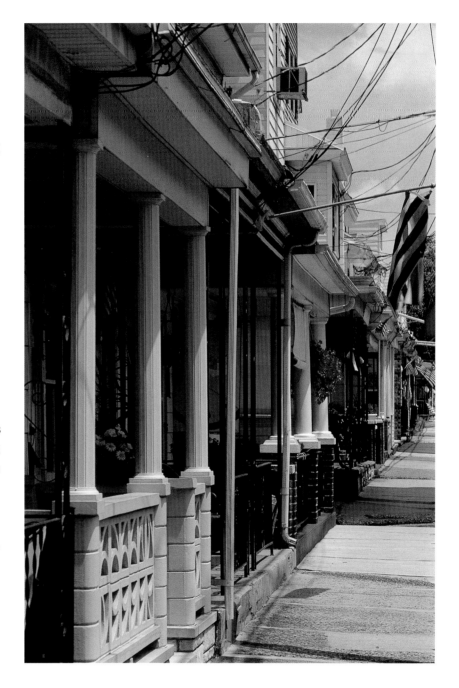

Front porches, Mahanoy City, Pennsylvania

**Pennsylvania church domes**

silk factories that employed the daughters and young wives of miners, and the railway stations and switching yards that gave access to a larger world.

Much of the history of the anthracite region focuses on the growth of industry and the ever-advancing technologies required to build the might of contemporary America. At times it seems as if the only history we accept is that defined by technology and expansion, yet we are all too ready to cast off these advancements as they become obsolete. The detritus of the latest technological or transportation advancement litters our landscapes. There are other histories, however, whose artifacts remain far clearer and equally compelling. Lansford, Ashland, and Mahanoy City remind us of those other narratives. They tell us about the people who brought into being our industrial wealth with their own hands. Still losing populations to better opportunities, these three towns remain but shadows of another time, not far distant, when people from foreign lands gathered together in the face of appalling exploitation to forge communities. As with so many similar towns in this study, it is the clarity of their decline that astonishes—because of the absolute pellucidity of their forms. They are spectral places whose urban fabrics lie netlike upon the valley floors anchored by deep holes puncturing black veins of the earth.

The study of Tamaqua, the last town of the anthracite coal region of Pennsylvania examined here, summarizes many of the preceding discussions about urban form and affords a link to the next chapter, on coastal Maine.

Fraternal Order of Elks building, Mahanoy City, Pennsylvania

**Diesel-engine truck, Tamaqua, Pennsylvania**

*Tamaqua* meant "land or waters of the beaver" to Native Americans who camped seasonally in the area. At Tamaqua, Panther Creek joins the Little Schuylkill as they both wind their way southward between openings in the Appalachian ridges. From the moment this land was settled, humans followed the streams into these mountains—first by foot, then by barge, then by railroad. The Reading Railroad tracks followed the same paths as had the Native American Tuscarora hunters.

Tamaqua sits on a flood plain between both watercourses and astride an early Native American north–south trading corridor. Europeans settled early in the eighteenth century on the advantageous flat land of Tamaqua, where they could use the abundant water power for sawmills that harvested the timber from green hills. Soon after the Native American Tuscarora disappeared, other Europeans arrived to strip the hills of earth and forests and expose the black seams of coal.

As mines and collieries surrounded Tam-

aqua and trains moved down Panther Creek from Coaldale and Lansford, Tamaqua became a railroad center with marshaling yards that gathered and stored the cars on ladders of track before heavy locomotives moved them southward to cities and industrial centers. Such enormous groupings of rolling stock required maintenance, and the Reading Railroad built a locomotive-repair facility at Tamaqua that serviced the entire region. The center structure was a roundhouse that could accommodate twenty-one steam locomotives under one roof. Tamaqua was a crossroads of watersheds, of paths, and then of rail lines. Because the Appalachian ridges surrounding Tamaqua tightly restricted its growth, no contemporary highway bypass has diluted its concise downtown center and surrounding residential neighborhoods. Consequently, its present-day urban form still evidences the previous influences of the railroad, watersheds, and Native American paths.

Tamaqua has a main street that lies rulerlike upon the landscape, crossing its topographic and cultural features and binding them into a coherent whole with a public space. Entering from the east down the widening opening of Panther Valley, East Broad Street bends slightly before dipping onto the flood plain and proceeding straight across Panther Creek and the Little Schuylkill River to a main intersection of five points, where five roads converge at the railroad tracks. Originally, the Reading Railroad maintenance shops and locomotive works sat one block away. Only unused stations and two tracks remain. Crossing these tracks, East Broad Street becomes West Broad, enclosed by

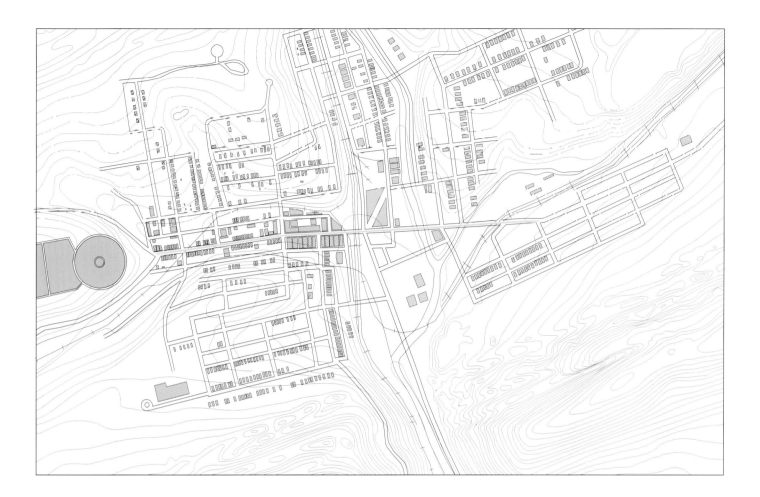

wonderfully scaled blocks of commercial structures and stately homes. A photograph of this defined urban space includes pumpers and fire engines cleaning up after a flood. As a transection through time and across landscapes, Broad Street touches all the transportation sinews that brought Tamaqua into existence.

West Broad Street and the town terminate at the splendidly formed Odd Fellows Cemetery, on a tilted hillside overlooking the downtown. A tall column capped by an eagle centers the axis of Broad Street. Concentric circles of soldiers' graves surround the column, their small American flags lifting in the early morning breeze, poignant reminders of Tamaqua's partic-

ipation in conflicts far distant from this grassy ridge.

As the railroads and mining companies of the anthracite region competed for markets far beyond these tight valleys, larger and more complex entities arose to process and transport coal. Bituminous coal from West Virginia and Virginia began to take market shares away, as did the newer fuels natural gas and oil. Labor strife interrupted supplies of anthracite coal and weakened its marketability further. Smaller companies disappeared or were absorbed into larger conglomerates. One of the oldest and eventually the largest was the Lehigh Coal and Navigation Company, known simply as the Old

Tamaqua, Pennsylvania. Broad Street is rendered in yellow.

West Broad Street,
Tamaqua, Pennsylva-
nia. (Courtesy of the
Tamaqua Historical
Society)

Company. Its red-dot symbol became synonymous with anthracite coal itself and was to be found throughout the Northeast on buildings and railroad cars. Faded red dots can still be found on abandoned warehouses in coastal Maine towns. Anthracite coal was vital for home heating and steam-driven industries in northern towns, so seemingly endless trains of brimming coal cars made their way to port loading facilities for the coastal schooners that plied the eastern seaboard filled to the decks with coal for cities and dock depots.

The final chapter of this study of urban form turns to those faraway cities and towns in coastal Maine that made the ships that carried the coal from mining towns in Pennsylvania. The Appalachians may be the spatial armature for our explorations of towns, but cultural connections soon overlaid their two thousand miles with activities that wonderfully accentuated the richness and variety of these settlements as ships from Maine carried cotton from the South and coal from the Middle Atlantic to distant places. Communities that were seen as isolated dots on a map soon became linked together in the larger network of this developing nation.

**Old Company red dot, mining car, Lansford, Pennsylvania**

# 7

# The Search for Norumbega

Maine Coastal Towns

Colossal wrinkles in the earth's crust 280 million years ago formed the Appalachian Mountains, which continue northeastward from Pennsylvania and New York across New England into the Canadian Maritime Provinces. This chapter explores those coastal towns of Maine that nestle among the coves, rivers, and hills that these tectonic forces brought into being. This study began with Camden, Maine, and now concludes with five additional Maine towns: Bath, Wiscasset, Rockland, Belfast, and Castine. These five communities teach us that beauty of urban form within a spectacular natural setting can become a town's greatest asset. Yet aesthetics played no role in their founding circumstances. Their narratives arose instead from a pragmatic exploitation of the environment. The precariousness of toiling against the sea legitimized the extraction of resources and grounded these towns firmly in their unique place on the edge of land and water. Their stories begin where the unfathomable sea meets the now familiar Appalachians.

Mount Katahdin, in the middle of the state of Maine, crowns the surrounding Appalachians, a massive granite cirque towering above its smaller neighbors. It is the northern terminus of the thirteen-hundred-mile Appalachian Trail.

The same folds we have seen in Alabama, Virginia, and Pennsylvania spread southward from Katahdin like rippled ridges of thick paint in cyclopean strokes. Millions of years of pressure and movement compressed the earth's crust in Maine into a finely grained, dense swath of low hills and valleys that spreads seaward. Even as the continents of North America and Europe-Africa pulled apart to form the Atlantic Ocean, they tore and ripped the coast into thousands of fragments and indentations that became the islands and bays so uniquely characteristic of this region.

It was during the Pleistocene Epoch that these hills received their final polishing as they lay beneath great sheets of ice more than a mile thick. Within the last million years, glaciers advanced and retreated across these ridges, grinding and scouring them down into gently rolling hills. At times the ice extended out into the ocean to the edge of the continental shelf, plowing the surface of what today is the bottom of the Gulf of Maine. Ice lay so heavily and thickly upon that surface that it weighted down the land mass and pushed it more deeply into the earth's crust and made the ocean extend farther up into the serrated bays. At other times, so much water was trapped within the blue glaciers that the

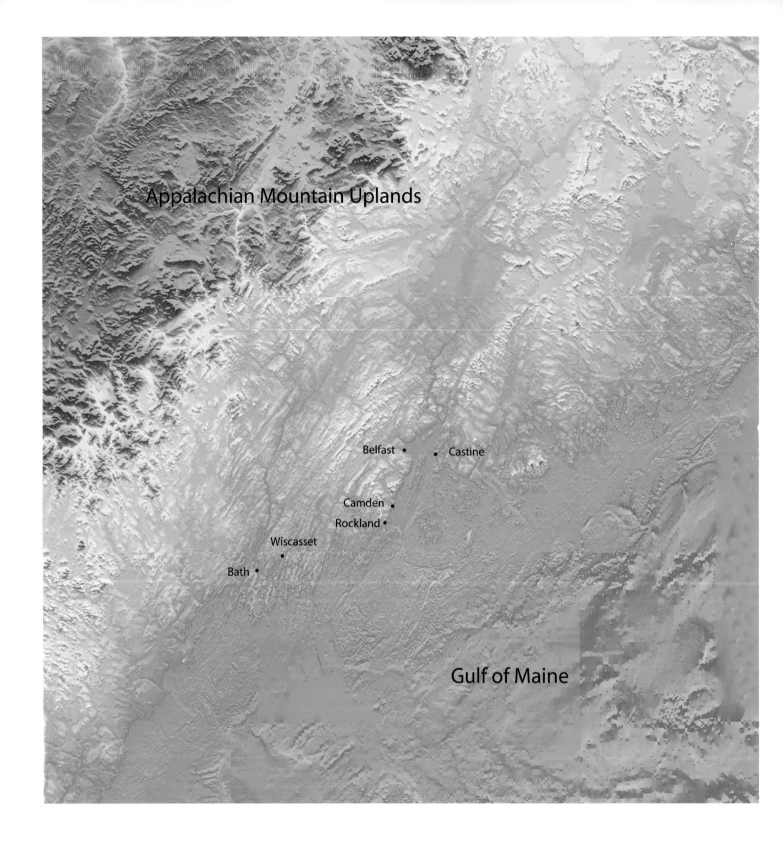

Appalachian Mountain Uplands

Belfast •   • Castine

Camden •

Rockland •

Wiscasset
•

Bath  •

Gulf of Maine

oceans fell and dry land reached out into the Atlantic until the Gulf of Maine became almost an enclosed inland sea. Nova Scotia stretched outward, and Georges Bank connected to Cape Cod and Nantucket. As ice and water eroded the rocky surfaces of the Appalachians into rounded folds, they made the bottom of the Gulf of Maine into a unique and varied topography comprised of more than twenty deep basins and innumerable shallow ledges that provide an incredible diversity of marine habitats. During the eighteenth and nineteenth centuries these waters became some of the richest fisheries in the world.

To understand the settlement patterns of the Maine coast is to grasp this mysterious underwater world—its depths, its currents, its shallow banks, and above all the massive breeding and feeding cycles and migrations of its once bountiful and seemingly inexhaustible schools of fish and flocks of fowl. The very earliest human inhabitants knew the complexities and seasonal rhythms of this biodiversity. Native Americans migrated in summers to the coast to partake in great feasts of clams and haddock harvested just offshore. Mounds of shells piled along hidden coves attest to the abundance of their food and the variety of their diet. Tales of haddock eight feet long and weighing more than three hundred pounds and of waterfowl darkening the horizon with their passing have come down to us through early accounts. It must have seemed that these riches would never end.

The shallow waters over the Georges and Browns banks protect an extremely intricate choreography of tides and currents. Water temperatures within the Gulf are considerably colder than those in the warmer northeastward-flowing Gulf Stream, allowing the Gulf of Maine to support an incredible richness of marine life. In marine habitats biodiversity is almost the reverse of that experienced on land, where the biomass increases toward the warmer latitudes of the equator. By contrast, the colder the water, the richer the nutrients that well up from the deep and the more complex and diverse the habitats. These nutrients nourish microscopic plankton that begin the expansion of the food chain. Tiny fish larvae feed on these plankton by moving through massive columns of cooler water, only to be eaten by ever-larger fish. The scoured glacial gravel bottoms of the Gulf offer an ideal habitat for the spawning of different species of fish. The deeply indented coastline and exceptional tidal surges provide amazingly productive marshes and mud flats, which are washed and refreshed daily by the fertile river systems that flow southward out of the eroded uplands of the old Appalachians. Each year those majestic and mysterious denizens of the deep, the humpback whales, return to the Gulf of Maine to feed and to take their place at the very top of this floating food chain. Very much aware of this bounty, Native Americans hunted seals, fished offshore, and gathered eels and salmon within the wetlands, and they built their summer settlements on the high ground along the riverbanks and inshore fisheries.

Europeans explored the Maine coast for two reasons. The first was modest: they wanted to establish fishing and fur trading settlements. The second was their imperialistic desire to acquire

(Opposite) Bathymetric map of the coast of Maine. This map splices together two different types of computer-generated contour renderings. The raised relief of the land is shown in reds, yellows, and greens; the depth of the ocean floor is shown in light greens to dark blue. Dry land and the ocean bottom are considered as one surface to emphasize their interdependence. The ridges that run 40 degrees east inland spread into the sea to become islands and underwater ledges, while the great river systems reach far out in deep trenches.

more territory. After Columbus's voyages and the buildup of the Spanish Empire in the Caribbean, other European powers sought an alternative northwest passage or direct route to the Far East around the northern edge of the American continent. In 1524 Giovanni Verrazzano's explorations along the eastern coast northward from Florida were disappointing because he had expected to sail through to the Indies. Instead, he found a vast and seemingly impenetrable land of bays and rivers. Early-sixteenth-century maps fostered this obsession with a northwest passage by emphasizing those routes that had been explored but found to be impassable. All the great river systems of the eastern coast—the Hudson, the Connecticut, and the Penobscot—are exaggerated. Thus, these beautiful cartographic examples map both expectations and frustrations. The French and English sent expeditions along this lengthy and richly indented coast and made grandiose, erroneous, and conflicting claims of sovereignty. And they drew elaborate maps that reveal more about what they wanted to find than the actual territory. It was not until 1607 that a Frenchman, Samuel de Champlain, produced a map of the Maine coast that accurately depicted its bays and rivers. Champlain was a keen observer and a talented navigator, and his map is amazingly detailed and correct. Its intent was to secure claims made by the Sieur de Monts for all of America from the fortieth parallel, now Philadelphia, northward to Montreal. In typical seventeenth-century fashion, Henry IV of France granted this immense area to the Sieur de Monts' charter without any knowledge of the extent of the territory, without regard to com-

peting claims by other countries, and most importantly, without any acknowledgment of the Native American populations already inhabiting it.

Champlain was methodical and determined and sailed the coast from Massachusetts to the Canadian Maritimes, recording his observations with notes and maps. His route took him to Mount Desert Island, which he named L'Isle des Mount Deserts because of its bare rugged granite mountains, and along Isle de Haute. Both islands are now part of Acadia National Park. Champlain sailed up Penobscot Bay into the Penobscot River, noting the site of Pentagoet, now Castine, and he made contact with the Native Americans, the coastal Wabanakis. He recorded on his map, but never found, the fabled city of Norumbega. This was reputedly an immensely wealthy inland city of gold located somewhere between the Kennebec and Saint Lawrence rivers. Norumbega was either a fiction of financial backers of earlier explorations or a cruel joke of the Wabanakis upon the naive Europeans. Champlain may have believed the Wabanakis, for he indicates Norumbega to be near present-day Bangor. Shortly after these explorations, its name disappears from maps of the Maine coast. It reappears again over time as the name for the entire New England region and for a mountain in Acadia National Park and various other geographical features. It survives as a mythical name with no location as its referent and is an anomaly in this study of real places.

Champlain's continued explorations of the deep estuaries took him up the Sheepscot River to the site of Wiscasset, which he noted with a cluster of structures on his map. How much of his information came from the Wabanakis and how much from direct experience remains uncertain. Regardless, his map is a wonderfully rendered commentary on the salient features of the Maine coastline and would play a dominant role in its eventual European settlement pattern. Its accuracy and Champlain's determined naming of major coastal features solidified France's claims to this region and, sadly, set in motion 150 years of strife between the French, the English, and the Wabanakis in which the Native Americans were the ultimate and definitive losers.

While not as dramatically documented, the second means of exploration was ultimately far more destructive for the Wabanakis, with territory usurped and fatal diseases transmitted. European, especially French, demand for felt for hats started a fur and hide industry that very soon depleted the stock of mammals along the coast and drove trapping deep inland. The French maintained good relations with their Native American trading partners, but this close association was the Wabanakis' undoing. Within a few generations their communities were decimated by smallpox. Profits and systematic trapping quickly exhausted the beaver population. The loss of a major species like the beaver was disastrous for the ecology of the northern forests. Coastal trading centers, Castine being the largest, sprang up along the coast as the Native Americans, and then the Europeans, directly gathered the rich but fast-dwindling bounty of the cold north woods. The exploitation and collapse of the American fur trade is one of the more depressing chapters among several in the history of the New World.

The English, the French, and the British Massachusetts Bay Colony contested the Maine coastal territory as its riches of timber and fur became evident. The grant by Henry IV of France extended "sea to sea"; it supposedly ran all the way to the Pacific and included whatever lay in between. Subsequent treaties between France and England put the boundary at the Saint Croix River, then the Kennebec, then the Penobscot. That the Penobscot with its wide approaches was the boundary line explains the location of a string of towns along its western shore. Belfast, Camden, and Rockland, were all English settlements on the English side. Castine was French in origin and sits across the bay on what was once French territory. All these treaties based the boundary on a natural feature of the coast, a major river, and then carried the territorial division inland on a straight line directly north to the Saint Lawrence River of New France. The present-day eastern boundary between Maine and Canada follows the Saint Croix River and then extends in a straight line north to the Saint John River.[1] Most importantly, every treaty between interested parties granted offshore fishing rights to both sides. While covetous of inland claims and resources, all parties perceived the sea as open to everyone. As the next century unfolded, Norumbega was discovered to lie beneath the tides and currents of the Atlantic Ocean.

Europeans had fished off the rich banks of Newfoundland from the early sixteenth century onward. To dry and salt their catch into

1. These boundaries were negotiated in the Aroostook War (1828–42) between the United States and Britain.

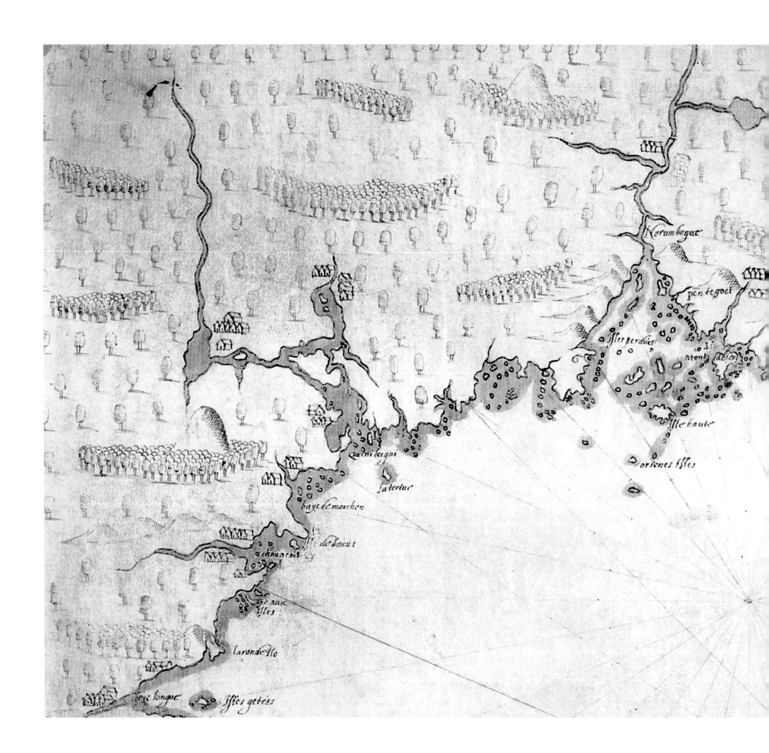

Norumbegue

pentegoet

Iller perdues

Monts deserts

Iller haute

Deortones Isles

quini begni

la tertue

bayt de marchen

Iller de boeut

achenacou

le nau Isles

larande Ile

oue longue          Isles geteos

192

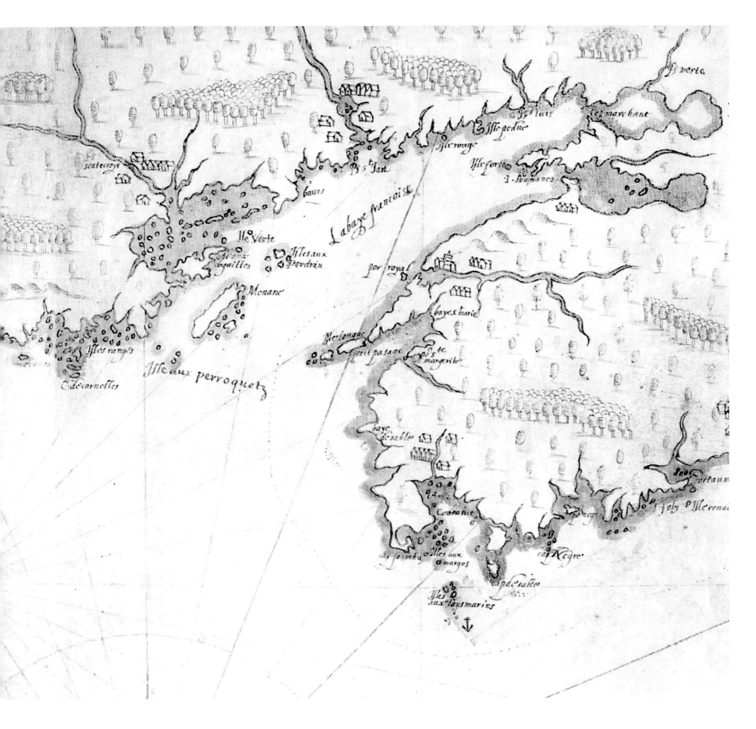

Facsimile of Champlain's
map of the Maine coast,
1607. (Library of Congress)

a preservable and marketable product, they needed codfish stations ashore. These were at first seasonal habitations with large areas, or *flakes,* for drying and structures for storage and habitation. The process of salting and the building of barrels for transportation of fish and fish oil required semipermanent structures. Other necessary conditions for such a station were a sheltered harbor with easy access along prevailing winds to fishing grounds, fresh water for drinking, wood for construction, and fuel and a beach, or *shingle,* for ease in drawing up boats. A shingle is a gently sloping beach of sand or small rocks deposited by earlier glaciation. It has a firm footing and is exposed at both high and low tide, making it an ideal place for landing a small boat safely. There is not a coastal town in Maine whose original setting did not meet these requirements. As the rich fishing grounds of Maine became apparent, these stations moved down from Nova Scotia to the outlying islands and promontories of the central Maine coast. Seasonal settlements gradually became permanent places to supply the growing demand for fish and to build the ships increasingly needed to ply these fecund waters. And thus were born the two industries that figured so prominently in the history and growth of these Maine coastal towns, fishing and shipbuilding.

The Native American Abanaki word *Kennebec* means "long quiet river." As it flows seaward out of Merrymeeting Bay, the Kennebec becomes just that, a straight, broad expanse of water that courses southward between a series of islands to enter the Gulf of Maine. Six rivers meet in Merrymeeting Bay, hence its name; two, the

Kennebec and the Androscoggin, provide access deep into the interior of the state. This area was historically a meeting place of many cultures: Native Americans came here on fishing or trading expeditions; Europeans too looked for fur or fishing territory. It was perhaps inevitable, then, that the protected land along the west bank of the Kennebec would become home to one of the most vital shipbuilding towns in America.

Ideally sited along a flat shoreline that expands gently inland between two ridges, Bath commands the most perfect location for ship construction. Protected from the open ocean, it faces a long stretch of deep water with a strong enough outward tide to float even the largest ship to the sea. A long shelf of land that runs north–south parallel to the waterway eventually became a continuous waterfront of shipyards. Low ridges rise behind this shelf and afford both sites and prospects for housing and other communal structures. Bath's urban form reflects this advantageous topography, as its long axis parallels the water and the ridges.

Timber for shipbuilding could be floated easily down the Androscoggin or the Kennebec from Maine's interior forests. Later, when the railroad pushed east from Boston and Portland, it extended to Bath with no major river or estuary crossings. The railroad enters from the north to snake southward in a deep cut parallel to the town's long axis before fanning out into the shipyards. Earlier a stage road and a ferry crossing took advantage of the dip in the topography on both sides of the Kennebec and allowed inhabitants to cross over to Woolwich and points farther east. Sadly, many of these natural attributes of the town's siting lie buried beneath the enormous contemporary concrete bridge abutments that bisect the city high above the shoreline.

The original form of Bath was deceptively simple. The largest shipyards grew to the south, on the land level with the water's edge. A series of streets parallel to the river's edge ran along the ridges; their names betray their locations: Water Street, next to the river; Front Street, next along the waterfront; then Washington, Middle, and High streets. Center Street gathers roads from inland at the courthouse and then runs perpendicularly down and up again to the town hall and the customs house. Commercial and retail establishments cluster around the courthouse and the town hall. An evocative photograph taken of Front Street in 1947 shows the civic engagement of Bath's citizens as they celebrate the city's centennial. The well-scaled commercial buildings frame the parade's activity in an intensely urban space. Farther back from the waterfront, lovely houses lined Washington, Middle, and High streets, especially next to the city green and the Patten Library. As in all these coastal towns, the grandest, most elegant houses represent wealth gained through shipping and trade.

What is unusual and unique about Bath is the way its two civic structures, the town hall and the courthouse, connect visually perpendicular to the town's long axis across the open space between two high ridges. There is a considerable drop from the courthouse down to the railroad tracks and then back up to the town hall, so that one can stand on the steps of either building and see the other across the valley. The customs house sits in the same block as the town hall on a promontory overlooking the waterfront. The town hall's beautifully rounded facade both terminates this spatial dialogue and deflects it to the left and right onto the retail street and the customs house. Bath, Maine, provides an ingenious example of "baroque" planning worthy of its namesake, the city of golden stone, Bath, England. Both towns use significant civic buildings as punctuation points to orient the public spaces of their streets.

The nineteenth century began with a fourfold explosion of Maine's population followed by an equally dramatic increase in shipbuilding. Maine seceded from Massachusetts in 1820 to become a state, and from then until the Civil War its coast was alive with shipyards building every conceivable type of vessel. Bath was a center for building and for control of great fleets of ships that sailed to every corner of the world. To give an idea of the magnitude of this industry, the Patten shipyard launched ninety vessels in the years 1816–69.[2] These were fast, full-rigged clippers for the Pacific routes, sturdy downeasters for the cotton and timber markets, and brigs for the West Indies trades. Later, from other yards, came the great schooners three hundred feet in length for the "coasting" cargo of coal. Any profitable cargo guaranteed huge fortunes, and vessels were quickly constructed for specific markets. Two types of vessels that have special relevance to our study were those for the cotton trade between Mobile and New Orleans and England and those that carried coal from railheads in Norfolk, Virginia, to all the great and

2. Martin and Snow, *Pattens of Bath*, app. B.

**Topography of Bath, Maine**

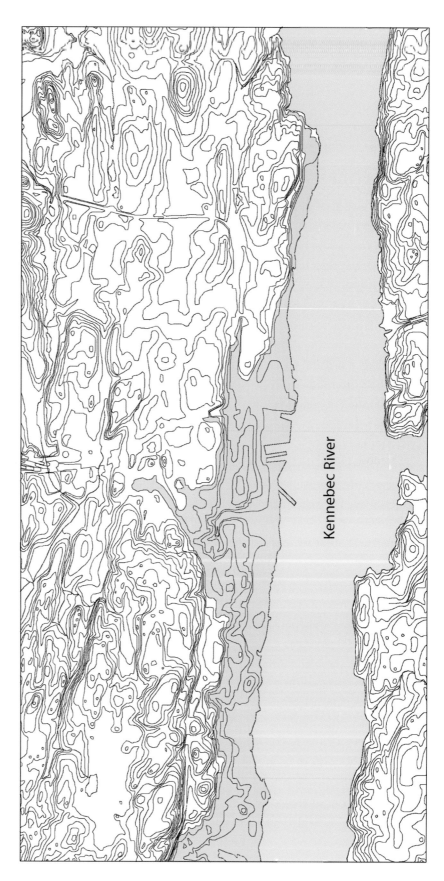

Kennebec River

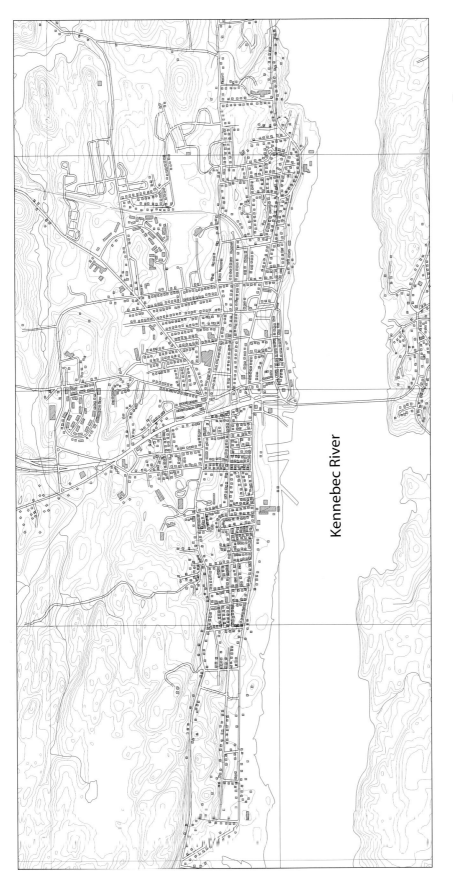

**Bath, Maine**

Kennebec River

197

**Front Street, Bath, Maine,
1947. (Courtesy of the
Pejepscot Historical Society, Brunswick, Maine)**

Figure-ground of Bath,
Maine

199

**Oakum Shop, Maine Maritime Museum, Bath, Maine**

small cities of the Northeast. These mark an interesting symmetry within the towns included in this study. Vessels from Bath, Maine, shipped cotton from Selma, Alabama, and Bath schooners carried coal from the mines of Lansford, Pennsylvania. Bath's ships connected all three towns and drew dependencies that were larger and more subtle than those conditioned by the spatial armature of the Appalachian Mountains.

During these years Bath's waterfront filled with wharfs and facilities for all the other industries necessary for shipbuilding, such as sail lofts, ropewalks, ironworks, and buildings for caulking storage. As wooden sailing ships began to be replaced by steel and steam-driven vessels, the enormous complex of the Bath Iron Works, whose cranes dominate the city today and dwarf

the new bridge spanning the Kennebec, began to turn out warships. To appreciate the contemporary efforts of this shipyard, consider that during the Second World War the Bath Iron Works built eighty-five destroyers, often going from the laying of the keel to launching in three months' time. Few cities or towns in America match Bath for the single-mindedness and longevity of its industry. For more than two hundred years this small place on the Kennebec turned out ship after ship and weathered each downturn in the world's economy.

From the very first property distributions, Bath maximized the interdependence of land and water. As we saw in chapter 2, long narrow lots running inland from the river maximized everyone's frontage in the Maine coastal towns. As Bath grew, it fastened more and more tightly to its very reason for existence, the long reach of the Kennebec. Wharfs and docks erased all traces of its natural shoreline and sculpted its edge. And yet embedded in Bath's urban form, like a template against the mirror of the Kennebec River, reside all those memories of launched ships and distant voyages to exotic ports; its wealth, like our recollections, gathered from the world.

The Sheepscot River, just east of the Kennebec, flows southward through fragmented pieces of this drowned coast into broad estuaries before spreading wide into the Gulf of Maine. Like so much of this coastline, its bays and inlets offered bountiful fishing and snug harbors.

European settlers took advantage of both and began their occupation early in the eighteenth century. Constant warfare with Native Americans postponed a major population boom until the late 1700s, when Lincoln County was created with the small river village of Wiscasset as its seat. In the nineteenth century Wiscasset developed a major shipbuilding industry. Yards and docks lined its waterfront, and fortunes lined the pockets of its inhabitants. It was during this period that so many of its stately homes and public buildings were constructed. The plan of Wiscasset is simple and elegant, for those who laid out its streets in the early eighteenth century took full advantage of its topography. Like all

**Bath Irons Works shipyard, Bath, Maine**

**Bell Haven (Nickels-Sortwell house), Wiscasset, Maine**

these coastal towns, Wiscasset was approached originally from the water. A broad street, Main Street, slopes gently up from the harbor to a village green surrounded by a courthouse, a church, and magnificent houses. This street is enclosed by brick and granite retail blocks at its lower end, forming the street edge. As one moves up the hill, the street is flanked by white neo-Palladian homes well set back from the curb. A tiny, fishbonelike grid connects residential streets perpendicularly to Main Street. Federal Street continues north along the Sheepscot River toward the even earlier settlement of Alna.

When the railway came to Wiscasset, it too

conformed to this elegant design and swept along the shoreline. Disembarking at the train station, one entered Wiscasset as one had from the coastal steamers. The plan of the town remains intact, so that even today when a locomotive slowly crosses Main Street at the base of the new bridge all traffic stops. To the consternation of many, Wiscasset has kept its form by forcing all the traffic of Route 1 north and east down Main Street and across the bridge to Newcastle. No bypass has been allowed to take energy from the center of this small jewel of a community; no urban compromise has been made to allow the fast flow of cars. Automobiles must concede the right of way to pedestrians, so anyone wishing to pass through Wiscasset must slow down and savor this wonderful example of obdurate urban form.

Names of streets are seldom random or haphazard and often offer an obvious clue to a use or place from the past. Main Street is always just that, the main retail and commercial center of a town; every northern village has an Elm Street that was once canopied by those nearly extinct beautiful overarching trees. A Mill Street undoubtedly lead to a gristmill; and a street name including the word *ferry* always connected to a river crossing. Examples abound, and we should heed their rich evocations of earlier functions. Running west out of Rockland's downtown is Lime Rock Street, which follows the gently rolling topography, first crossing the shallow arc of Broadway and then moving westward until it meets the corresponding arc of Old County Road. The figure-ground study of Rockland shows these arced roads connected to the shore

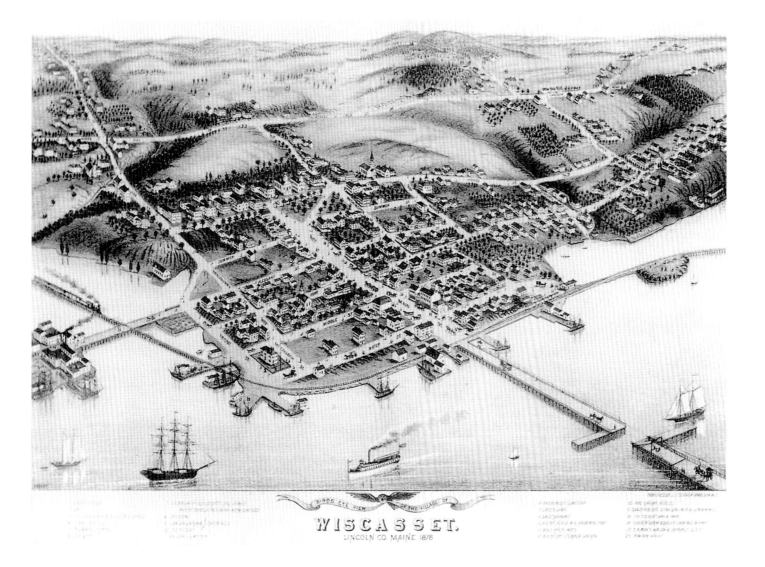

BIRDS EYE VIEW OF THE VILLAGE OF

# WISCASSET.
LINCOLN CO. MAINE 1878

by radial streets (see also chapter 2). Old County Road follows the line of one of the most productive limestone deposits in eastern America. With easy access to a natural harbor, blocks of stone were carried to the kilns lining Rockland's shore. They were then burned into lime, and the barrels of lime to be used for masonry mortar were shipped down the coast for the great building boom of early-nineteenth-century New York City. Thus, as its name aptly implies, Rockland's history and urban form come from the quarrying, burning, and shipping of rock.

In the early nineteenth century there were more than thirty wharfs and an incredible 160 lime kilns in Rockland and neighboring Thomaston. When Rockland, then named Shore Village, separated from Thomaston in 1848, 80 kilns lined its harbor. These were great structures with chimneys and piles of coal for fuel. Yearly shipments of barreled lime exceeded 1.5 million casks.

*Bird's Eye View of the Village of Wiscasset*, 1878. (Courtesy of the Wiscasset Public Library)

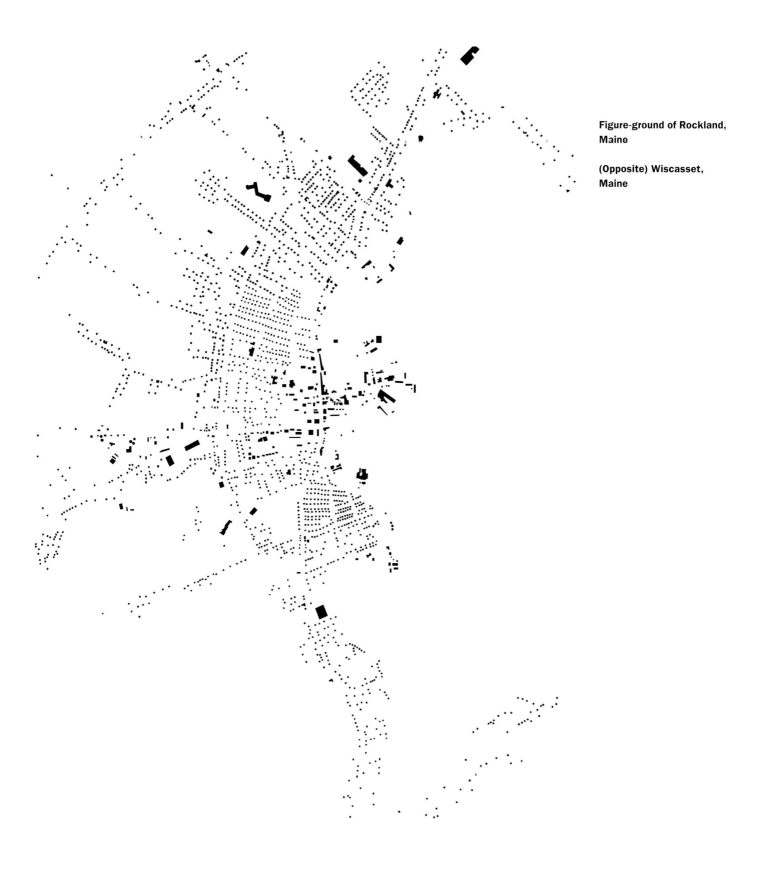

Figure-ground of Rockland,
Maine

(Opposite) Wiscasset,
Maine

Figure-ground of Rockland center

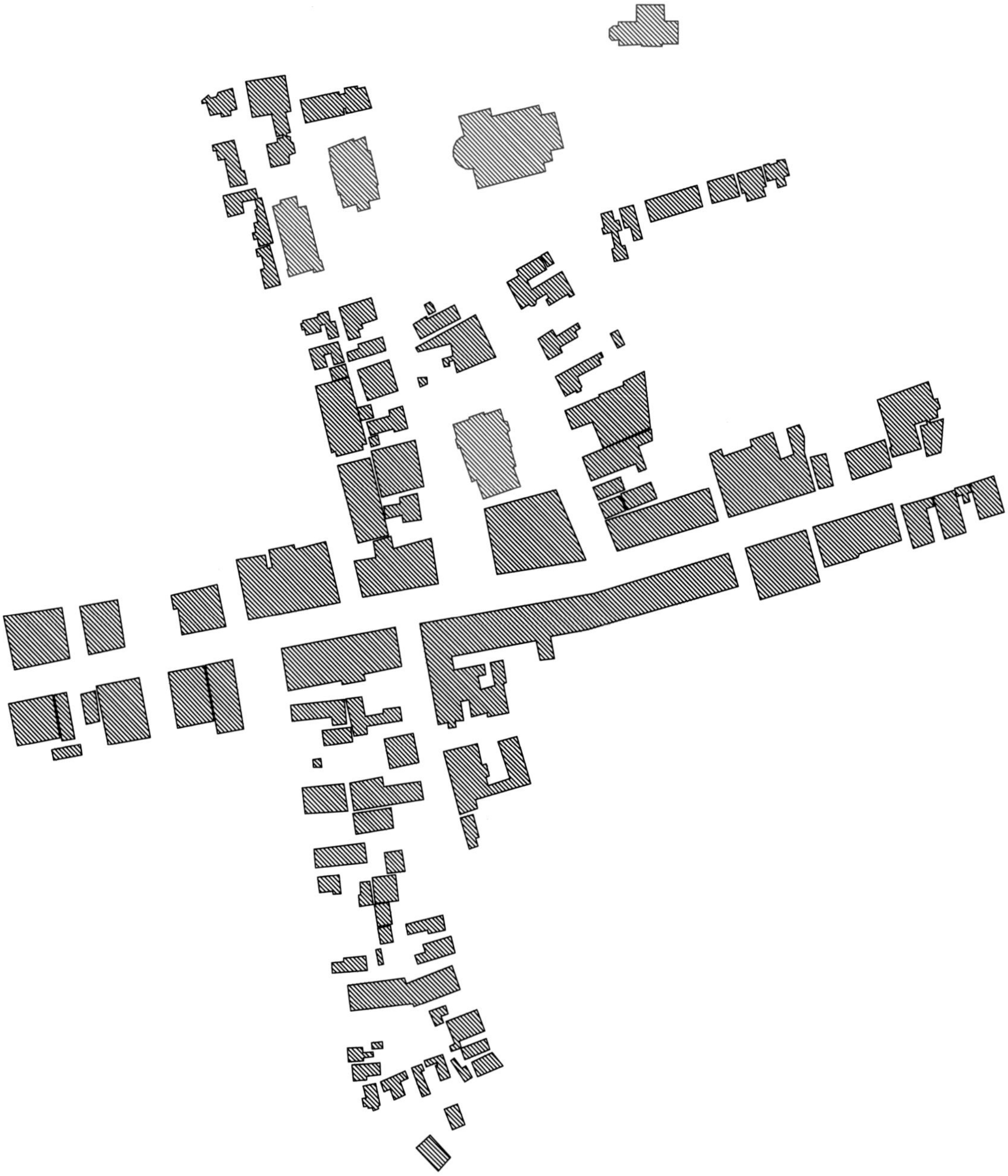

More than 150 schooners were involved in transporting this dangerous and expensive cargo.[3]

The lime quarries lie just west of Rockland.
First wagon roads connected these surface deposits to Lime Rock Street. Later, in the nineteenth century, the Lime Rock Railroad came
into the harbor on trestles, one branch from the
north, one from the south, like giant pinchers
bringing bulk rock from the quarries. This railroad, twelve and one-half miles in length, went
only between the quarries and the kilns. It was
not until later that the Maine Central entered

Rockland from the larger world. After it was
removed from the kilns, the lime was barreled
and loaded directly onto coastal schooners. The
entire harbor's edge bristled with the wharfs and
structures necessary for the dirty and demanding manufacture of lime. Coal for the steam
engines and the kiln fires came into Rockland
from the sea, as did wood for the barrel staves.
Whole industries, now forgotten, supported the
making of lime. There were coopers for barrels,
blacksmiths for the many teamsters, chandleries
for all the needs of shipping, and of course the

**Coast Guard station,
Rockland, Maine**

3. Harden, *Shore Village
Story,* 97.

shipyards that built the schooners to transport the casks.

Rockland, like all nineteenth-century towns, contained layers of manufacturing and supporting trades that have been replaced by contemporary uses. The heavy industries located directly on the waterfront have now disappeared along with the lime production, leaving vacant open lots. The next layer of space, Main Street, with its blocks of finely detailed brick and granite buildings, served the retail needs of a vital community. This beautiful street still remains for many blocks parallel to the shoreline. All the streets that formed the earliest property divisions terminate at Main Street and then radiate inland. Several churches and the gorgeous Rockland Public Library cluster at the intersection of Lime Rock Street and Main Street. (The beautiful building housing Rockland's customs house and post office, demolished in 1970, was an important component of this civic center.) Rockland offers a wonderfully clear example of a town once focused entirely on a single industry that depended upon the sea for transportation. Today its waterfront retains this connection with fishing wharves and a Coast Guard station.

The passage of time blinds us to the different values we attach to our civic structures. Churches remain through generations, although as we saw in the coal towns of Pennsylvania, they sometimes assume an almost mythic grandeur in an otherwise impoverished community. The southern courthouse, so prominent in a society obsessed with property ownership, retained its central position in towns across an entire region. The town hall and the post office

were ubiquitous buildings that northerners thought worthy of architectural expression in fine materials such as stone or brick. One of the forgotten important civic structures of coastal towns is the customs house, once the most important building in a community. Before income and property taxes fueled the nation's expansion, most federal revenue came in the form of customs duties: taxes on the import and export of goods and taxes on the movement of trade. To a young country just on the edge of solvency, customs duties represented the best possible revenue stream. The Tariff Act of 4 July 1789 authorized the collection of duties on imports, and Congress shortly thereafter set up districts and ports of entry. As the great commercial fleets of the United States plied the world's oceans, ports of entry became the places for counting and tracking these myriad exchanges. For nearly one hundred years thereafter, customs duties funded the entire budget of the U.S. government and paid for the nation's early growth and infrastructure, including the coastal lighthouses so necessary for safe maritime trade.

In 1853 the state of Maine had thirteen customs districts, of which Belfast's was fourth in total tons shipped. Belfast was the port of entry for the western half of Penobscot Bay, which included the ports of Camden, Islesboro, Vinalhaven, and Searsport. The collection of duties was no trivial matter and required the full weight of the fledgling federal government. The importance of this collection is expressed in customs services buildings, prominently located near the shipping wharfs in most ports. In a country as dependent upon trade as America was, every harbor was a thriving hub of bulk goods and raw materials. Lumber, furs, fish, and lime went out from Maine ports; molasses, sugar, salt, cloth, and coal, as well as most other consumer and manufactured products, came in. It was the business of the customs official to count, regulate, and impose duties on everything relating to shipping. Nathaniel Hawthorne was a customs official in the port of Salem, Massachusetts, where he worked in an elegant wooden structure at the head of Salem's wharfs. In terms of both its position in a town's plan and its materials of construction, the customs house became a community's most important building. Bath has a beautiful granite structure overlooking its shore; Wiscasset's customs house sits prominently on a hill, from where it commands the entire harbor. The very grandest of all, the customs house of the Port of New York, designed by Cass Gilbert, sits next to Battery Park at the very tip of Manhattan; it is a magnificently ornate structure built entirely of granite from the coastal Maine quarries of Penobscot Bay. (Few of these buildings continue to function as customs houses. New York's customs house is now part of the Smithsonian Institution.)

The entire town of Belfast frames the important relationship between the customs house and the sea. At the lower end of Main Street, the wharfs spread fanlike into the Passagassawakea River. Main Street is a wonderfully consistent prism of space formed of continuous blocks of brick and granite buildings. Uphill, at the other end of Main Street, channeled visually by the tightly enclosed commercial facades, sits the customs house. It is all the more prominent

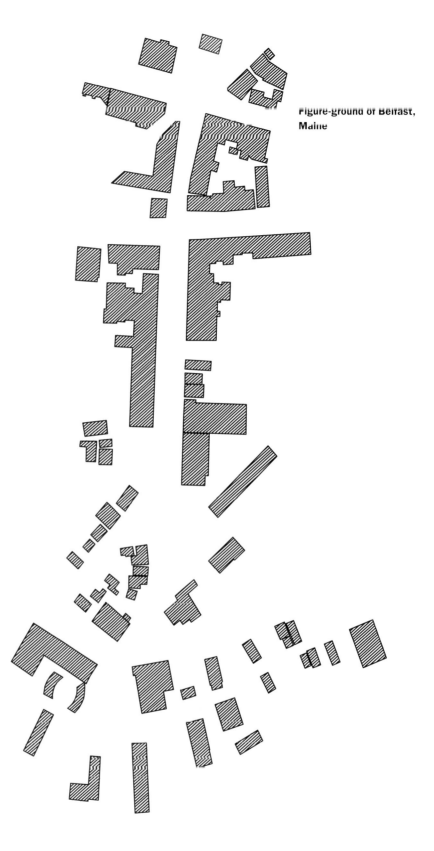

Figure-ground of Belfast, Maine

*Armistice Day Nov. 11th 1918*

**Customs House Square, Belfast, Maine, on Armistice Day, 11 November 1918. (Courtesy of the Belfast Historical Society)**

because its forecourt is the amazing intersection of six streets (see the discussion of this space in chapter 2). Main Street is crossed or intersected by streets with predictable names—Front Street, Washington Street, and of course High Street—in its journey from the wharf to Customs House Square. At the Customs House Square, Main Street deflects to join Church Street, Franklin Street, and the diagonal connector of Beaver Street. But these are not just random crossings: Main Street becomes the Augusta Road, now Route 3, and connects to

the state capitol, forty miles away. Long before, this was a path for Native Americans that linked the rapids at Augusta to Belfast Bay and the watersheds of the Passagassawakea and the Kennebec rivers. Church Street connects to High Street to become the important shore route from Rockland and Camden north to the former ferry crossing at the Passagassawakea and points east. The "Moosehead trail" branched northward from High Street to give access to the remote interior of the Maine woods. By shifting from one watershed to another at Moosehead Lake, one could return to Belfast by canoe on the Piscataquis and the Penobscot or, just as easily, paddle down to Augusta on the Kennebec and travel overland to Belfast.

Belfast is at the center of a radiating network of water and land trails that converge on the wonderful star-shaped space in front of its customs house. From the beginning of human inhabitation generations of Native American and European layered their histories onto this place, so that it has become a celebrated civic space in Belfast's downtown. The side streets intersect Main Street with acute angles that encouraged a number of ingenious architectural solutions. While approaching the customs house uphill from the wharfs along Front Street certainly is, and must have been, a clear procession, it is the view down into the town from the customs house that remains beautiful. With four roads radiating downhill away from the viewer, it is like a stage set with an exaggerated perspective creating a dramatic receding space.

Castine, on the eastern shore of Penobscot Bay, is a tiny town with the remains of four forts, which speak of a contentious history that far exceeds the town's size. Pentagoet, as Castine was originally named, was settled by the French in 1613 on the side of Penobscot Bay that was then New France. Because of its fine natural harbor and advantageous position in the middle of Penobscot Bay, it became a center for the French fur trade. Furs gathered from deep within the forests traveled down the wide Penobscot by canoe and then by ship to Europe. In 1667 the king of France granted Pentagoet and its surrounding territory to a French officer, Jean Vin-

cent d'Abbadie de St. Castine. St. Castine came to America and renamed the village Castine. Shortly thereafter the Dutch briefly occupied Castine in 1674 and 1676 and destroyed the first of the four forts, Fort Pentagoet. As the wars in America and Europe between the French and the British intensified during the eighteenth century, Castine changed hands repeatedly. During the Revolutionary War in 1779, an American fleet failed in a disastrous attack against the British, who then occupied Castine.[4] And during the War of 1812 the British seized Castine on numerous occasions and built the largest fort, Fort George, on the heights above the town. Castine owed its constant occupations to its advantageous position at the crossroads of several competing international interests. It was not until the border between British America, soon to be the "rebellious" United States, and British Canada was set at the Saint Croix River that poor Castine was finally left in peace. Through all the territorial vicissitudes the good citizens of Castine maintained an admirable neutrality and a brisk trade with the world at large. Salt was stored here for the great fishing fleets of eastern Maine, and shipyards produced a steady supply of vessels of all types. During the middle years of the nineteenth century Castine became one of the wealthiest towns on the northeast coast. It thus offers lessons in urban form and civic design that are belied by both its turbulent past and its ever changing sovereignty.

Castine sits on a peninsula at the very end of one of those long arms of fragmented coast thrust into the middle of Penobscot Bay. The land slopes gently up from its southeast fac-

4. For a detailed story of this naval battle, see Buker, *Penobscot Expedition.*

ing shore; a broad flat expanse provides an ideal site for streets and homes. The original French settlement chose well, for Castine is a magnificent location with a good harbor able to accommodate hundreds of ships. Water Street curves along the shore; Main Street rises perpendicular to it from the wharfs, passing stately homes and connecting the present-day Maine Maritime Academy to Battle Street, named for one of the many skirmishes between the British and the Americans. Castine's tight commercial center lies at the intersection of Main and Water streets, just yards from the bay. Today, shops and inns occupy what were once general stores and homes. Into the 1920s Castine had a busy canning industry surrounded by a waterfront

of coal and lumber warehouses. And of course there was a customs house, first in the three connected buildings facing the harbor, then farther uptown in what has become the post office. Much as in Wiscasset, residential streets with exceptionally beautiful and well maintained homes are perpendicular to Main Street and follow the contours of the hill. The space of Main Street, so consistently defined by a church, houses, and retail structures, as in all these towns, connects gracefully with the harbor. The Maine Maritime Academy's large oceangoing training vessel, the *State of Maine*, terminates the vista down Main Street toward the docks.

Castine's exquisite civic center, removed from its retail core, rewards study. Halfway up

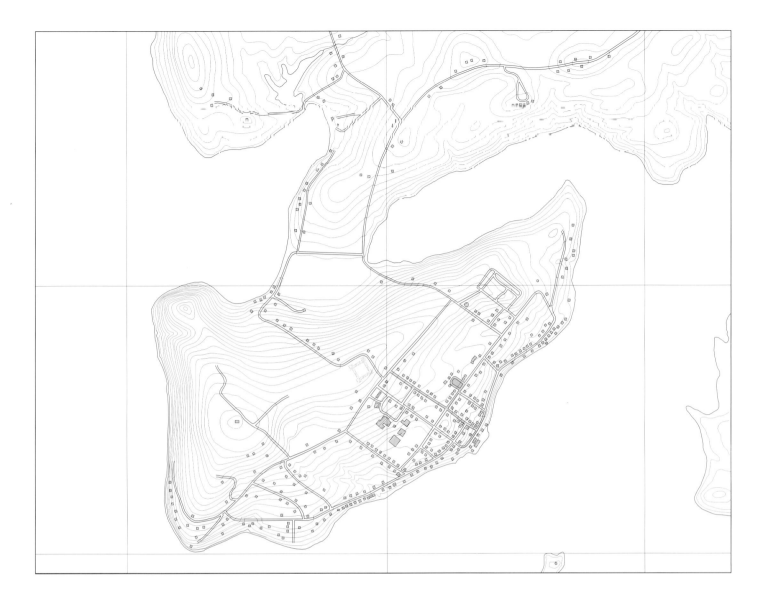

Main Street a turn onto Court Street takes one by the town hall to the beautiful, tree-lined village green enclosed by a church, a school (now the Historical Museum), three homes, and a library. The detachment of this civic composition from the commercial activities and the elegance of all its structures reflects a strong pride of place maintained through a long and turbulent history.

Castine ends our studies of Maine coastal towns. These examples have emphasized different salient characteristics of each town or city, yet all towns share parts of these disparate histories. While shipbuilding determined the location and form of Bath, it was a necessary part of the histories of all six towns. Wiscasset and Castine are small towns with similar urban armatures, distinctive civic spaces, and

Penobscot River and Bay, with the operations of the English fleet, under Sir George Collyer, against the division of Massachusetts troops acting against Fort Castine, August 1779, with full soundings up to the present site of Bangor, 1779. (Library of Congress)

Brigadier I.

Cape Jellison

South Creek

Orphan Island

Greyhound

Galatea

North

Albany

Landing of the Rebels

Blank

Rebel Battery

Rebel Battery

215

**Rendered Sanborn map of
Castine, Maine**

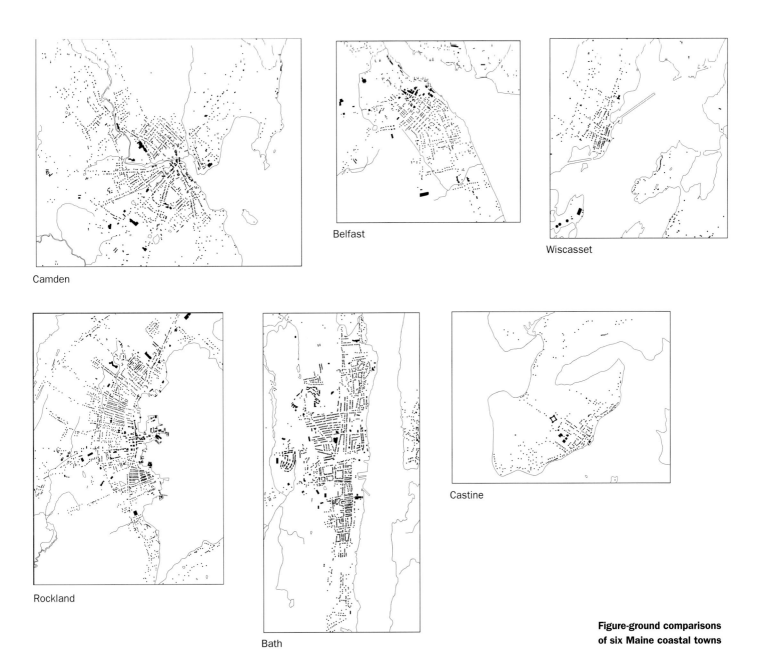

Camden

Belfast

Wiscasset

Rockland

Bath

Castine

**Figure-ground comparisons
of six Maine coastal towns**

**Schooner mast and lowered sail, Maine Maritime Museum, Bath, Maine**

the quintessential New England village greens. Bath and Camden also have lovely parks within their boundaries. Rockland's history depended upon a single resource, lime, yet all the other towns experienced similar dependencies and reinvented themselves with each new economic boom, including the most recent—tourism. Belfast, more than others, has been nimble in attracting different industries—from fishing to shoemaking to poultry and now a modern financial credit institution. All six coastal towns were, however, totally dependent upon the sea, and this dependency defined their physical structures. The interface of land and water confined their streets and their public spaces in small areas. This gathering of form left little room for elaboration or for expansion landward.

Nothing existed beyond a short walk or wagon drive from the docks. In fact, many towns had no road access in their early development, just access from the sea. Consequently, coastal towns are compact, with the retail core one street over from the waterfront. Dense structures organize this core with shared walls and with blocks of stores fronting directly onto the street. Gridded residential quarters correspond directly with a main street, because people walked to work. These tight urban centers form clear and identifiable public spaces, public streets with little concession to anything beyond accessibility. It is because of this conciseness of urban form that these towns remain so appealing still, in spite of their vehicular traffic and open parking lots. If only we could approach them today as they were intended to be entered, from the expansive sea, sliding landward among ghosts of masts and sails, and come ashore to walk the concentrated Main Streets of brick and granite instead of by car through long lines of strip malls and fast-food chains. Then perhaps we would discover that the changes of time and function have little diminished the solidity and integrity of their urban form. The forms of these towns still reflect their founding circumstances as coastal centers of trade and fishing, and they condense our expectations so as to remain succinct and concise summaries of a region's rich culture.

# Conclusion

## Cisterns of Culture

This exploration of towns settled within the spatial armature of the Appalachian Mountains covers an amazing array of unique places. We have discovered forty-two examples of urban form, from the shaded courthouse squares of Alabama to the gritty coal towns of West Virginia and Pennsylvania to the stolid villages of Maine. Few of these towns are well known outside their immediate region, and with the exception of several coastal villages, none are tourist destinations. Some are decidedly obscure and remote, yet this sampling of towns represents a rich and complex cultural history that deserves study. These towns' responses to their varied settings within the great Appalachian cordillera warrant recording and preservation.

Sadly, many of these towns are also poignant reminders of the transitory nature of human inhabitation. This impermanence raises difficult questions about urban form as an expression of a region's culture and about the sustainability of settlements. It also brings into sharp relief this book's thesis: that conciseness of urban form is the most sustainable kind of settlement pattern. Having examined and compared these many specific places, in this concluding chapter I reframe this thesis within a more general context. As the subtitle implies, these towns are cisterns,

or collectors, of culture, repositories of all aspects of dwelling. Inevitably, however, they either decline or radically change to accommodate both the present and the future. While they sustain our past, they are not necessarily sustainable themselves. Their uniqueness is also their undoing, for cultural distinctions are difficult to maintain in the face of the assimilating effects of a more dominant way of life.

Every town in this study depended upon the extraction of resources, either cotton, coal, or fish. In every case the resource was depleted or the environment degraded. The rapid growth and economic vigor of these towns during a period of incredible national expansion in the late nineteenth and early twentieth centuries suggests that cultural sustainability equates with economic development and its attendant resource exploitation. Towns come into existence because of a specific resource and derive their distinctive identity from that association, yet neither the resource nor the identity is sustainable. Before discussing these two complex dichotomies, however, I shall briefly summarize the settlement typologies encountered along this journey 40 degrees east, providing a series of simple diagrams as illustrations. Having explored the intricacies of these places in the

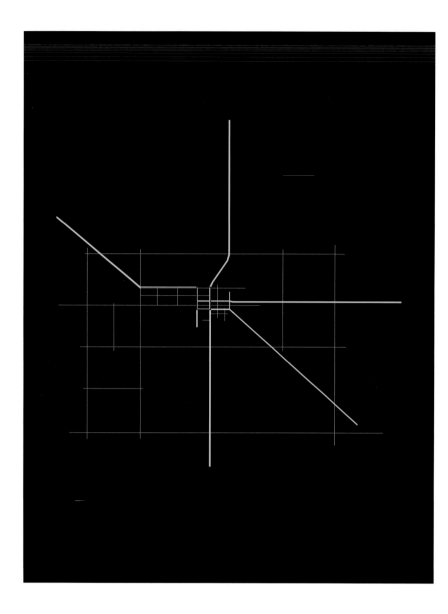

Placed upon ridges or on outwash plains of the lower Appalachians along the most viable trade routes, these towns functioned as tiny commercial centers for a limited area. Wagons or stagecoaches connected them to a larger world. Later, railroads and automobiles assumed importance as the major modes of transportation that bound them to a larger network. These wagon towns have a main street or commercial core tightly enclosed by well-crafted architecture that helped define the public space of the settlement. Many of these towns have been unable to survive the pressures of modern highway bypasses and strip malls. Their historic downtowns eventually succumb to the retail competition of national chain stores ranged along the newer perimeter roads. Ironically, one mode of transportation—the horse and wagon—brought these towns into existence, and another—the automobile—threatens their extinction.

Courthouse-square towns were also wagon towns, as they served as political centers for an area defined by a day's ride by horse. But the courthouse square, rather than a public street, is their focus. Ashland and Athens, Alabama, are two lovely representative courthouse-square compositions. These and other beautiful episodes across the southern landscape continue to function as small government nuclei. However, their retail cores, like those of wagon towns, suffer from competition with newer, automobile-accessible businesses that have located on the periphery of their downtowns. Nevertheless, courthouse squares remain exquisite examples of America's earlier ability to express its idealism through elegant yet modest architecture and

**Wagon town**

**(Opposite, top) Courthouse-square town**

**(Opposite, bottom) River town**

preceding chapters, we can now safely risk the reduction of their many different urban forms to types. It is important, however, to remember that these simple typological diagrams are distillations of towns and villages that contain many levels of complexity.

A wagon town brought roads together at nodes surrounded by small clusters of structures. Troy and Foley, Alabama, are examples.

urban design. Few societies have developed such consistent and frequent cultural markers as the South's courthouse squares. Unfortunately, their very regularity in the landscape means a division of scarce state preservation funds, and most counties have difficulty maintaining their courthouses and their surrounding retail frame.

River towns usurped the advantageous sites of earlier Native American settlements. River towns are found in the level coastal plains, where flat topography and lazy gradients allowed water travel. Selma and Demopolis, Alabama, are two examples located on rivers whose headwaters arise in the Appalachian cordillera. These towns sit on high bluffs safe from the inevitable seasonal flooding, and because of the mechanics of alluvial flow, these sites occur on the outside of bends within a shifting landscape. A central commercial space bounded by a regular grid of streets leads to the former river access. Like wagon and courthouse-square towns, river towns have not been able to respond to the changing demands of contemporary automobile infrastructure, such as strip malls and interstate highway intersections, and many of their downtowns have slipped into the stalemate of empty storefronts and weed-choked lots.

Railroad towns are examples of the enormous influence of nineteenth-century train transportation upon urban form. Sometimes linear in shape, these towns follow the geometry of the tracks. As rail travel decreased, the tracks were removed from the center of these towns, leaving vacant spaces in their compact grids, as in Cullman and Opelika, Alabama. Many towns in this study switched from one means of transporta-

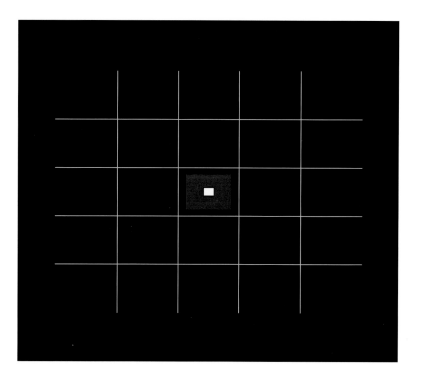

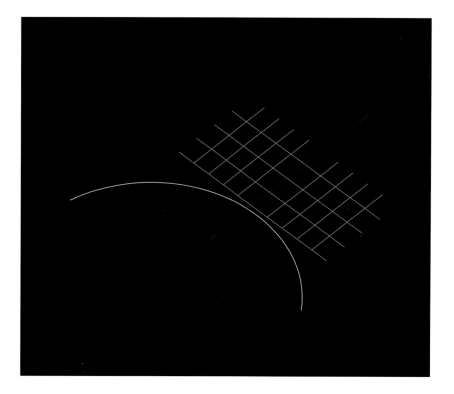

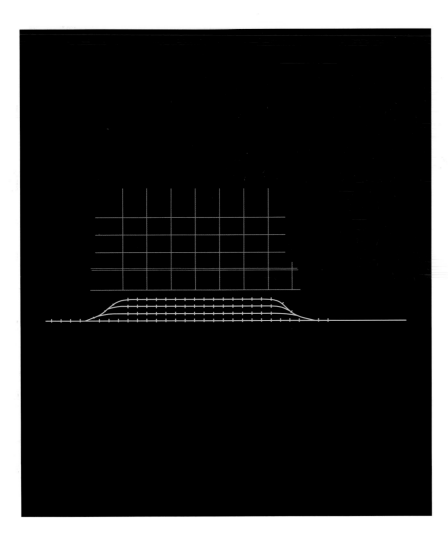

**Railroad town**

transported coal. These remarkable places illustrate the ability of urban form to conform to severely restrictive topographic constraints. The remoteness and relatively inaccessibility of these towns deep within the Appalachian Mountains makes them unknown beyond their adjoining regions. Their dramatic settings within steep mountain valleys gives towns such as Hinton, West Virginia, or Pikesville, Kentucky, an evocative power that lingers even as their populations decline.

The anthracite coal towns of Pennsylvania illustrate the rich history of coal mining, which parallels the development of this country's industrial growth. Their linear form superficially compares to that of other towns in this study, but as Lansford and Mahanoy City demonstrate, their urban configurations arose due to complex circumstances associated with the deep mines and collieries required to extract anthracite coal. In their long rows of worker housing these anthracite coal towns contain an intensity of urban fabric that is unmatched in other types of towns.

The coastal towns of Maine have managed to survive—even to thrive—and ensure their prosperity as tourist and summer destinations for visitors from places far beyond their immediate vicinity. Private yachts and pleasure boats still fill their harbors with activity and their downtowns with commerce. They have successfully reinvented themselves as recreational centers along the dramatic coast even as the demands of tourism impinge upon their original form with the proliferation of parking and congested automobile traffic.

tion to another, and with each change came a corresponding reorientation of their urban pattern. For example, both Eufaula, Alabama, and Wiscasset, Maine, successfully replaced river frontage with rail sidings and could be considered examples of a type of railroad town.

I have categorized settlements of the southern bituminous coal fields as alluvial towns because of the manner in which they respond to the shape of stream valleys. These towns were also completely dependent upon the railroads, which

The diagrams distill the differences between the forms of these towns, but they also emphasize a fundamental similarity. All the towns studied are tight, compact groupings of buildings. Every town has a clearly defined center with enclosed public spaces—either as streets or as courthouse squares. All have what has been referred to throughout this book as concise urban form. (I have used *concise* to mean "compact without excessive elaboration or superficial expression.") These towns are pragmatic in layout and vernacular in origin. Each uses forms particular and responsive to a place and a people.

Conciseness of urban form increases the potential for undisturbed and connected habitat in an increasingly fragmented world. These towns have been placed within a landscape as discrete episodes. This allows both the town and its broader context to remain distinct, so that neither is overwhelmed or diluted to the point that neither survives. Obviously, the more concise, the more compact, a settlement is, the more land remains outside and between towns for sustainable habitats. Settlement patterns imply spatial relationships that can either encourage diversity and continuity of open space or result in a homogenization of form across the earth's surface that progressively degrades distinctive opportunities for unique and contiguous habitats. A town or settlement is a concentration within the larger continuity of landscape and region. Built form and the natural world ideally should exist as a unity of complementary opposites.

A map of a portion of western Alabama indicates towns with their connecting infrastructure of rivers, railroads, and roads. The

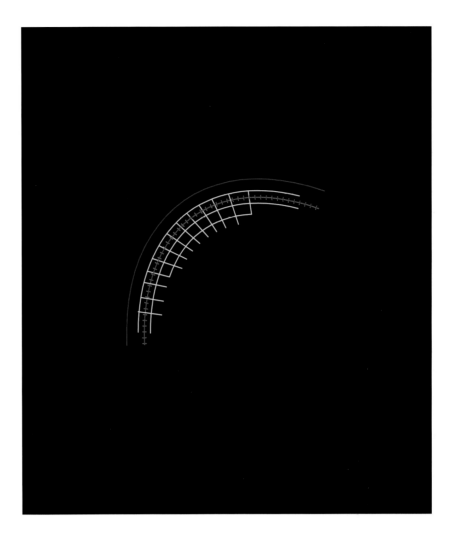

pattern that emerges is one of small, concise towns regularly spaced across the landscape. The towns are discrete entities within the larger agricultural countryside. They are tiny figures within an immense and undeveloped ground. This contrasts with the contemporary suburban patterns, where the figure and ground become indistinguishable—where the built world erodes the natural into smaller and smaller pieces until the built world surrounds and dissolves any possible continuities of the natural landscape.

**Alluvial town**

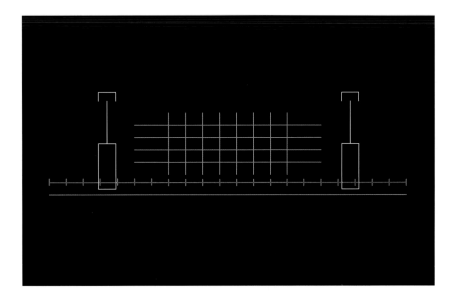

**Coal town**

Towns with their infrastructure exist as a network across the landscape; the way they are connected implies a larger order. The placement of towns in West Virginia corresponds to the placement of the rail lines that followed the watersheds up into the mountains and the coal seams. There is an order in the landscape that arises out of the location of mineral deposits, the associated settlements, and the tracks that accessed both. It is a natural landscape shaped by an ancient fluvial process and a cultural landscape that exists as a template imposed upon that same landscape.

The towns in Pennsylvania exhibit an order that arises out of the parallel folds or ridges of the Appalachians. This dendritic pattern contains the sharp angles and changes in direction of the drainage pattern. An 1857 map of the Mine Hill & Schuylkill Haven Railroad illustrates the congruity between waterways, railroads, and settlements. First railroads and then roads followed the valley floors in long straight lines. At

gaps in the ridges both transportation modes cut across the grain of the topography to connect to another valley. Because the coal companies still own most of the land surrounding these towns, one moves through a wooded landscape of deciduous new growth and then abruptly into the enclosed space of the town's long parallel streets. One travels down a valley floor from woods to town to woods, with nothing between but forests that cover a highly disturbed environment. Urban form and forested open space work in opposition, yet at the larger scale there is an order, a cultural web stretched tautly across the landscape that conveys both impact and richness. This separateness of town and country imparts drama to both.

The coastal towns of Maine present a very different diagram. They originally existed as dots along a sinuous coastline accessible only by boat from the ocean. The sharply indented coastline makes overland travel difficult even today, as the main highways curve inland and leave isolated towns on remote promontories. The transportation infrastructure of these villages was the wakes of ships over the surface of the sea.

These examples of larger regional settlement distributions serve to underscore the advantages of concise urban form in preserving habitat, although the planning of coal towns had no intention of sparing the surrounding hills. Concise urban form is one of the most sustainable things we can create to protect the future of this earth, ourselves, and our culture, and yet instances of compact organization are disappearing, and with them any hope of larger undisturbed habitats capable of sustaining the earth's necessary biodiversity.

How we settle this earth becomes the most important and far-reaching concern of the next millennium. As the world's population increases across the globe, as development spreads, our patterns of agriculture, industry, and housing will determine the fate of this planet. Ironically, it is less what we build than what we leave in between that matters. Unencumbered areas contract daily through logging, drought, or settlement encroachment. Habitat destruction threatens every corner of our world as we lose the biodiversity so necessary for the planet's long-term sustainability; thus, this book on settlement patterns poses uncertainties as well about a future beyond the confines of the Appalachian cordillera.

With the exception of the Pennsylvania coal towns, all the settlements investigated in this book are now contained by new spatial patterns of large parking lots and separated buildings. The normal sequence is an empty mall on one side of a town, a more recent, viable mall on the other, and a decaying historic downtown in the middle. In most instances, as the town's population declines, the county or regional population increases—a clear indication of sprawl. We in America are so profligate that we discard whole towns, yet as we do this, we lose our history, our places, and ultimately our culture. To be so wasteful of resources is certainly unsustainable; to lose our past is to lose ourselves.

But conciseness of urban form fosters another kind of sustainability that is less obvious than that of habitat integrity and resource con-

**Coastal town**

servation. I call this other kind of sustainability *cultural sustainability,* for these towns are repositories of cultural history. They act as cisterns that gather differences and concentrate them into one place. They gathered people from different cultures, including Estonians to Pennsylvania, Breton fishermen to Maine, and, tragically, African slaves to Alabama. (Slavery was obviously a profoundly inhuman method of

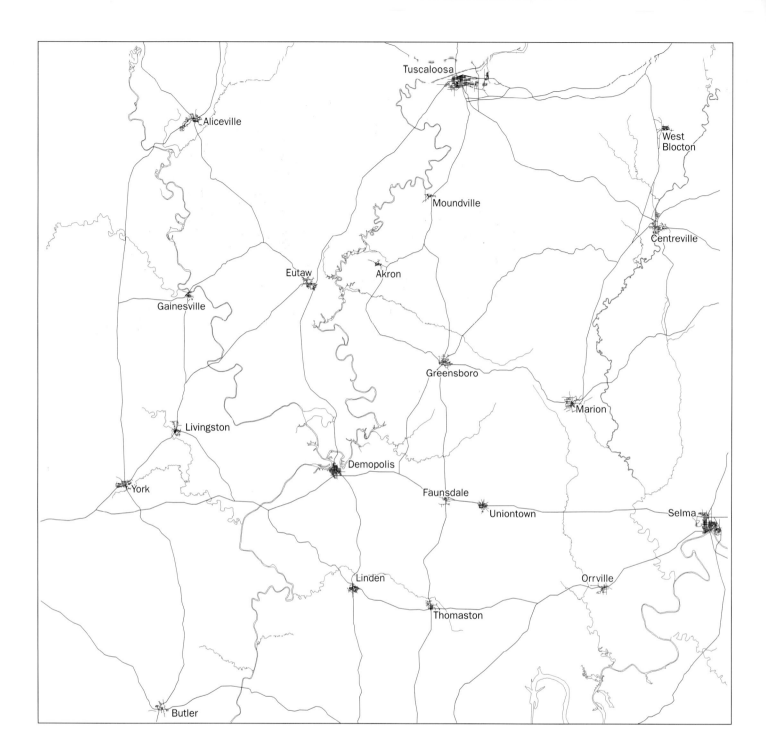

Western Alabama

(Opposite) Southern West
Virginia

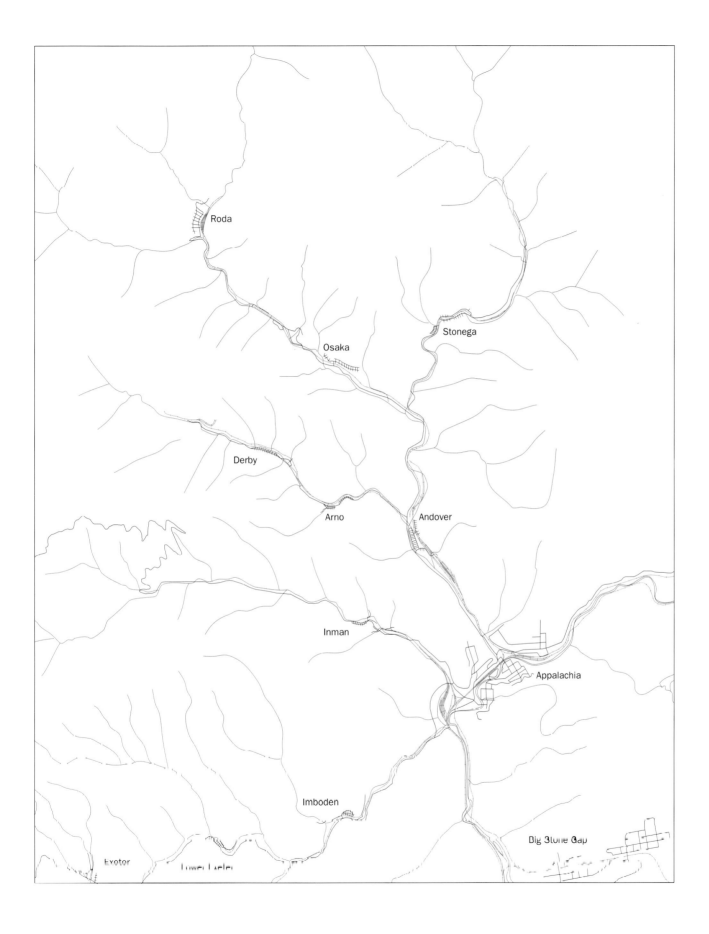

Roda

Osaka

Stonega

Derby

Arno

Andover

Inman

Appalachia

Imboden

Big Stone Gap

Exeter

Lower Exeter

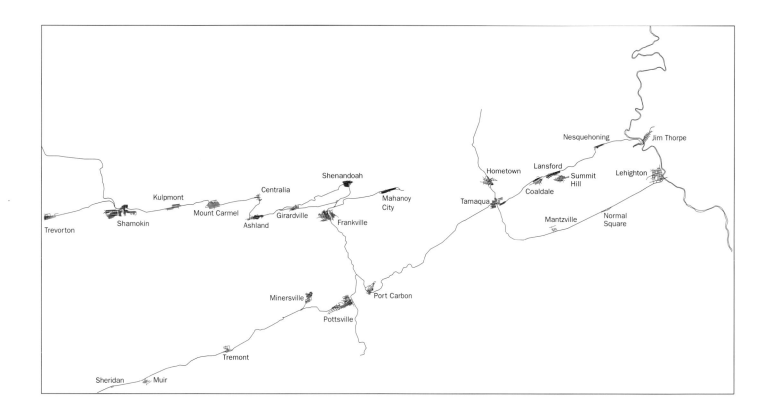

**Eastern Pennsylvania**

(Opposite) *Map of the Mine Hill & Schuylkill Haven R.R. & Branches,* 1857. (Library of Congress)

forcibly bringing people to America, yet African American culture has contributed immeasurably to this country.) These towns were places that once fortified and preserved such differences, which added to their richness and meaning. Cultural diversity on a national scale allows societies to adjust and respond to a shifting world, just as biodiversity enables complex ecosystems to change and adapt to subtle or cataclysmic climatic alteration.

As a homogenized landscape slowly spreads across America, our culture changes from one with a multitude of specific and unique places to one where all places are the same. As we lose this ability to embrace differences, this concentration of the other, we surely lose something

more valuable than just the physical forms of these settlements. These towns accommodated the reality of others as a dimension of human experience, and it is the perspective of the other—other kinds of people, other ideas, other cultures—that nurtures more tolerant and generous human beings.

There is a danger, however, in romanticizing the past of these towns, for they also teach a darker lesson about ourselves. They all depended upon extractive processes that proved unsustainable. Cotton exhausted the soil, coal no longer fuels our energy, and mining still pollutes our streams and hillsides. The Gulf of Maine is bereft of fish. In each case the earth has suffered irreparable harm. Certainly in the beginning

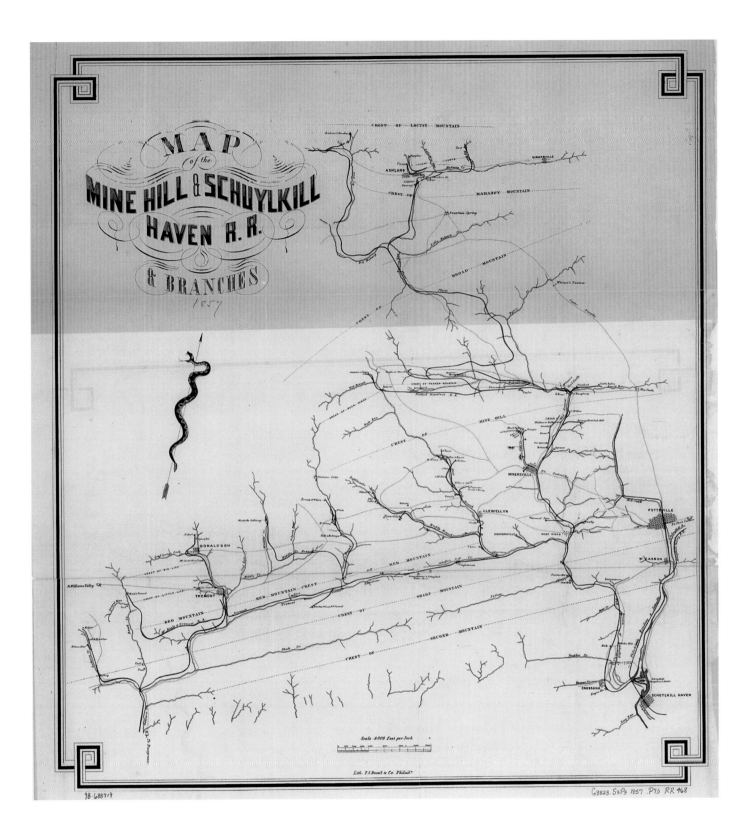

MAP
of the
MINE HILL & SCHUYLKILL
HAVEN R.R.
& BRANCHES
1857

Scale 4000 feet per inch

Lith. P.S. Duval & Co. Philad.ª

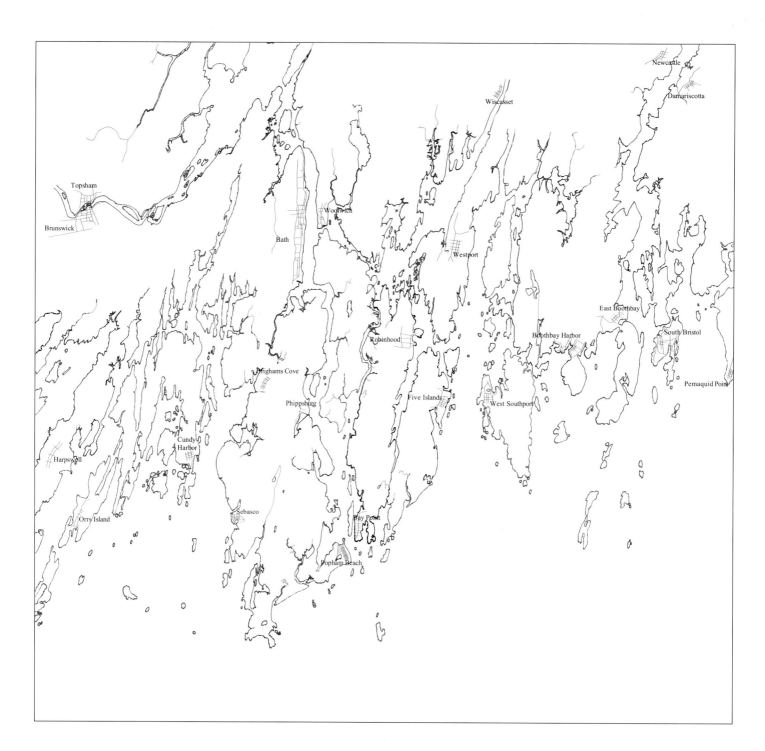

**Coastal Maine**

each town perceived its resources as unlimited and unbounded and their extraction as necessary for prosperity and the expansion of wealth. Contemporary America operates under the same illusion, except that we now deplete resources beyond our borders. It is sobering to reflect upon the world's riches necessary to sustain the automobile and emerging electronic culture of this country.

What makes the future doubly conflicted is the coupling of rapacious resource exploitation with the increasing homogenization of our built environment. Across America there is a persistent blending of urban form, so that a commercial strip in Los Angeles looks the same as one outside Atlanta, and Charleston, West Virginia, appears as a mirror image of Birmingham, Alabama. It seems that distinctive regional settlements will not survive their coalescence with the common aspects of American culture. Beauty of setting and contiguity to major population centers has allowed Maine coastal towns to flourish as tourist destinations, but the economic development of transient tourism extracts its own price in the same spatial dislocation that must accommodate automobile mobility. The seasonal influx of people strains the infrastructure and dilutes any authenticity of these places until they exist in the same uniform matrix of malls and open parking lots as most other tourist destination.

Uniform settlement patterns encircle our larger metropolitan areas as more and more people, enticed by better employment and aided by automobile mobility, migrate to their peripheries. When I asked elderly people in Penn-

sylvania coal towns where the younger families lived, the answer was Scranton or Philadelphia, where they had gone in search of jobs. What we have witnessed in the tiny towns of this study the length of the Appalachians happens at the macroscale in burgeoning regional centers. The edges expand in a new spatial configuration, and one massive conglomerate blends imperceptibly into the next. Montgomery, Birmingham, and Huntsville, Alabama, extend their grasps farther and farther into the surrounding landscape, devouring towns and habitat. Charleston, and Beckley, West Virginia, increase in population at the expense of small towns locked in neighboring valleys, their expansion hastened by the propensity of the state of West Virginia to use highway construction as an engine for economic development.

These forces change the spatial qualities of our spreading settlements into undifferentiated open space with buildings isolated by parking lots, so typical of our retail malls and office parks. This spatial change cannot, however, explain the uniformity of architectural and landscape architectural expression. Why must the housing, stores, eateries, and signs all look the same in Pennsylvania or Alabama? Is this emerging dominant culture only the result of the increased ease of communication and transportation? Or is it something we truly want?

I believe that we must take responsibility for the world we have brought forth. After two hundred years of turmoil and experimentation, what we have is now the universal expression of what we desire and what we have become. As I have argued throughout this book, we can-

Public library, Rockland, Maine

not separate form and content today any more than could the settlements of the past. Ours is a culture of easy mobility because, unlike those towns studied, we do not want roots or any attachment to a specific landscape. This lack of specificity is necessary in a mobile culture that fears the unfamiliar. If all places are the same, then we have co-opted the entire continent and can more freely move from location to location.

Perhaps the seeds of this uniformity were sown in the actions of those determined men on the Gettysburg battlefield in 1863. A year earlier, Abraham Lincoln had said that his "paramount objective in this struggle is to save the Union."[1] The United States was saved and joined together again. Having been torn apart by so horrible and singular an event as the Civil War, Ameri-

cans desired only to have a communal history, a single culture acceptable and accommodating to all. We hid our sectional differences beneath the idea of a national uniformity. After a period of unprecedented growth at the end of the nineteenth century, the two world wars drew us even closer together and opened the way for the homogenizing freedom of automobile mobility in the 1950s. Since then our assimilation of many cultures into one has succeeded beyond anyone's expectations.

My explorations of these small towns has taken me along the breadth of the Appalachians. I have talked with people in rowdy diners, in staid town offices, and in the elegant hushed

1. Abraham Lincoln to Horace Greeley, 22 August 1862, published in *New York Tribune*, 23 August 1862, clipping in Abraham Lincoln Papers, series 2, General Correspondence, 1858–1864, Library of Congress.

libraries that are such a part of our architectural
legacy. Always people were unfailingly courte
ous and open—and with their generous directions I found my way to hidden parts of their
histories. With their help, I searched each town
for the Civil War statues or monuments to the
comrades of the young men from both Camdens
who were at Gettysburg in 1863. These statues are
always to be found in a public square, cemetery,
or village green; their silenced lips and down-
cast eyes reproach those who might miss them.
I reflected upon their histories as I wrote about
the differences between these towns. Did these
soldiers perceive their differences—of North–
South, coastal–mountains, Atlantic–Western,
region against region—as so great as to go to
war? I cannot imagine pitting youth against
youth because of such disputes, for my journeys
found that these towns, although rich in their
diversity, are all quintessentially American. So
many mornings I drank coffee from a chipped
mug with my "breakfast all day" or lunched on
burgers and fries in a family diner. I obtained
cash from shiny ATMs tucked into local banks'
bastioned neoclassical facades, and I laughed
with retirees resting in rusted metal chairs on
dilapidated porches. I have seen American flags
of all sizes displayed—flags that beyond all else
symbolize our union. Perhaps that is the legacy
of each name carved in stone: that from such
myriad differences has been forged a common
heritage that must find its own expression in
new settlements and new places. If these towns
were maps of our culture, it is fitting that we
lose their "Tattered Ruins" in the deserts of our

Village green, Castine,
Maine

minds and allow those places partly of the future to become our new maps. We must invent a
culture that faces this future, yet we too remain
part of that same culture. This makes it difficult
to confront the reasoning and its expression in
the world we are in the process of creating. The
only alternative is to accept change as part of the
reality of our past as well as the harbinger of our
tomorrows. Perhaps the landscape was always a
blank slate marked by one generation and erased
by the next. Imperfect and transitory, this is our
history measured upon the earth.

Aczel, Amird D. *The Riddle of the Compass*. New York: Harcourt, 2001.

*Alabama Rail Plan Update, 1980.* N.p.: State of Alabama Highway Department, n.d.

*Alabama Urban Review, 1992: The Origin of Urban Alabama.* Vol. 1, series A103. Huntsville: Center for Research, Alabama A&M University, 1992.

Allen, T. F. H., and Thomas B. Star. *Hierarchy: Perspectives for Ecological Complexity*. Chicago: University of Chicago Press, 1982.

Ambroziak, Brian M., and Jeffrey R. Ambroziak. *Infinite Perspectives: Two Thousand Years of Three-Dimensional Mapmaking*. New York: Princeton Architectural Press, 1999.

American Friends Service Committee. *Wabanakis of Maine and the Maritimes: A Resource Book by and about Penobscot, Passamaquoddy, Maliseet, Micmac, and Abenaki Indians*. Philadelphia, 1989.

Appalachian Land Ownership Task Force. *Who Owns Appalachia? Landownership and Its Impact*. Lexington: University Press of Kentucky, 1983.

Armes, Ethel. *The Story of Coal and Iron in Alabama*. 1910. Reprint, Leeds, AL: Beechwood Books, 1987.

Badger, R. Reid, and Lawrence A. Clayton, eds. *Alabama and the Borderlands: From Prehistory to Statehood*. Tuscaloosa: University of Alabama Press, 1985.

Baker, Emerson W., et al. *American Beginnings: Exploration, Culture, and Cartography in the Land of Norumbega*. Lincoln: University of Nebraska Press, 1994.

Baker, William Avery. *A Maritime History of Bath, Maine and the Kennebec River Region, Volumes I, II and III*. Portland, ME: Anthoensen, 1973.

Barefield, Marilyn Davis. *Bessemer, Yesterday and Today, 1887–1888*. Birmingham, AL: Southern University Press, 1986.

———. *Records of Wilcox County, Alabama*. Easley, SC: Southern Historical Press, 1988.

Bartram, William. *Travels, and Other Writings*. 1792. Edited by Thomas P. Slaughter. New York: Library of America, 1996.

Basso, Keith. *Wisdom Sits in Places: Landscape and Language among the Western Apache*. Albuquerque: University of New Mexico Press, 1996.

Bath Historical Society. *The Sesquicentennial of Bath, Maine, 1847–1997*. Bath, ME, 1997.

Bigham, Darrel E. *Towns and Villages of the Lower Ohio*. Lexington: University Press of Kentucky, 1998.

Boeschenstein, Warren. *Historic American Towns along the Atlantic Coast*. Baltimore: Johns Hopkins University Press, 1999.

Bowsher, Alice Meriwether, and M. Lewis Kennedy Jr. *Alabama Architecture: Looking at Building and Place*. Tuscaloosa: University of Alabama Press, 2001.

Branch, Melville C. *An Atlas of Rare City Maps: Comparative Urban Design, 1830–1842*. New York: Princeton Architectural Press, 1997.

Brannon, Peter A. *Engineers of Yesterday*. Montgomery, AL: Paragon, 1928.

———. *Highways, Boats, and Bridges: A Story of
Ferryboats and Some Bridges of Other Days in
Alabama*. Montgomery, AL: Paragon, 1929.

Brigham, Albert Perry. *From Trail to Railway:
Through the Appalachians*. Port Washington,
NY: Kennikat, 1970.

Buisseret, David. *From Sea Charts to Satellite
Images: Interpreting North American History
through Maps*. Chicago: University of Chicago
Press, 1990.

Buker, George E. *The Penobscot Expedition*.
Annapolis, MD: Naval Institute Press, 2002.

Bunting, W. H. *A Day's Work, Part I*. Gardiner,
ME: Tilbury House, 1997.

———. *A Day's Work, Part II*. Gardiner, ME:
Tilbury House, 2000.

Campion, Joan. *Smokestacks and Black Diamonds:
A History of Carbon County, Pennsylvania*.
Easton, PA: Canal History and Technology
Press, 1997.

Campoli, Juli, Elizabeth Humstone, and Alex
MacLean. *Above and Beyond*. Chicago: Planners
Press, 2002.

Capra, Fritjof. *The Web of Life: A New Understanding of Living Systems*. New York: Doubleday,
1996.

Carnes, Mark C., John A Garraty, and Patrick
Williams. *Mapping America's Past: A Historical
Atlas*. New York: Holt, 1996.

Carver, Norman F., Jr. *Italian Hill Towns*. Kalama-
zoo, MI: Documan, 1995.

Castine Historical Society. *Castine*. Images of
America Series. Dover, NH: Arcadia, 1996.

*Cerda Urbs i Territori: Planning Beyond the Urban*.
Published in conjunction with the exhibition
"Mostra Cerda." Madrid: Electra, 1996.

Chapelle, Howard I. *The History of American Sailing Ships*. New York: Bonanza Books, 1935.

Chase, Fannie S. *Wiscasset in Pownalborough: A
History of the Shire Town and the Salient Historical Features of the Territory between the Sheepscot and Kennebec Rivers*. 2nd ed. Portland, ME:
Anthoensen, 1967.

Churchill, Edwin A., Joel W. Eastman, and Rich-
ard W. Judd. *Maine: The Pine Tree State from
Prehistory to the Present*. Orono: University of
Maine Press, 1994.

*Clay County Historical Commentary*. N.p.: Clay
County Historical Society with Clay County
Arts League, n.d.

Conkling, Phillip W. *From Cape Cod to the Bay
of Fundy: An Environmental Atlas of the Gulf of
Maine*. Cambridge, MA: MIT Press, 1995.

———. *Islands in Time: A Natural and Human
History of the Islands of Maine*. Camden, ME:
Down East Books, 1981.

Conley, Philip Mallory. *History of the West Virginia Coal Industry*. Charleston, WV: Education
Foundation, 1960.

Connelly, Thomas L. *Discovering the Appalachians*.
Harrisburg, PA: Stackpole Books, 1968.

Corner, James, ed. *Recovering Landscape: Essays
in Contemporary Landscape Architecture*. New
York: Princeton Architectural Press, 1999.

———. *Taking Measures across the American
Landscape*. New Haven, CT: Yale University
Press, 1996.

Cosgrove, Denis, ed. *Mappings*. London: Reakton
Books, 1999.

———. *Social Formation and Symbolic Landscape*.
Madison: University of Wisconsin Press, 1994.

Cronon, William. *Changes in the Land, Indians,
Colonists, and the Ecology of New England*. New
York: Hill and Wang, 1983.

Crumpton, Robert B., Jr. *Status of the State: Alabama 1974*. Montgomery: Alabama Development Office, State Planning Division, 1974.

Cullen, Gordon. *Townscape*. New York: Reinhold,
1961.

Cunha, Dilip da, and Anuradha Mathur. *Mississippi *Floods: Designing a Shifting Landscape.* New Haven, CT: Yale University Press, 2001.

Davis, Jay, and Tim Hughes. *History of Belfast in the Twentieth Century.* With Megan Pinette. Belfast, ME: Belfast History Project, 2002.

Deasy, George F., and Phyllis R. Griess. "Coal and Coal Mining, Part I, Bituminous Coal." *Atlas of Pennsylvania Coal and Coal Mining.* Bulletin of the Mineral Industries Experimental Station, no. 73. University Park: Pennsylvania State University Press, 1960.

———. "Coal and Coal Mining, Part II, Anthracite Coal." *Atlas of Pennsylvania Coal and Coal Mining.* Bulletin of the Mineral Industries Experimental Station, no. 80. University Park: Pennsylvania State University Press, 1963.

Dennis, Michael. *Court and Garden: From the French Hotel to the City of Modern Architecture.* Cambridge, MA: MIT Press, 1986.

Dietz, Lew. *Night Train at Wiscasset Station.* New York: Doubleday, 1977.

Doster, James F. *Railroads in Alabama Politics, 1875–1914.* Tuscaloosa: University of Alabama Press, 1957.

Drake, Richard B. *A History of Appalachia.* Lexington: University Press of Kentucky, 2001.

Drury, John H., and Joan Gilbert. *Jim Thorpe (Mauch Chunk).* Images of America Series. Charleston, SC: Arcadia, 2001.

Dubose, John. *The Mineral Wealth of Alabama and Birmingham Illustrated.* Birmingham, AL: N. T. Greene, 1886.

Dunaway, Wayland Fuller. *A History of Pennsylvania.* New York: Prentice Hall, 1935.

Dunaway, Wilma A. *The First American Frontier: Transition to Capitalism in Southern Appalachia, 1700–1860.* Chapel Hill: University of North Carolina Press, 1996.

Duncan, Roger F. *Coastal Maine: A Maritime History.* New York: Norton, 1992.

Durrance, Jill, and William Shamblin, eds. *Appalachian Ways: A Guide to the Historic Mountain Heart of the East.* Washington, DC: Appalachian Regional Commission, 1976.

Dyer, Barbara. *Home Sweet Home, Camden, Maine.* Rockport, ME: Camden Printing, 1996.

———. *More Memories of Camden, Maine.* Rockport, ME: Camden Printing, 1997.

———. *Vessels of Camden.* Images of America Series. Charleston, SC: Arcadia, 1998.

———. *Vintage Views of Camden, Maine.* Camden, ME: Camden Printing, 1987.

Eller, Ronald D. *Miners, Millhands, and Mountaineers: Industrialization of the Appalachian South, 1880–1930.* Knoxville: University of Tennessee Press, 1982.

Faulkner, William. *Requiem for a Nun.* New York: Random House, 1951.

Fenneman, Nevin M. *Physiography of Eastern United States.* New York: McGraw-Hill, 1938.

Foscue, Virginia O. *Place Names in Alabama.* Tuscaloosa: University of Alabama Press, 1989.

Frazer, Mell A. *Early History of Steamboats in Alabama.* Alabama Polytechnic Institute Historical Series. Auburn: Alabama Polytechnic Institute, 1907.

Freeze, Barbara. *Coal: A Human History.* Cambridge, MA: Perseus Books, 2003.

Gandelsonas, Mario. *X-Urbanism: Architecture and the American City.* New York: Princeton Architectural Press, 1999.

Giardina, Denise. *The Unquiet Earth.* New York: Ivy Books, 1992.

Griffith, Lucille. *Alabama: A Documentary History to 1900.* Tuscaloosa: University of Alabama Press, 1972.

Harden, Brian R. Chairman. *The Shore Village Story: An Informal History of Rockland, Maine.* Rockland, ME: Rockland Bicentennial Commission, 1989.

Harvey, Curtis E. *Coal in Appalachia: An Economic*

*Analysis*. Lexington: University Press of Kentucky, 1986.

Hatch, Louis C. *Maine: A History*. Somersworth: New Hampshire Publishing, 1974.

Heath, Kingston Wm. *The Patina of Place: The Cultural Weathering of a New England Landscape*. Knoxville: University of Tennessee Press, 2001.

Hebert, John R. *Panoramic Maps of Cities in the United States and Canada: A Check List of Maps in the Collections of the Library of Congress Geography and Map Division*. Compiled and revised by Patrick E. Dempsey. Washington, DC: Library of Congress, 1984.

Herr, Kincard. *Louisville and Nashville Railroad: 1850–1959*. Louisville, KY: L&N Magazine, 1959.

Hoben, Richard J. *Lansford: The First One Hundred Years*. Lansford, PA: Town of Lansford, 1976.

Hood, Jack B., and E. L. Klein. *Rivers of Alabama*. Huntsville, AL: Strode, 1968.

Hudson Coal Company. *The Story of Anthracite*. New York: Hudson Coal, 1932.

Hughes, Sarah S. *Surveyors and Statesmen: Land Measuring in Colonial Virginia*. Richmond: Virginia Surveyors Foundation and Virginia Association of Surveyors, 1979.

Hydro, Vincent, Jr. *The Mauch Chunk Switchback: America's Pioneer Railroad*. Easton, PA: Canal History and Technology Press, 2002.

Jackson, Harvey H., III. *Rivers of History: Life on the Coosa, Tallapoosa, Cahaba, and Alabama*. Tuscaloosa: University of Alabama Press, 1995.

Jackson, J. B. *Discovering the Vernacular Landscape*. New Haven, CT: Yale University Press, 1984.

Jubilee Historical Book Committee. *From the Rough: The Bessemer Story, 1887–1962, Diamond Jubilee*. N.p., 1962.

King, Geoff. *Mapping Reality*. New York: St Martin's, 1996.

Klein, Maury. *History of the Louisville and Nashville Railroad*. New York: Macmillan, 1972.

Knies, Michael. *Coal on the Lehigh, 1790–1827: Beginnings and Growth of the Anthracite Industry in Carbon County, Pennsylvania*. Easton, PA: Canal History and Technology Press, 2001.

Krier, Rob. *Urban Space*. New York: Rizzoli, 1979.

Kuchta, David. *Once a Man, Twice a Boy*. Nesquehoning, PA: Kiwi, 1999.

Lambie, Joseph T. *From Mine to Market: The History of Coal Transportation on the Norfolk and Western Railway*. New York: New York University Press, 1954.

Lantz, Herman R. *People of Coal Town*. New York: Columbia University Press, 1958.

Lee, Howard B. *Bloodletting in Appalachia*. Morgantown: West Virginia University Press, 1969.

Lewis, G. J. *Rural Communities: Problems in Modern Geography*. London: Davis and Charles, 1979.

Library of Congress, Geography and Map Division, Reference and Bibliography Section. *Fire Insurance Maps in the Library of Congress; Plans of North American Cities and Towns Produced by the Sanborn Map Company: A Checklist*. Washington, DC: Library of Congress, 1981.

Locke, John L. *Sketches of the History of the Town of Camden, Maine: Including Incidental References to the Neighboring Places and Adjacent Waters*. Hallowell, ME: Masters, Smith, 1859.

Long, John H., ed. *Alabama: Atlas of Historical County Boundaries*. New York: Scribner, 1996.

Low, Setha M. *On the Plaza*. Austin: University of Texas Press, 2000.

MacArthur, Pamela C. *John O'Hara's Anthracite Region*. Images of America Series. Charleston, SC: Arcadia, 1999.

MacLean, Alex, and Bill McKibben. *Look at the Land: Aerial Reflections on America*. New York: Rizzoli, 1993.

Maffi, Luisa, ed. *On Biocultural Diversity: Linking*

*Language, Knowledge, and the Environment.* Washington, DC: Smithsonian Institution Press, 2001.

Maine Historical Society. *Maine Bicentennial Atlas.* Portland, ME, 1976.

Marsh, Ben. "Continuity and Decline in the Anthracite Towns of Pennsylvania." *Annals of the Association of American Geographers* 77 (September 1987): 337–53.

Martin, Kenneth R., and Ralph Linwood Snow. *The Pattens of Bath: A Seagoing Dynasty.* Bath: Maine Maritime Museum and Patten Free Library, 1996.

McElfresh, Earl B. *Maps and Mapmakers of the Civil War.* New York: Abrams, 1999.

McMillan, Malcolm C. *The Land Called Alabama.* Austin, TX: Steck-Vaughan, 1975.

McMurry, Sally. *From Sugar Camps to Star Barns: Rural Life and Landscape in a Western Pennsylvania Community.* University Park: Pennsylvania State University Press, 2001.

McPherson, James M. *For Cause and Comrades: Why Men Fought in the Civil War.* New York: Oxford University Press, 1997.

Miller, Donald L., and Richard Sharpless. *The Kingdom of Coal: Work, Enterprise, and Ethnic Communities in the Mine Fields.* Easton, PA: Canal History and Technology Press, 1998.

Miller, J. Hillis. *Topographies.* Stanford, CA: Stanford University Press, 1995.

Mitchell, Robert D., ed. *Appalachian Frontiers: Settlement, Society, and Development in the Preindustrial Era.* Lexington: University Press of Kentucky, 1991.

Moore, Albert Burton. *History of Alabama and Her People.* Chicago: American Historical Society, 1927.

Nesbitt, Mark. *Through Blood and Fire: Selected Civil War Papers of Major General Joshua Chamberlain.* Mechanicsburg, PA: Stackpole Books, 1996.

Oleksyshyn, John. *Fossil Plants from the Anthracite Coal Fields of Eastern Pennsylvania.* Harrisburg: Commonwealth of Pennsylvania, 1982.

Olmsted, Frederick Law. *The Cotton Kingdom: A Traveller's Observations on Cotton and Slavery in the American Slave States, 1853–1861.* 1861. Edited by Arthur M. Schlesinger. New York: Da Capo, 1996.

Orme, Antony R. *The Physical Geography of North America.* Oxford: Oxford University Press, 2002.

Paine, Lincoln P. *Down East: A Maritime History of Maine.* Gardiner, ME: Tilbury House, 2000.

Parton, W. Julian. *The Death of a Great Company.* Easton, PA: Canal History and Technology Press, 1986.

Percival, Gwendoline E., and Chester J. Kulesa. *Illustrating an Anthracite Era: The Photographic Legacy of John Horgan, Jr.* N.p.: Commonwealth of Pennsylvania, 1995.

Picon, Antoine, and Jean-Paul Robert. *Les dessus des cartes.* Paris: Picard, 1999.

Pope, Albert. *Ladders.* New York: Princeton Architectural Press, 1996.

Porter, Eliot, and James Gleick. *Nature's Chaos.* New York: Viking, 1990.

Price, Edward T. "The Central Courthouse Square in the American County Seat." *Geographical Review* 58 (January 1968): 29–60.

Raitz, Karl B., and Richard Ulack. *Appalachia, a Regional Geography: Land, People, and Development.* Boulder, CO: Westview, 1984.

Rand McNally. *Rand McNally Handy Railroad Atlas of the United States.* Chicago, 1971.

Redington, Robert J. *Survey of the Appalachians.* South Egremont, MA: Taconic, 1978.

Remington, Craig W., and Thomas J. Kallsen, eds. *Historical Atlas of Alabama: Vol. 1, Historical Locations by County.* Tuscaloosa: University of Alabama Press, 1997.

Remini, Robert V. *Andrew Jackson and His Indian Wars.* New York: Viking Penguin, 2001.

Reps, John W. *Bird's Eye Views: Historic Lithographs of North American Cities.* New York: Princeton Architectural Press, 1998.

———. *The Making of Urban America: A History of City Planning in the United States.* Princeton, NJ: Princeton University Press, 1965.

Rice, Otis K. *West Virginia: A History.* Lexington: University Press of Kentucky, 1985.

Richards, John Stuart. *Early Coal Mining in the Anthracite Region.* Images of America Series. Charleston, SC: Arcadia, 2002.

Richardson, Jesse M., ed. *Alabama Encyclopedia: Volume I, Book of Facts.* Northport, AL: American Southern Publishing, 1965.

Robinson, Reuel. *History of Camden and Rockport.* Camden, ME: Camden Publishing, 1907.

Rogers, William W., Robert D. Ward, Leah R. Atkins, and Wayne Flynt. *Alabama: The History of a Deep South State.* Tuscaloosa: University of Alabama Press, 1994.

Russell, Howard S. *Indian New England before the MayFlower.* Hanover, NH: University Press of New England, 1980.

Scherer, Paul. *Musings of a Chronicler: Excerpts From Tamaqua's Past.* Vols. 1–4. N.p., 1983.

Schwieterman, Joseph P. *When the Railroad Leaves Town.* Kirkville, MO: Truman State University Press, 2001.

Shakespeare, William. *The Yale Shakespeare.* Edited by S. C. Burchell. New Haven, CT: Yale University Press, 1954.

Shifflett, Crandall A. *Coal Towns: Life, Work, and Culture in Company Towns of Southern Appalachia, 1880–1960.* Knoxville: University of Tennessee Press, 1991.

Simonton, T. R. *Tourist's Guide of Picturesque Camden on the Coast of Maine.* Camden, ME: Camden Herald, 1886.

Sitte, Camillo. *City Planning According to Artistic Principles.* New York: Random House, 1965.

Snow, Ralph Linwood, and Captain Douglas K. Lee. *A Shipyard in Maine: Perry & Small and the Great Schooners.* Gardiner, ME: Tilbury House, 1999.

Southerland, Henry DeLeon, Jr., and Jerry Elijah Brown. *The Federal Road through Georgia, the Creek Nation, and Alabama, 1806–1836.* Tuscaloosa: University of Alabama Press, 1989.

Stanislawski, Dan. "The Origin and Spread of the Grid-Pattern Town." *Geographical Review* 36 (January 1946): 105–20.

Stover, John F. *American Railroads.* 2nd ed. Chicago: University of Chicago Press, 1997.

———. *The Routledge Historical Atlas of the American Railroads.* New York: Routledge, 1999.

Tams, W. P., Jr. *The Smokeless Coal Fields of West Virginia: A Brief History.* Morgantown: West Virginia University Press, 2001.

Tilley, Christopher. *A Phenomenology of Landscape: Places, Paths, and Monuments.* Oxford: Berg, 1994.

Toppan, Andrew C. *Bath Iron Works.* Images of America Series. Charleston, SC: Arcadia, 2002.

Treese, Lorett. *Railroads of Pennsylvania.* Mechanicsburg, PA: Stackpole Books, 2003.

Van der Veer Hamilton, Virginia. *Alabama: A History.* New York: Norton, 1984.

Van der Veer Hamilton, Virginia, and Jacqueline A. Matte. *Seeing Historic Alabama: Fifteen Guided Tours.* Tuscaloosa: University of Alabama Press, 1996.

Walthall, John A. *Prehistoric Indians of the Southeast: Archaeology of Alabama and the Middle South.* Tuscaloosa: University of Alabama Press, 1982.

Ward, James A. *Railroads and the Character of America, 1820–1887.* Knoxville: University of Tennessee Press, 1986.

Webber, Melvin M., ed. *Explorations into Urban Structure.* Philadelphia: University of Pennsylvania Press, 1964.

Weightman, Gavin. *The Frozen Water Trade: A True Story*. New York: Hyperion, 2003.

White, I. C. "Supplementary Coal Report." In *West Virginia Geological Survey,* vol. 2A. Morgantown: State of West Virginia, 1908.

Williams, John Alexander. *West Virginia: A Bicentennial History.* Nashville, TN: American Association for State and Local History, 1976.

———. *West Virginia and the Captains of Industry.* Morgantown,: West Virginia University Library, 1976.

Williams, John R. *History of Camden, Maine.*

Vol. 1, 1907–1930. Rockland, ME: Courier-Gazette with Shoreline Graphics, 1989.

———. *History of Camden, Maine.* Vol. 2, *1931–1950.* Rockland, ME: Courier-Gazette with Shoreline Graphics, 1989.

———. *The History of the City of Belfast, Maine, from Its First Settlement in 1770 to 1875, Volume I.* 3rd ed. Rockport, ME: Picton, 1877.

Williamson, Joseph. *The History of the City of Belfast, Maine, from Its First Settlement in 1770 to 1875, Volume II.* 3rd ed. Rockport, ME: Picton, 1913.

Boeschenstein, Warren, 3
boll weevil epidemic, 108
Boone County, West Virginia, *131*, 141
Borges, Jorge Luis, vii, 13
Boston, 33, 163, 194
breaker boys, 5, *7*
Brewton, Alabama, *45, 46, 115,* 119, *122*
British colonies, 19. *See also* England
Brunswick, Maine, 18, *230*
Buker, George E., 211

cadastral organization, 42–64
cadmium, 172
Cahaba, Alabama, 33, 121
Cahaba Coal Field, 121–23
Calhoun, John C., 77
Camden, Alabama, 14, *17–42, 23, 24, 25, 26, 30–31, 37, 40*
Camden, Lord, 17
Camden, Maine, 14, 15, *17–42,* 66, *74–75, 77,* 187–88, 191, 208, 210, *217–18,* 233
Camden Anchor Works, 20
Cape Cod, 189
Cashtown Gap, 4
Castine, Maine, 18, 187–*88,* 190–91, *211–18,* 233
Central Georgia Railway, 119
Chamberlain, Lord, 18
Champlain, Samuel de, 190–93
Charleston, West Virginia, 131, 231–32
Chattahoochee River, 89, 90, 93, 103
Chattanooga, Tennessee, 117, 119
Cherokee Indians, 98, 102
Chesapeake & Ohio Railway, 158
Chicago, 98, 114, 119
Chickasaw Indians, 102
Chocktaw Indians, 102
churches, 5, 9, 178–*80,* 208
circuit courts, 71
civil rights, 65, 95. *See also* segregation
Civil War, 14, 18, 19, 24, 26, 34, 42, 66, 80, 95, 109, 110, 136, 159, 195, 232–33. *See also* Gettysburg, battle of
Clay, Henry, 77
Clay County, Alabama, 77, 80
coal: development of industry, 3, 4; mountain towns, 15, 110; and shipping, 207, 209. *See also* anthracite

coal; anthracite coal towns; bituminous coal; bituminous coal towns
Coaldale, Pennsylvania, *175,* 182
coastal towns, 5, 7, 9, 12, 14, 15, 17–42, 55, 185, 187–218, 219, 222–25, 230–31
Coffee County, Alabama, *74–75,* 76
Collyer, Sir George, 215
Columbus, Christopher, 190
Connecticut River, 190
Coombs Ship Yard, 20
Coosa River, 97, 104
cotton, viii, 23, 75, 87, 89, 90, 93, *107,* 108, 110, 185, 200, 219, 228
cotton gin, 24, *107*
Couch, Susan, 3
courthouse-square towns, viii, 4, 5, 12, 14, 15, 17, 22–27, 42, 54, 65–73, 208, 219–22
Creek Indians, 97, 102, 104
Cullman, Alabama, 47, 80, *88,* 115–16, 117, 120, 127, 221
Cullman, John S., 117
Cumberland Plateau, 75, 117, 119
custom houses, 57, 208–10, 212
customs tariffs, 208–9

Dallas County, Alabama, 33
Davey, West Virginia, *141,* 144, 155
DeBardeleben, Henry B., 125
DeBardeleben Coal and Iron, 125
Decatur, Alabama, *88,* 95, 97, 98, 99, 108
Decatur, Stephen, 95
Delaware River, 169
Demopolis, Alabama, *45, 46, 48,* 80, 90–91, *92, 94,* 95, 98, *102, 110, 221, 226*

East River Rail Road, 132, *134–35*
Elba, Alabama, 18, 66, *74, 75, 76, 78, 79*
Elkhorn Creek, 156–57
Elliott, S. G., 9, *10*
England, 17, 20, 29, 163, 190, 213–15
Enterprise, Alabama, 76, *107–8*
Escambia River, 90–91
Eufaula, Alabama, 18, *45, 46, 63, 88,* 90, *91, 92, 93, 96,* 98, 222
European public squares, 73, 87